The Letters of Sigmund Freud
to Eduard Silberstein
1871–1881

The Letters of

SIGMUND FREUD

— to —

EDUARD SILBERSTEIN

1871–1881

Edited by

Walter Boehlich

Translated by

Arnold J. Pomerans

The Belknap Press of
Harvard University Press
Cambridge, Massachusetts
1990

This book is printed on acid-free paper, and its binding materials
have been chosen for strength and durability.
Library of Congress Cataloging-in-Publication Data is on last page of book.

Contents

Illustrations

Editor's Preface

> The important point is not that the thing be done by myself
> or another, but that it be done and done well, whether by a
> scoundrel or by an honorable man.
>
> *Correspondance Littéraire,* XIV

THE LETTERS of Sigmund Freud to Eduard Silberstein, so often
quoted during the past few years, are now in the Library of Congress,
Washington, D.C. Thanks to the initiative of Dr. Kurt R. Eissler and
a donation from Muriel Gardiner, the Sigmund Freud Archives were
able to acquire the originals at the end of the 1970s.

For the transcription I have relied mainly on photographs. The
originals of the letters dated September 4, 1872; August 15, 1877;
July 22, 1879; August 10, 1879; and October 3, 1880, have not been
found, so that I had to work from unclear photocopies. The letters
dated July 10, 11, and 16, 1873, together with the letter dated April
22, 1928, exist only in unreliable copies by an unknown hand.

A few of the letters were published as early as the 1960s: the letter
of August 22, 1874, and extracts from the letter of April 28, 1910, in
Heinz Stanescu, "Unbekannte Brief des jungen Sigmund Freud an
einen rumänischen Freund" (Unknown letters by the young Sigmund Freud to a Romanian friend), *Neue Literatur* 16 (1965): 123–
129; the "Epithalamium" from the letter of October 1, 1875, in
Heinz Stanescu, "Ein 'Gelegenheitsgedicht' des jungen Sigmund
Freud" (An 'occasional poem' by the young Sigmund Freud),
Deutsch für Ausländer (January 1967): 13–18; and the letter of Au-
gust 22, 1874, once again, in Ernst and Lucie Freud, eds., Sigmund
Freud, *Briefe, 1873–1939*, 2nd ed., Frankfurt, 1968.

As we can tell from the context and from our knowledge of the relationship between the two friends, not all of Freud's letters have come down to us, either because Silberstein failed to keep some of them or because they were lost after his death. Any hope of recovering these seems remote. The diary mentioned in the letter of August 9, 1872, which must at one time have been kept with the bundle of letters, has also vanished.

In this edition, slips of the pen have been silently corrected; abbreviations that might have stood in the way of the reader have been spelled out. The treatment of Freud's first name, which he often shortened to "Sig.," needs special mention. Contrary to what used to be thought, it appears that Freud used the signature "Sigmund" as early as June 11, 1872, reverting to "Sigismund" for a short period only in 1874; I have therefore rendered "Sig." as "Sigmund" throughout.

The passages in languages other than German have not been corrected, for understandable reasons. Nor have they been translated literally; in other words, there has been no attempt to replace Freud's clumsy Spanish with a comparably clumsy translation. Instead, I have tried to capture Freud's style as closely as possible, which meant reconstructing what he probably wanted to convey in the foreign tongue rather than rendering what he actually wrote in it. It goes without saying that this method is necessarily based on assumptions that cannot be strictly proven, which is why I have refrained from remarking in every case on the way in which I have arrived at my solutions. The alternative, easier procedure would have reduced Freud to a stammerer and at the same time shifted the burden of interpretation onto the reader, who, when the going became hard, would not even have had the opportunity of deducing from the "false" premise to the "correct."

I have kept the notes as brief as possible where the reader may be expected to need no special guidance, and have expanded them slightly only where the subject matter is not common knowledge. Out of consideration for some readers I have noted certain facts which may be disconcerting for others because of their elementary nature.

The state in which the Wehrmacht and the black-uniformed representatives of the German master race left Europe has been anything but helpful to the work of annotation. Many things can never be explained, others I have failed to clarify. Without a great deal of advice and support I should have been unable to explain much of what has now come to light.

I must thank the ever helpful City and University Library of Frankfurt, the University Library of Vienna, the archives of Vienna University, the archives of the Karl Marx University, Leipzig, the Vienna War Archives, the Vienna City and National Archives, the Israelitic Congregation, Vienna, and the Wroclaw University Library; also, Rosita Braunstein Vieyra (New York), Guiseppe Cuscito (Muggia), the esteemed Kurt R. Eissler (New York), Gerhard Ficht- ner (Tübingen); Ilse Grubrich-Simitis (Frankfurt), who not only gave selflessly of her knowledge, but also showed great patience over many long years; Eva Laible (Vienna), Ingeborg Meyer-Palmedo (Frankfurt), Ursula Panzer (Cologne), Hazel Rosenstrauch (Vienna), Josef Sajner (Brno), Reinhold N. Smid (Cologne), Uwe Wesel (Berlin), and finally May Widmer-Perrenoud (Zurich) for so many conversa- tions "in this wasteland of ours, and yonder where they better dwell." Thanks are also due to Professor Dr. Clemens de Boor and the Sigmund Freud Foundation for their good offices.

Last but not least: the work on the letters, which the German publishers were unable to fund, has had the financial support of Pro- fessor Peter Schmitt (Frankfurt); to him, too, I am most grateful.

W. B.

Preface to the
English-Language Edition

SIGMUND FREUD wrote these letters in a variety of languages—
principally his native German and the schoolboy Spanish that he
and Eduard Silberstein shared, with a sprinkling of Latin, Italian,
and English. The German edition presented each letter as written,
with the necessary translations appended. In this edition, each letter
is presented complete in English, with the text of passages originally
in languages other than German given in the notes to each letter. In
the English text the beginning of such passages is indicated with ⸙
and the end with ⸕ . The translator has followed Walter Boehlich's
reconstructions of these foreign-language texts rather than translat-
ing them literally.

The form of the letters' dates has been standardized. Editorial interpolations appear in square brackets, and words that Freud under-
lined are in italic.

The annotation has been adapted for English-language readers.
The translator has occasionally added notes to clarify linguistic
matters or to supply additional information, identified by "Tr."

The publishers gratefully acknowledge the assistance of Deborah
Schneider in the preparation of this edition.

Introduction

Thou shalt, thou must abstain.
Goethe, Faust

SIGMUND FREUD AND EDUARD SILBERSTEIN are a disparate pair; about the first we know comparatively much, about the second disproportionately little, indeed one may say scarcely anything at all. Not a single line he wrote seems to have come down to us; his traces have been lost. That he played a role in Freud's life we have long since known from a letter to Martha Bernays,[1] but as that letter refers more to their gradual drifting apart than to their close ties, it fails to reveal that no other friend played a more important role in Freud's youth. The letter is misleading in many respects, for no matter how greatly the subsequent paths of the two friends may have diverged, Freud remembered Silberstein all his life with friendship and affection and never forgot what they once shared.

What they shared was what they did together: the learning of Spanish, the founding of the Academía Castellana (or Española), the inventing of a private mythology, the writing of humorous texts. And there was their correspondence, one half of which has in large part come down to us thanks to Silberstein, who preserved it carefully, thus granting us unexpected glimpses into Freud's youthful development. What we learn as a result is quite new, but since it is Freud's words alone that we see, it is he who is in the spotlight, his

---

1. Ernst L. Freud, ed., *Letters of Sigmund Freud, 1873–1939*, trans. Tania and James Stern, London: The Hogarth Press, 1970, pp. 112ff.

recipient remaining in the dark. Because he does not speak we cannot see him.

What has been established about him is not a great deal. Eduard Silberstein was born on December 27, 1856, in the Romanian city of Jassy, a fairly important trading center with a large Jewish community. During the second and third decades of the nineteenth century, pestilence and cholera halved the population, which, however, quickly climbed back to a figure of sixty thousand, though it continued to suffer from the ravages of war and a series of occupations. The Jews suffered more than anyone else, particularly in the pogrom of 1866, during Charles von Hohenzollern's visit to Jassy. Perhaps that was the reason why Eduard's father, Osias, whom Freud called "half mad,"[2] moved to Braila, a town near the mouth of the Danube, where he built up a business whose profits allowed him to send his sons to the Higher School in Vienna. He had at first intended to give them an orthodox Jewish education, but this plan evidently foundered on their opposition.

Together with Freud, Silberstein attended the Leopoldstädter Real- und Obergymnasium for many years, matriculating in 1874 and going on to study law in Leipzig for two semesters. In the winter of 1874 he enrolled for eight courses, including those in history by Karl Biedermann and in English by Richard Wulker; in the summer of 1875 he enrolled in just three, one of them by Wilhelm Roscher on the history of political and social theories, which no doubt reflected the interest in social democratic politics he maintained throughout his life. Following this second semester he withdrew his name from the university register and discontinued his Leipzig studies.

Starting in the winter semester of 1875 he studied in Vienna, attending Franz Brentano's lectures in particular, along with a few lectures on jurisprudence, and was made a Doctor of Jurisprudence in 1879—unfortunately, as was then the custom, without being obliged to submit a written thesis, so that we do not even have a dissertation by his hand. He does not appear to have worked as a lawyer at any time. He returned to Braila, where he remained a highly respected citizen until his death in 1925. His first marriage was to Pauline Theiler (July 22, 1871–May 14, 1891), a young

2. Letter to Martha Bernays, February 7, 1884, in ibid. Tr.

woman from Jassy, whom because of her melancholia he sent to
Vienna so that she could be treated by Freud. When she arrived she
told her maid to wait downstairs, and instead of going to the con-
sulting rooms, threw herself to her death from the third floor (Amer-
ican fourth floor) without having seen Freud.[3]

We do not know when Freud and Silberstein first became friends,
but by about 1870 they must have been close enough for Freud's
parents, no doubt for economic reasons as well, to propose taking
the brothers Eduard and Karl Silberstein into their new apartment
as boarders, although in the event nothing came of this plan. It
seems reasonable to suppose that the two boys met at school, but
there may be another explanation. The ailing Amalie Freud was in
the habit of visiting Roznau, a health resort not far from Freiberg, at
fairly regular intervals, usually taking one or more of her children
with her. In 1869, Amalie, accompanied by a child, perhaps Sigmund, and a Frau Anna Silberstein from Braila, accompanied by a
sister and a child, perhaps Eduard, were there at the same time.[4] We
cannot be sure, of course. Did the two mothers become acquainted
on that occasion, or did their sons know each other so well by then
that Eduard recommended both the health resort and the mother of
his friend to his mother? These are hypotheses; what is certain is
that relations developed between the two families that must have
centered on Sigmund and Eduard. By 1871, when the boys' regular
correspondence began, the Spanish Academy had already been
founded and the joint study of Spanish started, without teacher,
grammar, or dictionary, and based on the reading of a primer I have
been unable to trace.

This primer appears to have contained texts by Cervantes and by
Cecilia Böhl de Faber, including an extract containing the conversation of two dogs, Cipión and Berganza, from which the friends
took their "academic" names, Freud opting for the critical, peda-
gogic, and clever Cipión, and Silberstein for the more garrulous and

3. A report of the incident was published in the *Neue Wiener Tageblatt* for May
15, 1891, but did not mention any names. At the time Freud's practice was at 8 Maria-
Theresienstrasse. See also the biographical note by Rosita Braunstein Vieyra in the
Appendixes.

4. Joseph Sainer, "Die Beziehungen Sigmund Freuds und seiner Familie zu dem
mährischen Kurort Rožnau" (The connections of Sigmund Freud and his family with
the Moravian spa of Rožnau), in *Jahrbuch der Psychoanalyse* 24 (1989): 73–96.

adventurous Berganza. Occasionally they mixed up their names; at other times Freud wrote Braganza—the name of the Portuguese and Brazilian ruling house—instead of Berganza; and the most curious fact remains that Freud always referred to himself as a "dog at the hospital of Seville," whereas Cervantes speaks of the hospital at Valladolid. The fragment with which Freud was familiar must therefore have dealt with Berganza's stay in Seville, and Freud seems never to have read more than this extract from the *Novelas Ejemplares* because he never corrected himself.

The Academy, which had just two members but nevertheless boasted a seal, was not called the Academía Castellana from the outset but was originally referred to as the SSS, possibly for Spanische Sprach-Schule (Spanish language school). In addition to everything else both friends were accomplished linguists and immediately applied whatever they had just learned to their correspondence. The first attempts, as is only to be expected, were extremely clumsy, but the vocabulary and the mode of expression quickly expanded, though Freud never wrote anything like correct Spanish. Even so, he forgot so little of what he learned that, many years later, he was still able to write a letter in Spanish to his Spanish translator.[5] So long as he kept in practice he made noticeable progress, but whenever he wrote letters only in German for a time, he had first to get his hand in again.

His method of learning the language, together with the distraction of his other studies, explains why Freud's Spanish letters are not always perfectly plain. The more elegant his German, the more clumsy his Spanish can seem. What went wrong was not so much the syntax as the vocabulary, the entire correspondence reflecting the lack of a dictionary. Not surprisingly, Freud often failed to find the right word; what is surprising is how often he succeeded. Only when he did not know a word but thought that he did, or came up with a word by associating freely from a more familiar language, does he leave us puzzled. Thus he coined many words that do not exist in Spanish, or used words to mean something completely different from what the context demands.

The puzzles are most easily solved when he playfully hispanicizes German words, for instance rendering *büffeln* (to bone up on) as *bu-*

---

5. *Standard Edition* (hereafter S.E.), XIX, p. 289.

felar, or *Geige* (violin) as *geigolina*. Often he also hispanicizes Latin words, turning *desiderium* into *desiderio* (instead of the correct *deseo*), or *ostendere* into *ostender*; more frequently still he hispanicizes French words, turning *livraison* into *libracion*, *anéantir* into *aneantir*, *vacances* into *vacancias* and *chemin de fer* into *camino de hierro*. It makes little difference to us whether he got there by conscious or unconscious association—that is, whether he merely hoped that his hispanicized words corresponded to Latin and French words he knew, or whether his associations were, so to speak, mechanical, with Freud himself failing to realize how he arrived at the word he eventually used.

The problem is best illustrated by an actual case. In October 1875 Freud wrote: "My father used a Russian to invite your brother on an inspection." He could hardly have meant that; first, because it seems odd for a Russian to have appeared out of the blue, and, second, because Jacob Freud knew Karl Silberstein well enough not to need an intermediary. What then are we to make of this Russian? Freud must have been searching for a word with which he was not familiar, come up with a French one and then turned it into Spanish. What he probably meant to say was "my father used a ruse" (*une ruse*)—hence *ruso*, a Spanish word with quite a different meaning. And so we get the Russian, to whom Freud could not possibly have been referring, which is also borne out by the fact that, had Freud really meant a Russian, he would have capitalized *Ruso*. My solution to this puzzle is, of course, a conjecture; it cannot be proved. There are many similar instances.

The Academy was the setting Freud and Silberstein created for the furtherance of their friendship and common interests. It embraced their literary efforts, their need to give voice to the joys and sorrows of puberty, and their fondness for disguising things from others by giving them secret names. Thus they referred to the girls to whom they felt attracted as "principles," and developed a private mythology whose beginnings seem to go back to a shared journey from Roznau to Freiberg in the summer of 1871. In Freiberg, they were the guests of the Fluss family with whom the Freuds had been closely acquainted since their own Freiberg days. One of the seven Fluss children was Gisela, then not yet twelve years old, who came to take up the central place in their mythological web. Some six months later we meet her in the correspondence as "Ichthyosaura," a most misleading name for a clearly attractive young creature. Its meaning emerges from several other indications, for instance from Freud's signature of one of his letters as "Lord of the Lias and Prince of the Cretaceous" and from his referring to one Salter, an otherwise unidentified character, as "Iguanodon." These three jigsaw pieces provide us with the solution. Ichthyosaura as well as Iguanodon, the Lias as well as the Cretaceous, were taken from a poem by Josef Victor von Scheffel that was very popular in schoolboy and student circles at the time and later.[6] The key scene is played between Iguanodon and Ichthyosaura, and involves a kiss. It may be that Freud and Silberstein observed Herr Salter—no doubt in perfect innocence—kissing little Gisela one day, and thus arrived at their private mythology.

Freud later encountered Gisela again, in the summer of 1872—this time without Silberstein, a lucky circumstance to which we owe the letters of August 17 and September 4. Freud had fallen head over heels in love with her, but feigned near-indifference, hiding his true feelings behind the biblical quotation that people are altogether "brutish and foolish." A day after he had written the first letter, Gisela traveled back to Breslau, but that was not the end of the story. In his next letter from Freiberg, Freud returns to her, but now uses quite a different tactic to conceal his motives for writing. His early eruption of sexuality seems to have frightened him, as also happened later. On this occasion, he pretends that his affection lies with the mother, not with the daughter, that he has transferred his esteem for the mother to friendship for the daughter. Whereas he had originally admitted that his feelings were more than mere friendship, he now corrects himself and no longer admits to infatuation or love, having decided to renounce and abstain. We cannot believe him—least of all the claim that what he feels for the daughter is really intended for the mother. Even so, Eleonore Fluss, the daughter of an innkeeper from Karlsbad, must indeed have made a great impression on him. She was worldly, liberal, and modern after her own fashion, especially when it came to her children's education, and so had qualities Amalie Freud lacked. And because Freud valued these

6. The poem is reprinted in the Appendixes. K. R. Eissler has previously drawn attention to the connection with Scheffel, in "Creativity and Adolescence," *The Psychoanalytic Study of the Child* 33 (1978): 470.

qualities, Frau Fluss must have struck him as the kind of mother he would have preferred, a woman who had turned her back on the ghetto, who was capable of moving in the social circles he himself hoped to enter one day, and who, moreover, had no qualms about displaying her maternal love before the stranger who at the time felt like her son. He found it much easier to confess this admiration to Silberstein than to live with his feelings for Gisela.

We cannot tell if Gisela noticed what was happening to Freud. She went away, disappearing from his sight for many years, although not from his memory. He was able to impose abstinence on himself but not to erase his memory of her. Very much later, in 1899, he tried to interpret what had happened to him in his paper "Screen Memories."[7] Siegfried Bernfeld, without any knowledge of the letters to Silberstein, has remarked that the experiences and memories of the alleged patient were in fact Freud's own.[8] We can now tell that Freud's first experience of love was bound up not only with the wish for another mother but also with the wish that his father might have weathered the crisis in the wool trade as well as father Fluss, that they could have stayed on in Freiberg, that Jacob Freud could have been as successful as Ignaz Fluss, that he could have grown to know a life of bourgeois prosperity and would not always have had to abstain or deprive himself—economically at first but then sexually too. He did not love his poverty but came to terms with it; the effort needed to accept the renunciations imposed simultaneously by society and by himself was disproportionately greater.

In the summer vacation of 1875 Freud finally went to England to visit his two half-brothers in Manchester. The journey had been often planned and often postponed, perhaps because of the expense. While Freud wanted to go because he loved England, his father had quite different hopes for the visit. He hoped to wean his son from his high-flying scientific dreams and promised himself two things from the stay in England: that Sigmund would find business, which the two half-brothers pursued with greater success than their father, appealing, and that he would take a fancy to Pauline, whose story is

7. S.E., III, pp. 301–322.

8. In Siegfried Bernfeld and Suzanne Cassirer Bernfeld, *Bausteine der Freud-Biographik* (Foundations of Freudian biographical study), ed. I. Grubrich-Simitis, Frankfurt, 1981, pp. 93–311.

merged with Gisela's in "Screen Memories." Neither hope was to be
fulfilled; on the contrary, Freud dreamed dreams of a future in England where he would work miracles, supported by the press and by
rich benefactors. Perhaps practical work was to be preferred to theoretical studies after all. In any case, he was concerned about what
was to become of him. His mind was fully taken up with the search
for a vocation and the possibilities of extricating himself from his
pecuniary misery. The search for love does not seem to have preoc-
cupied him. However, when he returned to Vienna, something happened for which we have been unable to find a satisfactory explanation. In a strange way Freud put a stop to his youth, to his
youthful dreams and to everything connected with the Academy. He
buried the magic wand and moved forward into a new age "that has
no need of poetry and fantasy."

The trigger was the marriage of a "principle," that is, of a girl
whom he had once admired. The geological formation to which she
belonged, the Lias, had come to an end, and with it what Scheffel
called "the whole of the Saurian age." That girl was Gisela. He took
his leave from her, forever, gently alluding to *The Tempest* and hiding behind Prospero.[9] What had given him infinitely more pain than
pleasure was consigned to the past. Only now can we see how great
a hold his early infatuation, which he had taken so much trouble to
deny, had over him. All his concealed sorrow was as nothing compared with the sorrow of this separation. The "Epithalamium," with
its deliberately clumsy hexameters, lets us into the secret by turning the object of his love—at least partly—into an object of con-
tempt. To be able to forget, Freud must first destroy Gisela's image.
He turns the Thracian beauty into a blonde with a pumpkinlike
head; her once radiant eye now has never been pierced by learning's
rays. Ichthyosaura has become a conventional woman, a housewife,
no more—not desirable, in any case, and her interest in kosher
cooking, which Freud was in the habit of mocking, did not render
her more attractive to him. She seemed to be endowed with everything that Freud could not bear, so she was welcome to marry another and share his bridal couch.

But was all that really as it seemed? Was the parting really as pain-
less as his verse alleges? By chance, the letter to Silberstein contain-

---

9. See Eissler, "Creativity and Adolescence," p. 475.

ing the "Epithalamium" also contained a sheet of paper on which Freud had noted his first draft of the poem (see the Appendixes). Here everything is wild despair. Thoughts of suicide abound, and the idea of beholding "the faithful bride in another's arms" enrages him. So at least he claims, and his only solace is that she has married a descendent of Jacob, by which Freud meant not his father but the people of Israel.

Instead of the riddle now being solved, fresh and even more intractable, problems arise. From the letter he sent it is plain that Freud was conveying a piece of news—the marriage of a principle—to Silberstein, but the draft states that a letter from Silberstein (or from somebody else?) had cast "wretched abominable despair" into Freud's heart. Only one of the two can be correct. But which? Matters become even more complicated, because the sheet of draft paper contains further notes that refer to a planned journey to Lemberg. These lead to the supposition that Silberstein (whose relationship with the Fluss family was more straightforward) had also been invited to the wedding in Lemberg, and that Freud wanted to meet up with him at the station early in the morning. Silberstein would have been traveling there from Braila. In any event, nothing came of Freud's journey, either because of the death of Wahle's father or else because he did not have enough money for his ticket. The multiplication which is also to be found on the sheet of draft paper could have been an attempt to work out how much the rest of his English currency was worth.

If all this is correct, then Gisela would have been given away in marriage at the tender age of sixteen to a Lemberg businessman by the name of Rosenzweig. Now, no records of that marriage can be found, not even in Vienna, where Gisela lived later, on the evidence of "Screen Memories." No children from such a marriage appear in the register of the Israelitic Congregation. But an entry in the marriage records of the Leopoldstadt Congregation reveals that the spinster Gisela Fluss was married on February 27, 1881, to Emil Popper, a businessman from Pressburg.[10]

So it was all quite different. Either the marriage was called off at the last moment, contrary to all appearances, or else Rosenzweig

10. See Ernest Jones, *Sigmund Freud: Life and Work*, 4th ed., London: The Hogarth Press, 1980, vol. 1, p. 36, n. 3.

the businessman never existed and the trip to Lemberg must have had a different reason. In that case, the person Freud wanted to meet at the station could not have been Silberstein, but might have been a cousin from Cracow, or some other member of the family. In short, Gisela was neither to be married nor did she get married at that time; Freud invented the whole thing to rid himself of Gisela, to render her unattainable. He could not kill her off, not even poetically, and if someone had to be done away with then it had best be himself, but not even that in earnest. And so he married her off in order finally to forget her—but in vain, since "Screen Memories" indicates that he continued to feel deeply perturbed even after thirteen years of marriage. Because she seemed dangerous, Gisela was consigned to the dungeon of mythology from the very outset, yet the pattern of Freud's behavior did not alter even when the threat must have seemed less, as we may see from the following example. Before concluding his studies, Freud received a grant to do research into the reproductive organs of eels[11] in Trieste. It was his first stay in a southern country and he avidly absorbed the new impressions. On the first day he saw nothing but beautiful women, but after that he saw none. The beauties admittedly had a flaw: they adorned themselves with a lock of hair hanging over one eye, a fashion that was spreading to the "more dubious classes of society." Freud obviously decided that he must not allow himself to see any more beautiful women, and when he did all the same, quickly dismissed them as prostitutes—that is, escaped from them by rendering them untouchable, much as he rendered the rest of them ugly and hence undesirable. He had so internalized the constraints of his upbringing as to turn them into anxieties, which he could only counter with defense reactions and, of course, with instinctual renunciation.

Two and a half weeks later he went on an outing to Muggia and again told Silberstein at length about the women he saw there. The girls and children were very pretty and the women pleasing to behold, unlike those in Trieste. But then Trieste was close by, Muggia far away; he would not be returning there. Nevertheless his defenses were aroused, even in the little fishing village, in the form of so

11. The resulting study was published as "Beobachtung über Gestaltung und feineren Bau der als Hoden beschriebenen Lappenorgane des Aals" (Observations on the form and finer structure of the lobed organs of the eel, described as testes), *S.B.Akad.Wiss.Wien* (Math.-Naturwiss.Kl.), part I, 75 (1877): 419–431.

many midwives and pregnant women. That could only mean that they had to be avoided since the consequences were so patent. The price of possessing them was the disgrace of pregnancy, which affects both men and women, particularly in a region where the women seemed to be unusually fertile. Propagation, after all, was the subject with which he was occupied day in and day out.

The "Italian goddesses," he admitted, frightened him—as long as he saw them as such; he defended himself from that fear, steeled himself against temptation, and decided on abstinence, that is, self-deprivation. Later, during his long engagement, he came up against the southern world once again during a performance of *Carmen*, and this time his reaction was if anything even stronger, for self-evident reasons: "The mob gives vent to its appetites, and we deprive ourselves. We deprive ourselves in order to maintain our integrity . . ."[12] While deprivation never became a key concept of his theory, it cannot be ignored in his work. Thus he was to write of the individual in *The Future of an Illusion*: "The civilization in which he participates imposes some amount of privation on him."[13]

Freud was much harder on himself than he was on Silberstein, who had an altogether different temperament, did not suffer from constant lack of money, and seems to have had far fewer anxieties. Occasionally their differences led to tensions and opened a certain gulf between them. With his liking for flirts and worse, Silberstein must have struck Freud as something of a gay blade, and no doubt Freud considered his friend's inconstant heart a paltry thing on this faltering earth. He accordingly tried to lead him back to the path of virtue by many an admonition, changing into the pedagogue whenever he could not play the psychologist, as if he were just not months but generations older. What he voices on those occasions is a set of thoroughly bourgeois views on the relative freedom of men and the weakness of women who have "no inherent ethical standard." Even so, he is perspicacious enough to seek the cause of this weakness not simply in the essence of women but also to relate it to the role bourgeois society has assigned to them: they are punished longer and harder for the transgression of ethical norms than are the equally guilty men.

12. *Letters*, p. 65
13. S.E., XXI, p. 16.

One admonitory letter to Silberstein contains a biblical allegory with a double purpose. First, it draws Silberstein's attention to the fact that, if he does choose a wife, he must do so from among the daughters of Israel, and that one of the few commandments binding upon every Jew is Abraham's instruction to his servant not to "take a wife unto my son of the daughters of the Canaanites, among whom I dwell: But thou shalt go unto my country, and to my kindred." Second, Freud uses the allegory to express a wish that can only be understood by comparing it with the biblical passage. Freud, not Genesis, brings in mention of a portrait ("of one of the maidens that dwell in the land of my fathers"). What Freud is asking Silberstein for in this way is a photograph of Gisela.

Freud was proud of his allegory; it brought up something not otherwise mentioned between the two friends, namely his Jewishness, which he never denied as long as he lived. True, he was a "completely godless Jew,"[14] even in his youth, but an avowed Jew nonetheless. Not because of the creed, the countless commandments and prohibitions, albeit they did leave some slight impression upon him, but because of his conviction that someone born a Jew could never cease to be one. Jewishness was, so to speak, an indelible characteristic.

The Leopoldstadt Gymnasium he attended was a mixed school. In the lower classes Gentiles predominated, and in the higher classes there was a preponderance of Jews, but Freud's friends were all Jews without exception, and the same was true of his university years, even among Brücke's assistants. Silberstein, it seems, followed a slightly different pattern. Freud did share in the slow process of emancipation and the incomplete extension of civic equality which made possible his gradual advancement until 1938, but in his youth he made no attempt to break out of what was always a kind of ghetto. This came later, and was not always propitious for him.

He was attached to his people, though not to their religion, with which, right up to *Moses and Monotheism*,[15] he never ceased to take issue. Unlike his father, he did not learn Hebrew, and he had no more than a smattering of his mother's Yiddish. His biblical quota-

14. Heinrich Meng and Ernst L. Freud, eds., *Psycho-Analysis and Faith: The Letters of Sigmund Freud and Oskar Pfister*, trans. Eric Mosbacher, London: The Hogarth Press, 1963, p. 63.

15. S.E., XXIII, pp. 7–137.

tions suggest that he read the Bible in Luther's translation, when he might have been expected to be more familiar with Philippson's version. And though he did remember some of the Jewish high holidays, he hardly did so in a way suggesting Jewish orthodoxy.[16] But then, even Jacob Freud must have moved a long way from his own father's piety, which is not to say that Jews at the time did not prefer to keep their own company. Despite outward appearances, this remained the same a generation later.[17]

A limited Jewish education was imparted to Freud at home; all other forms of education evidently at school. It was there that he must have developed his passion for reading, and the foundation must have been laid for his love of belles-lettres. However, his letters to Silberstein do not reveal that that he was assimilating more than the curriculum demanded. References to his reading matter are at first sparse and do not become more common until his university years.[18] But even then, his reading of Schiller, Goethe, Heine, and Shakespeare, and also of Freytag and Auerbach or even Hebbel's plays, in no way differed from what the educated world at large was reading in Germany at the time. At best it is his predilection for the two atheists, Börne and Lichtenberg, that sounds like his own choice. Macaulay, on the other hand, whom he held in such high regard, was a favorite writer of the educated middle class. The dialogue of the two stars may suggest that Freud had read Leopardi's *Dialogo della Terra e della Luna*, but this seems unlikely because that work had not yet been translated into German; more probably it was prompted by his favorite author, Dr. Mises, of whose writing many more of its ideas are reminiscent. Naturally the letters to Silberstein do not contain full details of what Freud read from 1870 to 1880, but we can infer a great deal from his unacknowledged quotations. Most are scattered in the body of the letters without the

16. See Peter Gay, *A Godless Jew: Freud, Atheism, and the Making of Psychoanalysis*, New Haven, Conn.: Yale University Press, 1987, p. 125. Gay depicts the Freud household as more secular. See his bibliography for further references.

17. See Gershom Scholem, "Zur Sozialpsychologie der Juden in Deutschland, 1900–1930" (On the social psychology of the Jews in Germany, 1900–1930), in *Judaica IV*, Frankfurt, 1984, p. 242.

18. See Peter Brückner, *Sigmund Freuds Privatlektüre* (Sigmund Freud's private reading), Cologne, 1975. Brückner confines himself to a few authors from a later period.

slightest hint that they are not Freud's own words. And often they
are not entirely word-perfect, which did not prevent quite a few of
them recurring regularly, as a kind of stock-in-trade, in Freud's later
writing.[19]

Freud extended his store of general knowledge during his pro-
longed university studies much more energetically than when he
was at school. Besides literature, he was particularly attracted to philosophy, a subject he read systematically with his friend Paneth.
How great an impression Brentano made on him is shown by the
extensive treatment of the problem of God's existence in the correspondence. It was probably only during that period that Freud ever
wavered and wondered whether God might exist after all, whether
what he had but recently declared dead might yet be alive and sus-
ceptible to proof. However, it was apparently not Brentano who left
the deepest impression on Freud, but Feuerbach. "Feuerbach," he
wrote to Silberstein in March 1875, is "one whom I revere and admire above all other philosophers." For all that, Freud later denied
his debt to him, as he denied his debt to others. To a question by
Ludwig Binswanger, he replied in 1925: "I certainly read David
Friedrich Strauss and Feuerbach with enjoyment and enthusiasm in
my younger years. But it strikes me that the effect has not been a
lasting one."[20] More remarkable still is the omission of Feuerbach
from *The Future of an Illusion*, in which he is dismissed with the
remark that "I should not like to give an impression that I am seeking to rank myself as one of them" (Feuerbach, certainly Strauss,
probably Nietzsche, and possibly Marx).[21]

Which of Feuerbach's writings Freud read, apart from Karl Grün's
compilation, we cannot tell for certain, though they undoubtedly
included *Das Wesen das Christentums* (The Essence of Christian-
ity) and very likely *Theogonie* as well. Not only his critique of religion but also his dream theory are fed from this source. In Feuerbach's "God is the manifest soul, the expressed self of man; religion

19. For Freud's use of quotations, see Walter Schönau, *Sigmund Freuds Prosa* (Sigmund Freud's prose), Stuttgart, 1968, pp. 98ff.

20. Wilhelm Hemecker, *Philosophiegeschichtliche Voraussetzungen der Psychoanalyse Sigmund Freuds* (The philosophical and historical assumptions of Sigmund Freud's psychoanalysis), inaugural dissertation, Graz, 1987, p. 82.

21. S.E., XXI, p. 35.

the solemn revelation of man's hidden treasures, the confession of his innermost thoughts, the public avowal of his love secrets," he needed only to replace God or religion with the unconscious to arrive at a basic concept of psychoanalysis.

Walter Boehlich

Letters

Overleaf: Seal of the Academía Española. The reversal of letters during printing was presumably not taken into account by the friends who made the seal.

Official Section

The sender has just been instructed to request Herr Eduard Silberstein to make the following suggestion to his mother: Herr and Frau Freud[1] would be prepared* to lodge him and his brother Karl** and to provide them with a room in the new apartment[2] to which they will be moving in two months' time, and also to sign their sick notes for school*** and to establish whether our luncheons, etc., are to their liking. The sender accordingly requests that the recipient bring this application to the notice of his mother.

Sender

*As far as the sender knows, the others have no objection either.
**who is said to be a proper little terror.
***which will not be required, I hope.

1. Jacob Freud (1815–1896) and Amalie, née Nathanson (1835–1930).
2. Freud is presumably referring to his family's move from 30 Glockengasse to 5 Pfeffergasse, which took place in 1869 or 1870.

Vienna, July 12 or December 27, 1871[1]

To the Birthday Child

My teeth are giving me great pain and prevent me from keeping my promise. Please come to my house so that the lessons in the x x x language are not disturbed, and I shall not be without your company. Neither I nor the others will bother you much with congratulations.

I remain your devoted servant
Sigmund Freud

Postcard; in Latin
    1. Eduard Silberstein's birthday was on December 27; the card is postmarked July
12.

Viennae, 12.7. oder 27.12.1871

Ad Jubilarem

Magnis doloribus me dentes afficiunt atque ne—promissa teneam, impediunt.
Venias quaeso ad domicilium meum, ne instructio x x x linguae turbetur, neve ego
consuetudinis tuae caream.—Neque ego, neque alteri felicitationibus te multum mo-
lestabimus.

Quedo su atento servidor
Sigmund Freud

[Vienna,] December 12, 1871

I beg Your Honor to go down to the seventh class tomorrow, as I
shan't have the time to go to it.

I remain your devoted servant
Cipion

[in pencil, probably by another hand:]
    Guillaume de Champeaux et ses écoles[1]
    Lettres sur l'histoire des français par Thierry[2]
    Paul et Virginie par Bernardin de Saint-Pierre[3]

Postcard; in Spanish
    1. E. Michaud, *Guillaume de Champeaux et les Ecoles de Paris au XIIe siècle*
(Guillaume de Champeaux and the Schools of Paris in the twelfth century), Paris,
1867.
    2. Augustin Thierry, *Lettres sur l'histoire de France* (Letters on the history of
France), Paris, 1827.
    3. First published in 1787.

12.12.1871

Le ruego á Vm, que vine mañana debajo á la setima clase, porqué no habrá tiempo de venir á el.

Quedo su atento servidor
Cipion

———————

[Vienna, December 31, 1871]

Dear Eduard,   *Official*

Mother was very cross when she heard that you did not want to come over. She had already told your mother that you would be with us on New Year's Eve. We expect you without fail. Remember how glorious it is to bring oneself to do something for others.

Amalia Freud[1]

Please *do* come

Postcard
1. Not in Freud's handwriting (except for the address); probably written by Amalie, or perhaps by Jacob, Freud.

———————

Vienna, January 19, 1872

It is with great pleasure that I take the opportunity of writing you the first letter of this year.

I am ill and cannot go to school.

I beg you to come and see me at four o'clock. I have another commission for you. Please pay Theuman[1] thirty maravedis for the first delivery. It will be returned to you with many thanks.

Please bring it to me (the delivery)

Yours
Braganza

Postcard; in Spanish
  1. Jacob Theumann (b. 1855), one of Silberstein's classmates.

Vienna, 19.1.1872

Asgo con mucho gusto la ocasión de escribiros la primera carta en este año—
Estoi enfermo, no puedo andar á la escuela—
Os ruego, vengais á mi a las cuatro de la tarde—Tengo aun otra comision para
vosotros. Pagád á Theuman treinte marav. para la primera libracion, que ha de
traerme—Se le volverán á vosotros con grandes gracias—
  Traedmalo (la libracion)

Su
Braganza

[Vienna, January 30, 1872]

I have chanced upon the two sisters, one of whom is Löw's[1] celebrated love. How wrong I have been! Because the picture of her Your
Honor painted for me was all wrong! I expected to see a heroic and
vengeful maid and what I found was a plain, plump, and cheerful
girl. In short, she does not compare with Ichth.[2]

Your Honor's friend
Cipion

Postcard; in Spanish
  1. Konrad Löw (b. 1856), one of Silberstein's classmates.
  2. Ichthyosaura, code name for Gisela Fluss (b. September 26, 1859). See the Introduction.

Acaso he visto á las dos Hermanas entre las cuales está la celebrada querida de
Löw—¡Que estoi engeñado! ¡Que no está adecuada la imagen, que me pintaba Vm.
de ella! Esperaba á ver á una virgen heroica y vengativa y ví á una moza sencilla, gorda
y alegre—En conclusion no se la puede igualar á Ichth.

Su amigo de Vm.
Cipion

Vienna, March 25, 1872[1]

Today I chanced upon Ichth.'s brother, Ichthyosaurus communis L. He greeted me with a finger. I cannot tell you how sorry I am that it wasn't "her"—as seeing him wasn't worth a brass farthing.

Yours
Cipion

Please forgive the nonsense I have just written.

[on the other side of the card:]
    fressen: cañamo [to feed: hemp[2]]
    trinken: agua [to drink: water]
    schreiben: zapato [to write: boot[3]]
    Muse: loba [muse: she-wolf [4]]

Postcard; in Spanish and Italian
    1. Freud wrote *martes* (Tuesday) instead of *marzo* (March).
    2. Meaning a meager diet, a reference either to bird seed or to the hemp soup of Eastern Europe.
    3. The German *Stiefel* (boot) also means nonsense. Tr.
    4. The Spanish word also means a plain woman.

Vienna, 25 Martes 1872

Hoi me topé casualmente con el hermano de la Ichth.—Ichtyosaurus comm. L.— Saludaba de un dedo—No puedo decir, cuanto me pesa el no haber sido—"ella"— Pues no recibiré un cuarto por haber vistole.

Su
Cipion

Que me tengas perdonado que he escrito tal zapato.

    Oggi incontrai per istrada il fratello della "Ichthyosaura."
    Salutava d'un ditto—
    Non posso dicerle quanto mi rincresce ché non era ella—
    Non riceverò un quarto por aver vistolo—

Vienna, July 27, 1872

Dear Berganza,

How can you tell that you were the first?[1] And, if you can, why blame my sisters for telling me? Are you mocking me? Or is it true? I wish it were, and thank providence for having removed all the causes you might have had for killing yourself. To think that you were "the chosen and the first without knowing it." How well off you are! You have just visited your aunt and I have not seen Ichth. for two weeks.

Your unfortunate
Cipion

Postcard; in Spanish
   1. Probably the first to have been kissed.

Vienna, el 27.7.1872

Querido Berganza
   ¡Como puede V. saber que está el primero?[1] ¡Y si V. lo sabe, porqué reprobar á mis hermanas de decirme el motivo? ¿Se burla V. de mí? ¿O es verdad? Deseo, que fuese, y digo gracias a la fortuna de haber abstraido todas las causas que V. tuviese para matarse. V. fué "diputado y primero sin una noción de serlo"—¡Que V. está feliz! V. acaba de visitar á su tia y yo no he visto á Ichth. desde dos semanas.

Su desgraciado
Cipion

Vienna, August 3, 1872

◦§ Before the departure

Dear Berganza,

I am writing promptly after receiving your most pleasant letter, availing myself of what little time is left before I leave. I am very pleased that you accept my proposals, except for the articles involving Ichth. and the foreign connections. Regarding these I am not very sad to learn that they do not suit you, the first concerning myself alone and the third being your business. You can imagine in how much of a hurry we are, doing the packing and making all the necessary preparations, but let us say no more of that as it is neither cheering nor amusing.

As to my traveling companion, I have the most amusing things to report. I intend to make him fall in love with his presumed sweetheart, Amorska,[1] and to that end I spend all day telling him things about Roznau that have to do with her. He already thinks of nothing but her, sighing and perishing with love. He can't wait to get to Freiberg, but only as a springboard for reaching Roznau. You already know whether or not I shall introduce him to the true Amorska, who, moreover, is not even there!

You will shortly receive detailed reports on my (or our) stay in Freiberg (Montelibre, as it will be called in the records of the Spanish Academy) but first I await your news, believing as I do that in the peace and quiet of our homeland (Montelibre and Braila) we shall find much to write about, provided desire so prompts us. I hope that now, as in the future, you will keep the promise you have made to your

Cipion

My letters will look better once I am in Montelibre. If you have not yet been tired out by my wretched Spanish, turn over and you will discover a memorable piece in German: 🙦

Description of our adventures after the departure of D. Berganza.

Our situation on the small vessel Ebersdorf was indeed desperate. We had the misfortune of first addressing a short man with a white cap as a porter and then, having realized our mistake, as Captain. Incensed, the little fellow bridled, informed us that he was the navigator and, in revenge, filled our imagination with such terrible scenes that we were convinced we would be marooned on the island as fodder for wild animals. It turned out otherwise, however, for the captain, sensible of his worth and hence a man of civility, had two sailors take us to the other bank of the Danube Canal, and granted us the pleasure of a "dinghy" crossing after all those alarms. Disembarkation was our sole desire, in order to wet our whistles, for both

of us were parched. And lo! "God does not desert the honest Jew,"
as the Jews have it, or "God does not desert the honest German," as
the Germans have it, or "—the honest Frenchman," as the French
have it etc. etc., in short, we chanced upon a thicket filled with
pitch-black and plum-blue blackberries. "Let us spread a veil over
what happened next; anyone who has been in a like situation may
easily imagine the scene," as they say in novels. When we had had
our fill, we bounded off to the nearest Freudenau[2] hostelry, where
we both ate three helpings of bread and butter—and came upon a
party of small boys from St. Joseph's School, with all the familiar
teachers: Teufelsberger, Schopf[3] & & &—the little tummies coped
with the bread and butter as if it were bonbons. Two of the teachers
had brought their wives along to help with the spreading; I took
them for the landladies, and asked for buttered bread. Since, however, I struck them as being too tall to be numbered amongst their
little company, they refused me politely and referred me to the
kitchen. Once we had done [Remainder missing.]

First portion in Spanish
    1. Probably from "amor" with a made-up Czech feminine ending, intended to
mean "beloved."
    2. Southeast of Vienna, between the Danube and the Danube Canal.
    3. Probably Alois Teugelberger and Johann Schopf.

Vienna, el 3.8.1872

Antes del partido
Querido Berganza

    Os escribo pronto despues de recibida vuestra carta gratísima, aprovechandome del
poco tiempo, que me queda antes del partido. Estoy mui alegre de que aconsentais á
mis propuestas, escepto los articulos de la Ichth. y de los enlaces ajenos. Que cuanto
á esos no me atristo mucho de que no os convienen, los primeros tocan solamente a
mi, y el tercero es cosa vuestra. Ya podeis imaginaros, cuanto estamos de prisa para
encajonar (einpacken) y preparar todo lo necesario, pero de eso no hablemos, pues no
es cosa, que os pudiese alegrar ó divertir.
    Mas de mi compañero de viaje, os tengo que referir las cosas mas chistosas—In-
tento hacerle aficionarse á su querida presunta, la Amorska y a ese fin le cuento todo
el dia acaecimientos de Roznau tocantes á ella. Ya no piensa que en ella, ya suspira y
se perece de amor. El está apasionado de irse á Freiberg pero soltanto lo cree un pied-
à-terre para lograr á Roznau. Vosotros ya sabeis, si le monstraré la Amorska verdadera
ó no, ademas que ni siquiera está allí!!
    En poco tendreis relatos muy minuciosos de mi (ó nuestra) demora en Freiberg

(Montelibre como se llamerá en l.p.d.l. A.E.) pero antes estoy aguardando vuestras nuevas y creo, que en la quietud y ociosidad de la patria (Montelibre y Braila) ya tendremos materia de escribiros, puesto que el desiderio nos precise á hacerlo—Espero, que esa vez como todas las vinideras cumplireis con el aconsiento, que habeis hecho á la ventaja de vuestro

Cipion

Tendran mejor facha mis cartas cuando estaré en Montelibre—Si aun no estais cansado del miserable Castellano, volvais la hoja y hallaréis en alemán un escrito muy memorable:

Freiberg, August 9, 1872

Dear Berganza,

A week has passed since your last letter and I have heard nothing from Your Honor since. I do not know what to make of that; I cannot take offence as Your Honor has not written to the Italian master or to any other of our acquaintances; there is nothing left to me but to fret at your fickleness, or to shudder at your fate. Though I am not so squeamish as to be disturbed by such neglect, I cannot help thinking that you may have been stricken by something, the nature of which I cannot guess. For that reason, and because I do not know whether this note will reach Your Honor, I do not propose to tell Your Honor about my diversions and pastimes; there are more important things at present to concern me, and the most important of all is to know whether Your Honor has gone to Hell. If so, I do not want a reply, but if not, may Your Honor remember his promise to see to the matters I charged him with on board the Neptune.

To keep Your Honor informed about my own life, I am preparing a small travel diary into which all the outings I shall ever make will be crammed. I think of Your Honor every day, and yesterday, finding myself at the inn in Hochwald[1] (a paradise without equal, as you will soon observe), I scored two Spanish lines on the table to perpetuate your name "D. Berganza."

Once I have received confirmation that you are alive and have read my letters, I shall cover some six quarto sheets of paper, so much do I have to tell you. I have still not seen Roznau.

Looking forward to lengthy and detailed letters
D. Cipion
member of the S.S.S.[2]

In Spanish
1. A popular tourist spot twelve miles north of Roznau, with a famous ruined castle.
2. Possibly an abbreviation for Spanische Sprach-Schule (Spanish language school). See the Introduction.

Freiberg, den 9. August 1872

Querido Berganza,

Ya hay una semana que recibí la ultima carta suya y desde ese tiempo no he sentido nada de Vm.; no sé que hacer de eso, no puedo ofenderme, pues ni ha escrito Vm al maestro italiano, ni á otro de nuestros conocidos; no me queda otra cosa que apurarme de su ligereza ó estremecerme de su suerte. Aunque no soy hombre melindroso para inquietarme de tal descuidado, no puedo yo detener el pensamiento, que se lo haya encontrado un mal, de maniera, la que no puedo adivinar—Y por esa razon, por no saber yo, si ó como Vm recibirá esa cartilla no quiero referirle á Vm de mis divertimientos y pasatiempos, ahora me tocan cosas mas importantes y lo mas importante es saber ¿si Vm ya ha bajado á los infiernos ó nó? Si aquello, no quiero respuesta, pero si no, recuerdese Vm. de su promesa de cumplir con los articulos, que le he dado en borde del Neptun.

Para informar á Vm. de mi vida, preparo un librito de viaje, en qué se hallarán borradas todas las partidas, que jamas emprenderé—Pienso á Vm todos los dias y ayer, estando en la venta del lugar Hochwald (paraiso sin semejante; de lo que sentiréis en seguida), escribí en la mesa dos renglones castellanos y hice memoria de vuestro nombre "D. Berganza".

Recibida una vez la aseguracion, que vivís y leéis mis cartas, os escribiré unas de 6 cuartos de papel, tanto tengo que contar. Aun no he visto a Roznau.

Espero vuestras cartas estendidas y exactas
D Cipion
de la S.S.S.

Freiberg, August 17, 1872

Dear Berganza,

Your last letter showed me how wrong I have been to accuse you of neglecting your friend, but I hope you will forgive my impatience, which cannot get used to the idea that news from one takes five days to reach the other. Let me say in advance that I shall not make mention of my travels in our correspondence; I have more important matters to relate. All the same, I am keeping a travel diary just for you from which you will gather more than you really ought to know. Your letter gave me great pleasure, on the one hand because it tells me that you have been converted to ice cream, and on the other because I am delighted at your brilliant championship of the S.S.S. The sample of Turkish money, which you meant to enclose, was not there. I notice that you have only let me have a selection from your experiences, but you have kept your thoughts to yourself. I hope that your telling of them will more than make up for this. My position here would be splendid were I a different sort of person; I was given a warm reception, have been on pleasant outings, and have been well entertained. However, I tend toward some slight dissatisfaction; our evening saunters and nocturnal visits have so accustomed me to communication that I find it hard to do without it now. That Rosanes[1] is a poor listener is something you do not need to be told. He is, incidentally, becoming very popular among the young people here, whom I shall describe to you anon, and has many of our Mascial's characteristics, save his vitality. It is my need for communication which is causing me to write the diary you will be reading in the first week of the school year. It contains little you will find incomprehensible; yesterday and the day before I wrote so frankly in my annoyance as I would never have thought myself capable of. I shall try to be just as frank now, in the confident belief that no one else will catch a glimpse of this letter. I shall try to make my confessions easier by framing them in our official language.

Your Honor may remember a youth by the name of Emil, head of the dyeworks,[2] who tried to render relations with Ich. palatable to me even then. That young man is a favorite of mine; I find him honest, very discreet, capable of noble sentiments and quite devoid of those materialistic principles that only elevate man by minimizing his pettiness. One day, or rather: one night (Your Honor will find the details in my diary), I made him privy to the saurian myth of Roznau, asking him if he still hankered after Ichth. He denied it in good faith and in exchange told me the story of his declaration of love to a certain Ottilie.[3]

This amusing story, told with the utmost naivety, delighted me greatly, and I believe that for as long as I stay here I shall not be wanting for entertaining material. Moreover, although he tried to provoke me, I did not feel hurt by his taunts, for reasons Your Honor will soon come to know.

There is another youth here, by the name of Richard,[4] our constant traveling companion, rather lazy, rather slow, rather droll. He has done his lower studies at the Gymnasium, was a good pupil, and will continue his education in a place called Seldnitz or Segnitz[5] in Bavaria. The third son[6] I might call the little one, he is sensible and rather timid.

Now for the girls. There are four of them and we shall be speaking of three. However, I have tired myself out writing of things in Spanish that do not deserve it and must now speak of other things which deserve it more, in German. Why then should we speak of only three girls when there are four? Did I not promise Your Honor to open myself up to you? Let us be frank, who could read this short letter except Your Honor? ⊱

I regret that I have divided my forces and do not intend to repeat what is, in any case, recorded in my diary, so let me just say, ⊰ that I took a fancy to the eldest, by the name of Gisela, who leaves tomorrow, and that her absence will give me back a sense of security about my behavior that I have not had up to now. Knowing my character, Your Honor will rightly think that instead of approaching her I have held back, and nobody, not even she, knows any more about it than His Majesty, the King of the Turks. I am not afraid of making myself ridiculous by telling Your Honor all this because Your Honor knows that people are altogether brutish and foolish, and would to God it were the last of our foolishness! But remember your duty not to let these notes fall into anyone else's hands if you want me to speak of my feelings again. When we reach the end of the road, we shall be laughing at all this as at everything else, because that is all it is worth, but I trust that my friendship merits a prompt reply, what with a distance of two hundred miles between us. ⊱

And now—I have had enough of this dry tone—isn't life one of the strangest things in the world?

⊰ The news has just reached me that Herr Iguanodon (Salter)[7] is with us. I still haven't been to Roznau, but have decided to go this week. Your Honor may have gathered that all is not well. ⊱

I conclude this letter, the greatest piece of nonsense the A.E. has ever produced, with cordial regards to your parents, and remain

Your

Cipion

I have had one letter from home. Everyone is well. Anna wrote to me "since that is all I may impart to a brother, I send you cordial greetings and remain . . . ["]

Portions in Spanish

1. Horaz Ignaz Rosanes (1857–1922), one of Silberstein's classmates, later director of the Stephanie Hospital in Vienna. In 1895 he assisted Freud in the Emma Eckstein case; see Jeffrey M. Masson, ed., *The Complete Letters of Sigmund Freud to Wilhelm Fliess, 1887–1904*, Cambridge, Mass.: Harvard University Press, 1985, pp. 116ff.

2. Emil Fluss (b. October 8, 1856); the reference is to Emil's work in his father's textile and woollen factory.

3. In 1891 Emil Fluss married another Ottilie, namely Ottilie Mandl, née Prosnitz (b. March 19, 1867). See Freud's letter to Emil Fluss dated February 7, 1873, in Ilse Grubrich-Simitis, ed., *"Selbstdarstellung": Schriften zur Geschichte der Psychoanalyse* ("Self-Representation": Writings on the history of psychoanalysis), Frankfurt, 1971, pp. 111ff.

4. Richard Fluss.

5. Near Kaufungen on the Main river. Italo Svevo (1862–1928), who took an early interest in psychoanalysis—as witness his last novel, *La coscienza di Zeno* (1923)—attended the same institute from 1873 to 1878. See J. Pouillon, "La conscience de Zeno, roman d'une psychanalyse," *Les temps modernes* 10 (1954).

6. Alfred Fluss.

7. Not identified. See the Introduction.

Vm se recuerda de un joven llamado Emil, jefe de la tintura, el cual ya entonces tentó embocarme enlazos con Ich.—Ese joven es mi favorito, le hallo hombre de bien, muy discreto y capaz de sentimientos nobles, con no poseer él esos principios materialisticos, que solos elevan el hombre, humillando su pequeñez. Un dia, es decir: una noche (los pormenores hallará Vm en el Tagebuch) le he descubierto el mito saurico de Roznau, preguntandole, si todavia tuviese inclinacion por Ichth. Lo ha negado de buena conciencia y de trueque me ha contado la historia de sus requiebros á cierta Otilia.

Esa historia chistosa, referida con la mayor naividad, me ha deleitado muchisimo y creo que por el tiempo de mi morada no me faltará materia de divertimiento. Por ademas ensayando él provocarme, no me siento herido de sus pullas (Sticheleien) por razones, que en poco tiempo Vm sabrá.

Otro joven hay, llamado Ricardo, compañero perpetuo de nuestros viajes, un poco perezoso, un poco lento, un poco chistoso. Ha acabado la parte inferior del gimnasio,

era buen alumno y continuará sus estudios en el lugar de Seldnitz ó Segnitz en la
Bavaria. El tercer hijo puedo llamar chiquito, es cuerdo y un poco temerario—
Vamos a las niñas. Cuatro hay y de tres hablaremos. Pero me ha cansado mucho el
escribir tales cosas, que no lo merecen, en lengua castellana y me veo precisado á
decir otras que mas lo mereciesen en aleman. Y porque solo hablariamos de tres, si
cuatro son? ¿No le he prometido de abrirme a Vm.? Hablemos francamente. ¿Quien
podria leer esa cartilla escepto Vm?

... que he tomado inclinacion para la mayor llamada Guisela que partirá mañana y
esa ausencia me devolverá una firmedad de la conducta que hasta aqui no he conocido—Vm, considerando mi caracter proprio, se imaginará con razon que en vez de
avicinarme, me he alejado de ella y nadie, ni ella misma siquiera, sabe de eso mas que
su majestad el Rey de los Turcos. No temo seros ridiculo informandoos de eso, porque
sabeis, como todos somos locos y tontos y necios y ojalá que fuese la ultima necedad
nuestra! Pero ahora os toca el deber de no dejar mis cartillas en mano de ninguno,
supuesto si quereis, que continue hablar de mis sentimientos. Y, llegados á la fin
reiamos de eso, como de todo otro, porqué no merece mas, pero espero, que mi amistad merece una respuesta veloz, pensando á la distancia de doscientos miliares entre
nosotros.

En ese momento me viene la nueva, que el Señor Iguanodon (Salter) está en la casa
nuestra, aun no he sido en Roznau, pero he tomado la resolucion de ir acá esa semana.
Vm concibe que no buenas estan las cosas.

Freiberg, September 4, 1872

Queridisimo Berganza!

It is only with reluctance that I forgive you for writing me so little
about yourself, but a touching resignation reflected in every line of
your letter makes me refrain from asking more of you than you can
accomplish. Perhaps things are much the same with you as they are
with me. You feel suddenly torn out of your familiar and beloved
circle, and no doubt are not busy enough in Braila for the pain of
your loss to be dulled.

You do me an injustice when you call my mood gloomy and sad—
blame it upon my nonsensical style, which, if that indeed is the
impression my last letter conveyed, never allows me to say what I

Sigmund Freud in 1872,
at the age of sixteen

mean. I am more lighthearted than ever and only in unguarded mo-
ments am I seized by that forlorn mood. I have spared no means to
keep you informed of my life in Freiberg. You will find me an informative oral source and my notebook and diary a written source, and
these will relate the events of this month more than amply. [I] expect the same from you by word of mouth, and hope to meet you in

Vienna before October first; I myself shall be leaving on the fifteenth, so please send your next letter to Vienna and let me know the precise day of your arrival. Then we shall continue our secret studies with renewed strength and forge a new bond. I am weary of all those evenings spent strolling around the town in the company of others; as long as I have time to spare, I should prefer to spend it with you alone. I suspect we have enough to tell each other to dispense with a third for an audience. These days, I get hardly any Spanish practice. You write your nocturnes to me in German and I myself have long since written the last Spanish word in my diary. I felt the urge to speak my mind fully and that I could only do in the mother tongue.

A strange letter, you will exclaim, not a word about what has been occupying me most of the time, not a mention of the ideas that above all I associate with thoughts of him. Let me tell you everything straightaway. On Wednesday, after I had written to you, she departed, not without playing me a trick that annoyed me for some time. I said good-bye sadly and walked to Hochwald, my little paradise, where I spent a most pleasant hour. I have soothed all my turbulent thoughts and only flinch slightly when her mother mentions Gisela's name at table. The affection appeared like a beautiful spring day, and only the nonsensical Hamlet in me, my diffidence, stood in the way of my finding it a refreshing pleasure to converse with the half-naive, half-cultured young lady.

One day I shall explain to you the difference between my affection and another passion at some length; for the moment let me just add that I did not suffer any conflict between ideal and reality, and that I am incapable of making fun of Gisela. So please avoid all allusions to her in the presence of Rosanes or others. His wit is like a distorting mirror; he must ridicule everything in order to render it ridiculous; he has no feeling for frankness or purity; where others find children lovable, he invariably finds them ridiculous; he has no aspirations, but is a coarse egoist; his ideal would be to live well, to be held in high regard, and to mock at the unfamiliar. I must add, however, that he is quick to respect that which is beyond his understanding, or at least that it is easy to instill respect in him. He could never feel passionate, has never fathomed our friendship, and if he ever discovered our hearts' affections his first reaction would be to laugh and his second to be astonished. I get along with him quite well, but we are never really close. I have put you in his place a thousand

times, thinking how differently you would have behaved toward the
others. But I have strayed from the subject dear to me; it would seem
that I have transferred my esteem for the mother to friendship for
the daughter. I am, or consider myself to be, a keen observer; my life
in a large family circle, in which so many characters develop, has
sharpened my eye, and I am full of admiration for this woman whom
none of her children can fully match.

Would you believe that this woman from a middle-class back-
ground, who once lived in fairly straitened circumstances, has acquired an education of which a nineteen-year-old salon-bred young
thing need not be ashamed? She has read a great deal, including the
classics, and what she has not read she is conversant with. Hardly a
branch of knowledge not too remote from the middle classes is foreign to her, and though she cannot, of course, have a solid grounding
in everything, she has sound judgment. Yet she frankly admits that
in Freiberg one can unlearn everything and learn nothing new. She
is even knowledgeable about politics, participates fully in the affairs
of the little town, and, I think, it is she above all who is guiding the
household into the modern mainstream. But don't therefore take
her for a frustrated bluestocking. I have seen for myself that she
plays as large a part in running the business as Herr Fluss, and I am
fully convinced that all the factory workers obey her as they do him
and that she can give orders equally well and even more decisively.
And you should see how she has brought up and continues to bring
up her seven children, how they, the older more so than the younger,
obey her, how no concern of any of them ceases to be hers. None of
the children has a horizon beyond her own. I have never seen *such*
superiority before. Other mothers—and why disguise the fact that
our own are among them? We shan't love them the less for it—care
only for the physical well-being of their sons; when it comes to their
intellectual development the control is out of their hands. Frau
Fluss knows no sphere that is beyond her influence. And you should
see the love of the children for their parents and the eagerness with
which the servants do her bidding. I cannot blame her for liking
Gisela best; she is the first of the daughters to enjoy a broader education and was, so to speak, a guest in the house. I have never seen
her in a bad mood, or rather, vent her mood on the innocent. She
punishes the children with looks and by withholding little favors,
working on their sense of honor and not on their behinds, the
youngest alone occasionally enjoying the benefit of the maternal

hand; she herself is the first to admit that this is not the way to keep the child under control, and that besides she never strikes her on the right place. She keeps a house that is hospitable beyond all measure, and is so kind a hostess that she has drawn us into her most intimate family circle. After supper we always stay on upstairs, until everyone sinks into the arms of sleep. A few days ago I had a terrible attack of toothache. I was raving the whole day, and having tried every remedy in vain, I took some pure alcohol to deaden the pain. This occurred downstairs in Emil's dye shop; she knew little of my indisposition. I soon fell asleep, or rather, passed out. Emil had me taken upstairs, the severe shock on an empty stomach did the rest; I vomited violently but lost the toothache as I'd wanted. Not that the hangover or the vomiting had been deliberate, but once it had happened she cared for me as for her own child. The doctor was called, I slept upstairs that night, and got up the next morning well and without toothache. She asked me how I had slept. Badly, I replied, I didn't sleep a wink. Or so it had seemed to me. Smiling, she said, I came to see you twice during the night, and you never noticed. I felt ashamed. I cannot possibly deserve all the kindness and goodness she has been showing me. She fully appreciates that I need encouragement before I speak or bestir myself, and she never fails to give it. That's how her superiority shows itself: as she directs so I speak and come out of my shell. I shall carry away an insight [?] and memories of a good and noble person, and show my gratitude, in my way, by making you privy to the high regard in which I hold her.

She can never have been beautiful, but a witty, jaunty fire must always have sparkled in her eyes, as it does now. Gisela's beauty, too, is wild, I might say Thracian: the aquiline nose, the long black hair, and the firm lips come from the mother, the dark complexion and the sometimes indifferent expression from the father.

But enough; you can see how the words pour from my heart and the letters from my pen. Let me say a word about the history of the SSS [?]. That Iguanodon dined with us you know from my last letter; it merely increased my desire to come to Roznau but my lazy traveling companions postponed the outing from one day to the next. When I arrived there last Sunday, I was greeted with much the same news as Ritter Toggenburg:[1] they left this morning. You may imagine my irritation. I have long since consigned the contentious articles to maldiccion [malediction], and went there with the intention of feeding my aversion. Gisela's image refused to budge from my mind. Caramba!

I could tell you infinitely more, but Rosanes assures me that they would not accept the letter and that you would have to pay excess postage, and so I conclude in haste. As I look over what I have written, I cannot but beg your forbearance for half of it. One thing I hope is that your next letter will make up for the sparseness of your last and that you will reply at once, while still under the influence of these lines. In that case your obdurate heart and indurate mouth might open up to let me know that you are not yet dead to me.

Your Cipion

Kindest regards to your parents.

P.S.   G. had long since left when I fell ill. If you ever get to Breslau, look up Tauenziengasse and if you should come across the nameplate of an institute,[2] greet it for me.

Your
Sigmund Freud

No mano otra toque esa carta. [Let no other hand touch this letter.]

1. Ritter Toggenburg is the eponymous hero of Schiller's ballad (1797) about a knight who returns from the Holy Land to learn that his love entered a nunnery upon hearing the rumor of his death.

2. Not identified. There was an institute of music at 22 Tauentzienstrasse, and a school at 58.

Vienna, July 10, 1873

I take the liberty of informing you herewith that, with God's help, I passed my examination yesterday, July 9, 1873, and that I was awarded a matriculation certificate with distinction.[1]

Yesterday was exciting indeed; my report is splendid: one excellent, seven very good, and a commendation in geography. Last night I, poor fellow [?] slept peacefully for the first time in four weeks. If the truth be told, I don't really feel like relating the rest of the story, for I want to be properly idle, and that requires time above all. Perhaps, if you ask in your next letter, I shall report on a few episodes from the day of pitched battle. The letter you sent me as soon as you arrived never reached me, but if you never wrote it, then do so now. Your duties, I hope, leave you time enough. My hand is very slapdash today, which is because it was so put upon yesterday.

I cannot unfortunately produce the promised biblical story, I feel the "urge no more to give poetic voice to experience"; *that* interest has been replaced by another. I have just learned that my trip to England is no longer an impossibility. Say nothing about it for the moment; I shall let you know as soon as I have further news. Needless to say, I expect both more, and more interesting, news from you than I myself can impart. I feel a sort of state of intoxication, *light-*headed as one always is after shedding such loads. Forgive the brevity of this letter. Your modest expectations do you credit today; your frugality is always a fraud, for whenever you withhold letters on which I have counted, you cheat me. So please be more bountiful and you will soon receive interminable epistles from me. If fortune should smile upon you, seize it by the crown, you whom I shall call πολυμήχανος,[2] if only you find the means of increasing your glory by writing me a weighty letter.

In expectation of all that may come, be it a letter or a picture or an allegory or whatever else you may care to write

Your Sigmund Freud

Spanish next time, I am pressed for time today. Greetings to your mother if you should have a chance to convey them.

To Herr *Eduard Silberstein*
most personal

1. For details of the Matura, or graduation examination, see Freud's letter to Emil Fluss dated June 16, 1873, in Grubrich-Simitis, ed., *Selbstdarstellung*, pp. 118ff.
2. *Polymechanos* (resourceful), an epithet that Homer applies to Odysseus.

Vienna, July 11, 1873

Dear Berganza,

I received your letter early this morning and, as a man of honor, I hasten to reply the same day. I did not enjoy your news, save for learning that my mother and sisters and the mischievous Alexander[1] are in good health. As for yourself and your good wishes, which once more give me proof of your warm friendship, you will have gathered from my first letter that our hopes for a meeting in Roznau are vain because it seems to be my father's firm intention [not] to let me go to Roznau, and because I am neither able nor willing to go against his wishes. Regarding my English visit, I repeat my request that you tell no one about it. My mother would be the last person I would want to know until it is definitely settled. You have no right to be annoyed, for though I, too, miss you now and would miss you in similar circumstances, I have learned, in the absence of pleasant companions, to enjoy my solitude, which makes very agreeable company. Roznau has the most marvelous walks, the most secluded woods, an extensive and high mountain range and the tastiest of strawberries, and yet you manage to be bored in Roznau? Do on your own what we should do if we were together: walk, toy with your thoughts, drink water from the springs, and gather strawberries in the fields.

Perhaps you are unfulfilled, have nothing to think about? I keep silent about other matters to which you could turn your thoughts; is there not an Abraham who left you, saying: "Eliezer, thou knowest what the Lord hath bidden me: thou shalt not take a wife from amongst the daughters of this land which is a land of idolaters and sinners: but thou shalt go unto the land of my fathers where I was born, and which the Lord bade me leave, and bring me the portrait of one of the maidens that dwell in the land of my fathers. And the pious Eliezer replied, saying: Trust thy faithful servant Eliezer to do as thy Lord hath decreed."[2]

I hope the allegory is clear. [Remainder missing.]

In Spanish
   1. Freud's younger brother (1866–1943).
   2. Based on Genesis 24.

Querido Berganza,

He recibido tu cartilla hoy por la mañana y como hombre de honra[do] me apresuro á responder el mismo dia. No he gozado con tus nuevas escepto que mi madre y hermanas y el picaronzuelo Alejandro son en buena salud. Lo que es tu y tus deseos que me prueban de nuevo tu tierna amistad, ya habrás sabido por medio de mi carta primera que en vano deseamos hallaros á Roznau porqué parece intencion fijada de mi padre [no] dejarme ir á Roznau; y yo ni puedo ni quiero oponerme. Cuanto á mi viaje ingles, reitero mis ruegos, de no manifestar nada á nadie. Mi madre sería la postrera á quien yo quisiera comunicarlo antes de ser un hecho. Tu fastidio no es justificado, tambien yo siento y sentiría en tu posición tu ausencia, pero cuando yo no tengo agradables compañeros gozo de la soledad que es compañía muy estimable. Roznau tiene los paseos mas deleitosos, las selvas mas solitarias, una motaña grandísima y altísima y las fresas mas sabrosas ¿y tu puedes aburrirte á Roznau? Lo que haríamos si fuesemos unidos hazlo solitario: pasear, jugar con tus pensamientos, beber agua de las fuentes y coger fresas de los prados.

Quiza no eres ocupado? no tienes á qué pensar? Que callo de otras cosas á que han de volverse tus pensamientos, no hay un Abraham quien separándose de ti ha dicho: "Querido Elieser sabes, lo que me ha mandado el Poderosísimo Diós: que no debes eligir entre las mozas de ese país, que es país de idólatras y desalmados; mas ve en el país de mis padres, donde yo he tomado nacimiento, de donde me ha hecho salir el Diós mío y traeme el retrato de una de las mozas de el país de mis padres. Y el piadoso Elieser ha dicho: Te fíes en la fidelidad de Elieser que hará lo que te ha mandado tu Diós."

Espero, que tu entiendes esa alegoría.

Vienna, July 16, 1873

Yesterday afternoon I girded my loins, seized a stick in my right hand, and went up into the mountains. I intended to take the steamer to Nussdorf[1] and to climb the Leopoldsberg[2] from there, but the boat had already gone, leaving me with the bitter necessity of walking in the heat. You know my galloping stride. In an hour I had progressed so far along the Danube that the mountains were lost to view; since I was finding the detour annoying I turned off toward the Kahlenberg, [arriving] there after a long and arduous walk, with my heart beating like a clock striking and with sweat pouring for the first time in my life; my heart [the mountain?] was reached from the escarpment. It was the worst possible approach.

July 17

I interrupt the rather tedious account of my walk in order to reply to your letter, which has just arrived. First of all, my short and sweet advice to you is to intercept Rhea Silvia[3] tonight and to empty her basket thoroughly—*fundibus*[4] since you will scarcely be able to consume those delicacies with me, you may eat them on my behalf. You undoubtedly have a hold over her, but should you still feel bashful, then I herewith solemnly and ceremoniously assign to you what is mine, and call upon you to consume whatever I might have eaten up myself, had I been present—out of pure consideration, lest poor Rhea Silvia be conscious of my absence. For I am unlikely to visit Roznau. God knows how it happened, but this year it has become a question of principle. I am resigned to it, the day passes by quickly, I must confirm the observation, but indolence does not suit me. Something will be decided soon, and I will let you know the outcome.

As for Mme Lipska, it will be necessary to deny everything she accuses you of, even if it were the very truth, lest you find yourself in a great quandary.

On this occasion, my regards to Herr and Frau Hilferding[5] and Frau Lipska, since accursed Fate, as you write, will not grant me the pleasure of a reunion. I am aware of Fate's purpose, and am to some extent grateful to her for repeatedly introducing me to new circles. Finding the past beautiful is pure luxury in most cases.

My year, which used to have the longest days before I took the Matura (twenty-two hours) now has the shortest (eleven hours). If you do not write to me regularly, I shall retire to bed at seven o'clock. I don't have to ask you specifically to inform me of what you hear about conditions nearby, nor need I repeat the other request tending in the same direction; you know, don't you, why the Jews do not doff their hats to God in the Temple. Because he is omnipresent.

I would not advise you to read Homer, for though you are told in Werther that the young man, returning from a gathering that was as distinguished as it was tasteless, started to read Homer's song about the Suitors gorging themselves on the pigs they had slaughtered,[6] that young man was all alone and abandoned—without Mama, aunt, new and old friends—which is not the case with you. Nor do I find any mention of dictionaries in Werther . . .

You should have arrived earlier at your decision to go mountain climbing, if it is at all practicable. My own contentment here has a large hole that cannot be patched and that, as happens with holes, grows bigger by the day; I am often tempted to look for a remedy— but then—.

Of the next, my first university, year, I can give you the news that I shall devote all of it to purely humanistic studies, which have nothing to do with my later field but will not be unprofitable for all that. So, if you decide to become a physician, you can easily catch up with me and make your first cut on a human cadaver in my company; if you opt for diplomacy, of course, no one will ever catch up with you, not even history. To this end, I shall be attending the philosophy faculty during my first year. So, if anyone [?] asks me, or you on my behalf, what I intend to be, refrain from giving a definite answer, and simply say: a scientist, a professor, or something like that.

Cholera[7] is raging in some outlying districts, if we are to believe what people are saying, but please do not mention it to my mother or to anyone else, and if need be refute the rumor, which is bound to be exaggerated.

I trust you do not show my letters to anyone, if they should ask to see them, because I want to be able to write with complete candor and about whatever comes into my head.

Yours sincerely
Sigmund Freud
Cipion

Portions in Spanish

1. At the time not yet part of Vienna, lying west of the junction of the Danube Canal.

2. To the east of the Kahlenberg, on the Danube.

3. Presumably a girl met selling fruit in the forest.

4. An error for *funditus* (to the bottom).

5. Friends of the Silberstein family.

6. An imprecise recollection of the entry dated March 15 in Goethe's *Sorrows of Young Werther* (1774).

7. In the summer of 1873, cholera reached Vienna by way of Galicia.

Cuanto á Mme Lipska será menester, negar todo lo que ella te imputará, aunque fuese la verdad misma, si no llegarás en un mucho embarazo.

La Cólera está muy fuerte en algunos arrabales supuesto que se puede creer á las relaciones de la gente, pero no digas nada á mi madre ni á otro hombre, mas contradice á las exageraciones que por cierto se hacen de muy poca cosa.

Espero que ni muestras mis cartillas a nadie si alguien se las pide de ti, porqué quiero escribir con toda ingenuidad y sobre todas las cosas, que [se] me empeñan.

Tu sincero
Sigmund Freud
Cipion

Vienna, July 24, 1873

Dear Friend,

I am wretched and annoyed at the news in your letter that you have received neither book nor letter from me. I want you to know that I posted you the Zeplichal,[1] for which I had paid 2.50 guilders, the day after I received your order on the sixteenth of July, and that two days later, that is on the eighteenth (or nineteenth or twentieth) of July, I followed it up with a letter weighted with the remaining fifty kreuzer. Admittedly, I didn't register the book, but only to save on the cost, since as it was the postage came to ten kreuzer, and since I thought it was safe enough anyway and that it would be a remarkable thing if an unregistered letter or book had no chance of reaching its destination. I am rather more worried, I confess, about the letter—the fifty kreuzer in two twenties and a ten-piece coin may have been noticeable and attracted the attention of the post office staff. But even then, it should have reached you—you would only have had to pay a small excess fee. Since neither of the two has arrived they must, in the opinion of the post office here, and in my own as well, be *waiting in Roznau.* So please apply to Halumiczek, whose genius is probably responsible for the delay, and to [the] postmaster, who is, after all, an amiable fellow, and ask them for what I sent you. I have no doubt that it must be there and if you only pursue the matter with zeal, it will turn up. For in all honesty, if it is not found, the loss would be great. Not that of the book and the money, for three guilders can be made good, although with great difficulty, but the letter—if the letter is lost it cannot be replaced. And just this letter, oh, jealous fate! You see, this letter contained a short essay, a biblical study with modern themes, something I could not write again and of which I am as proud as of my nose or my maturity.[2] It would have refreshed you like balm; one could not tell it was concocted in my den. It was so sensitive, so biblically naive and forceful, so melancholy and so gay—it's the very devil that it's been lost, it grieves me. Since postal communication between Vienna and Roznau is as safe as it is, I would also like to know if Dolfi[3] received her four issues of Hofmann.[4] If they did not arrive, the same applies.

Write to me *by return mail* to tell me the results of your efforts; until the matter is cleared up you will receive no *decent and sensible* letter from me. The form and content of this letter can be excused only on the grounds of haste and vexation.

Your
Sigmund Freud

If you reply on the wings of an eagle, or like a flash of lightning, you will not have done too much. All further news, including several items of importance, on receipt of your letter.

1. A stenography textbook: C. Zeplichal, *Lehrbuch der Gabelsberger'schen Stenografie*, Vienna, 1870.
2. *Maturität* could also refer to his recent matriculation. Tr.
3. Freud's sister Adolfine (1862–1943). She died in Theresienstadt concentration camp.
4. A series of books about children's parties: Friedrich Hofmann (1813–1888), *Kinderfeste*, 1853–.

Vienna, July 30, 1873

Dear Friend,

It appears that you received my last letter, in which I informed you about the missing order, no more than you did my first letter and the item itself. It is remarkable—I cannot explain it otherwise than that we have a friend in the post office with a special interest in our correspondence, and who perhaps also has a son studying Gabelsberger's shorthand.

Take note, therefore, 1. that I wrote you a letter on (about) the seventeenth, in which I told you I would send the book and the remainder of the money. (You received this letter)

2) that I dispatched the Zeplichal in a wrapper on the nineteenth

and 3) that on the twenty-second I wrote you a long letter weighted down with the fifty kreuzer left over from the three guilders (the same day that we sent off Dolfi's birthday present)

4) that on about the twenty-fourth, by way of a reply to your letter which indicated to me that you had received neither the book nor my first letter, I wrote again, advising you to make enquiries with the Roznau postmaster and to send me a speedy reply.

To this last letter I have had no answer, nor do I gather anything about you from my mother's and sisters' letter, so that I am now writing by registered post, lest the same mishap that has befallen me two or three times occur again.

I must, however, confess that I am much more anxious to hear whether you have received my consignment and why you do not write, so that I can provide you as soon as possible with another book and other letters to make up for the loss. Alas, enclosed in the letter that has gone astray was a masterpiece of a biblical idyll, to which I am not likely to turn my hand again, as my innocuous good humor has long since gone to blazes.

What I would like best is to hear that you received my last letter and, due to whatever impediment, failed to answer it. In any case, reply promptly, no matter what has happened. I shall write back immediately and in full, also in Spanish, snowing you under with all sorts of news, which I am in too depressed and uncertain a mood to do at the moment.

In hopes of a speedy reply
Your Sigmund Freud
D. Cipion

Whatever reason you may have had not to write, please write immediately upon receipt of this letter; if I cannot read and write letters, I am afraid I shall catch + + + cholera + + + out of deadly boredom.

––––––––––––––

Vienna, August 2, 1873

Dear Friend,

It is in vain that you try to console me upon the loss of my biblical study; I have not suffered a similar loss for years. The disaster is in no way mitigated by the fact that you do not know what *you* have missed, for it was intended for your perusal. Although I cannot tell what my letter and the Zeplichal are doing in Hungary,[1] and can swear an oath that I in no way commissioned their journey, I am hopeful that they may find their way to you. If not, then the loss of the letter can never be made good, but I shall certainly let you have another Zeplichal, should the former not have reached you by August tenth.

I have nearly two weeks' news to report to you, and therefore make bold to scribble the items down haphazardly, as they spring to mind.

(You complain about my unclear script, adding that you yourself have become used to it. To whom else do you show my letters?)

I can only hope that the one so favored is not Herr Hilferding. How did *that* Saul come to be amongst the prophets, and how do you come to be one of his disciples? Is philosophy his major subject, does he hope to earn his living from it, or does he live on the manna our Lord rains down on him, merely practicing philosophy for the love of it? Far better he were a philosophical lover, he who will need it to console himself over the gap separating his brilliant genius from the simple sense of his unphilosophical wife. Does he really aim to be a second Christ, redeeming mankind for a second time? And does he really imagine that he can bring redemption with philosophy? Believe me, if anyone wishes to turn himself into so great a fool, he must be born to it; it cannot be acquired very easily by study. A strange man, indeed, this Joshua Χριστός [*Christos*], far better he returned to playing cards than studying Baco of Verulam[2] and Descartes. In particular, how can you possibly become his famulus[3] while the groves of Roznau still stand, in which grow the strawberries I so love?

You ought to be ashamed of yourself, it is for your sake alone that I wish I were there. How could you stray so far from the path?

Alas, *I* am unable to show you the way. You will have to make that effort yourself. For I cannot come to Roznau, that road is barred to me forevermore (as they say in Die Räuber,[4] a play I have seen twice). I can hardly believe that I kept the reason from you; indeed I remember specifying the obstacle quite clearly. My father does not wish it, and though I long for the place for one hour each day, I cannot seriously plan to do what he for good reasons opposes. In order to tie myself down here and to burn my bridges, I have enrolled in swimming classes. I regret it, however, not because it puts fetters on my possible journey, but because the low water level has turned the classes into a mudbath. One cannot possibly drown, can barely dive anywhere, and with the danger the whole thrill has gone.

For the rest, I have little cause for jubilation or for complaint either. I am not going to the Exhibition, but in a short two weeks I have seen Rossi[5] as Othello in the Wiedner Theater,[6] Die Räuber in the Burg and in the Laubetheater, and Caius Gracchus[7] as well. The Shah[8] arrived yesterday, but he is a boring brute and leaves me indifferent. Rosanes's favor was withheld from me for some time, and now again, for numerous reasons but not out of enmity. Revolutions are occurring in him, too, but of a liquid sort, not fiery as with us.

My day is very short, from twelve to two o'clock; if you keep writing to me diligently, I shall soon forget the date, just like you. Incidentally, it is one year since my trip to Freiberg. If you have the time, do consult the diary daily for what happened to me a year ago. I did a great deal of living in those six weeks. But that you know, for I have told you a good many things over and over again.

I had a conversation with an ass of a bureaucrat (or rather I spoke and he hee-hawed), who can bray in his kind of Castilian as well as in Spaniolish.[9] I am glad to impart several results of my investigation to you, the great linguist. Instead of para qué they say para *lo que,* for aprender they use "embesar" (literally translated as "to enkiss"), they do not use the perfect, but usually employ the preterite: "Yo no tuvé nada," moreover pronouncing the final é as i.

I think I have seen your Swedish schoolmaster. Quite a long time ago I visited the Exhibition and peered into the Swedish schoolhouse through a window, in the company of my precious sisters, when— up came a man to the window and said to one of them in a foreign accent: "Not today, tomorrow at nine, my dear child." What a pedant, don't you agree?

I read in the papers that Palacký[10] was in Roznau. Did you see him?

There is much I could tell you about the four plays I have seen. Rossi, you ought to know, is an Italian actor whom the Viennese praise to the skies, while leaving actual theater attendance to salami eaters and Danube regulation workers. I do not wish to pass judgment, but only to make a few comments. As Othello, he spoke in Italian, at times so fluently that I could not follow him, was more brown than black, and whenever he disapproved of something would grunt like a Kaffir. He gave Desdemona, who rather resembled Virginia in the illustration, short shrift and made horrible earnest of the throttling. I feared for the poor lady, the more so as she did not stir at the end of the act, but then she curtsied briskly and seemed quite reconciled with her African. The notorious handkerchief was a tiny fazzolettino, the size of Desdemona's palm, probably so as to render it more easily stolen. After the performance everyone clapped, the Italians who did not know Shakespeare no less than the Germans who did not understand Italian. The robbers at the Stadttheater are a down-at-heel crew, while those at the Burg are on the government payroll and thus stout and well-fed fellows. In the Stadttheater, the robber chief wore an ugly light-blue coat and Franz, in fair retribution for his artistic lapses, was consigned to the tower; in the Burg Theater, Lewinsky[11] had the privilege of being allowed to hang himself. But then, he did give a thrilling performance. To think that an honest man can see right through a villain! The Caius Gracchus is by Wilbrandt; he has a mother, Cornelia, and a wife, Licinia, who do not leave him alone for one minute, because they fear his childish pranks. He speaks most eloquently though I doubt he knows his own mind, and finally dies on the Aventine, abandoned by all save Cornelia and Licinia. His death is so boring that not even the worst oligarch would claim he deserved it. Licinia, as well as Amalia in Die Räuber, was played by Fräulein Precheisen,[12] a tall beauty with fair hair, who must have a heart of stone, for, try though

she might, she could manage neither tears nor raptures. The ability
to say or shout "dead" is not part of her repertoire, an advantage that
unfortunately she displayed brilliantly in both roles. She ought to
take care not to recite her own obituary, lest all the mourners burst
into fits of laughter.

So much for today. Reply soon, I am in a corresponding mood.

Your Sigmund Freud

❧ It seems unnecessary to assure you that I have been deeply
touched by Mrs. L.'s misfortune; I could not tell from your letter
whether her husband died in Roznau or in his homeland. I hope she
lacks neither friends nor parents; they may console her. Tell her that
I shall carry out her small commissions with pleasure, but that I
shall not know the price of the book for another two days, because
tomorrow is Sunday. Write me the details of this sad happening. ❧

Cipion

Postscript in Spanish

1. Probably through confusion of the Moravian Roznau with the Hungarian
Rozsnyó.

2. Francis Bacon (1561–1626), Baron Verulam.

3. A student assisting a professor during lectures. Tr.

4. J. C. Friedrich von Schiller, *Die Räuber* (The Robbers), act 1, scene 1: "the path
thereto is barred to him, as Heaven is barred to Hell."

5. Ernesto Rossi (1829–1894) came to Vienna during the World Exhibition to per-
form his most famous role.

6. The Municipal Theater.

7. Adolf von Wilbrandt (1837–1911), *Gracchus, der Volkstribun* (Gracchus the
Tribune), 1872.

8. Nasir ad-Din (1831–1896), Shah of Persia.

9. Ladino, the language used by Jewish communities of Spanish origin; *embezar*
means to teach or to learn, but it is derived from the Latin *invitiare*, not from *basiare*,
which becomes *bezzar* in Ladino.

10. František Palacký (1798–1876), Czech politician, member of the Frankfurt Par-
liament of 1848, later leader of the Czech faction in the Austrian Upper House, author of the five-volume *Geschichte Böhmens* (History of Bohemia), 1836–1867.

11. Joseph Lewinsky (1835–1907).

12. Olga Precheisen (b. 1855) married Joseph Lewinsky in 1875.

No me parece necesario el asegurarte, que la desdicha de la Señora L. me da en el
corazón; no podía entender si por tu carta si ha muerto su marido á Roznau ó en su
patria. Espero que á ella no faltarán amigos ó padres; qué la consuelen. Le digas, que
con mucho gusto efectuo sus pequeños encargos, pero que el precio del libro no sabré

antes de dos dias porque mañana es domingo. Me escribas pormenores de ese infeliz accidente.

Cipion

Vienna, August 6, 1873

Dear Friend,

Your Jeremiads please me greatly, the more so as I could dream up a Chapter II to add to your Chapter I.[1] Your resignation is most laudable—after all, no one has yet invented a lantern to light up God's dark ways. Though, unlike you, I have not taken to philosophy out of despair, I have other vices that threaten my salvation. If this were to go on, I shall get the "English disease"[2] rather late in life. I read English history, write English letters, declaim English verse, listen to English descriptions, and thirst for English glances. To be sure, the main thing, my trip to England, is off; I am bound by contractual, indissoluble ties to the Viennese swimming club. And even if I were not, I doubt whether a favorable wind would waft me across the Channel. I dare not go on lest I write a chapter of Job, mutatis mutandis.

One reproach I cannot spare you. You forget that man must be himself.[3] Get up into the mountains by yourself and let books and society rot. Get into the mountains, I say, and eat strawberries. Eat strawberries, I say, and forget you are by yourself.—A few days ago, when I myself picked strawberries and raspberries on the Sofienalpe near Dornbach,[4] I was overcome with nostalgia. Since you went away, I have been up in the mountains four times; but my heart's in the highlands,[5] down here I find not one step is worth the trouble. A single muddy rill in exchange for three mountains, how ridiculous! The vegetation sparse, not a berry for miles, what a contrast! Not a single pine or fir, only beeches and willows, what a terrible shame! But bear in mind that I must either spend forty kreuzer or else must cover a most unrefreshing stretch of road before I escape, and that an entire day is usually required for an insignificant out-

ing—so just think how I would feel were I by myself in Roznau instead of you! Do likewise, get up into the mountains. I am beginning
to share Herodotus' view of the malevolence of fate.[6] Why couldn't
ten of my other scribblings have been lost, and the one incomparable [letter] be saved! How much elevating thought would you not
have found in it, especially in respect of this instruction to you.
Don't speak to me of substitutes. If the sun should explode one day
and we should dwell in darkness, what substitute could you find for
it? If the sea dried up and the heavenly sources, what substitute for
water would you prescribe? So don't speak to me of substitutes; it is
irretrievably lost and will never return.

⊰ I disapprove of your reserve in affairs of the heart. In the circumstances, it is your duty to please Mrs. L., not to avoid her. If you
fail to absorb some of her tenderness, all her love will be focused on
her husband and she will suffer terribly when she hears of his death.
But were you to reduce some of that love in your favor, then her pain
will be the less and perhaps you will have saved the life of Mrs. L.
and her health. It is your bounden duty to make that sacrifice.

Rosanes is staying at his friend Bettelheim's[7] country estate for
the second time. I don't know what they talk about, but it would
seem they have some common business. ⊱

I have a small favor to ask, which may well seem peculiar to you.
In the first field of the meadowland opposite the house in which my
mother stayed last year,[8] and before that as well, there is a tree that
looks like a cypress or an arbor vitae and whose twigs and small
needles have a marvelously spicy and acrid taste. As you know, I am
quite an expert on the grasses of the field and the herbs of the woods
and have tasted all sorts of greenery, but nothing ever pleased me
more than the twigs of that tree. So please be good enough to seek
it out—you won't find that difficult; it is one of the first in a small
copse in the above-mentioned field—taste it and enclose a sample
in your next letter, or if possible send me a small packetful, for
which service I shall remain obliged to you until ten years after the
Resurrection. Don't abandon hope that you may still receive my letter and the Zeplichal, make enquiries about them once more, but if
they do not turn up I shall at least acquire another copy of the book.

⊰ I am very sad that neither you nor I observe the law of the A.E.
which stipulates that we make use, in fact constant use, of the
Noble Castilian Language. As you can see, I have begun to remind

us of that duty. Several silly thoughts keep floating through my head and, provided my mood does not change completely, I may well follow them up. During the days of my utmost exertions, that is, a week before the now + defunct + matriculation, I earnestly pondered the possibility of creating a system of numbers, having observed that everything in the real world has its equal, or equivalent, in the world of numbers.[9] Numbers are born, die, marry, and destroy one another like men. Their estates comprise nobles, soldiers, genealogical tables, just as happens with the estates of mortal man. Numbers even have a mythology and gods! I know how astonished you must feel at this discovery, but when I have finished the work and present it to you, you will have to concede that it is a marvelous proof of human perspicacity in general and of that of your friend, its creator, in particular. I realize full well that the subject merits the attention of a thousand men cleverer than myself, but though my talent be sparse, my efforts will be praised,[10] and the eternal glory of the idea will be linked with my name, albeit my successors and those who will stand on my shoulders will outshine me in carrying it out. ✳

"Presentient of such great good Fortune,"[11] I conclude,

Your Sigmund Freud

Needless to say, I await your contributions to my numbers system.

Cipion
miembro vitalicio de la
famosa A.E. Señor del
Lias y Principe de la
Greda.
[life member of the famous Spanish Academy,
Lord of the Lias and Prince of the Cretaceous]

Portions in Spanish

1. After Heinrich Heine's *Atta Troll* or *Deutschland, ein Wintermärchen* (Germany, a winter's tale).

2. The phrase *englische Krankheit* refers to rickets; here it also means his weakness for things English.

3. Goethe, *Faust*, II.4.

4. Northwest of Vienna.

5. Robert Burns, "My Heart's in the Highlands."

6. Not found in Herodotus in this form; probably a reference to the life of Croesus (Herodotus I.32) or that of Polycrates (III.40).

7. Josef Bettelheim (b. 1856), one of Silberstein's classmates.

8. 441 Brückengasse.

9. For further details of Freud's numerology, see D. Bakan, *Sigmund Freud and the Jewish Mystical Tradition*, New York, 1958.

10. Ovid, *Epistulae ex Ponto* III.4.79.

11. Goethe, *Faust*, II.5.

Tu encogimiento en las cosas de galanteria no apruebo. Es tu deber en esas circunstancias complacer à Señora L. no á esquivarla. Si tu no te apoderas de una parte de su tenereza, todo su amor se concentra en su marido y será terrible el dolor, cuando sabrá su muerte. Pero si tu diminuyes ese amor en favor tuyo, el dolor será menor y acaso habrás salvado vida y salud á Señora L. Porque es tu deber y tu has de sagrificarte á el.

Rosanes está en la hacienda de su amigo Bettleheim ya la segunda vez. No sé, sobre qué tratan, pero parece que tienen un negocio que efectuar.

Me pesa mucho que ni tu ni yo observen la ley de la A.E. que prescribe hacer uso y uso frecuente de la Noble Lengua Castellana. Ves, que yo he comenzado, á recordarlos en nuestro deber. Unos tontos pensamientos me pasan por la cabeza, que acaso seguiré, supuesto, que no se muda totalmente mi humor. En los dias del grandisimo trabajo es decir una semana antes la + difunta + Maturidad me ha ocupado muy de veras la tentativa de costruir un sistema de los números, porque hé notado, que todo lo que pasa en el mundo real tiene su igual, quiero decir su equivalencia en el mundo de los numero[s]. Los numeros nacen, mueren, se casan y se matan como los hombres. El estado de los numeros tiene su nobleza, sus ejercitos, sus tablas genealogicas como el estado de los hombres mortales. ¡Hasta una mitologia y dioses tienen los numeros! Yo sé bien, que tu te estrañaras de esta descubrimiento, pero cuando yo habré finido la obra y tela propondré, conoscenderás [?], que es una prueba maravillosa de la penetracion humana y especialmente de la de tu amigo, el autor. Sé tambien, que el objeto es digno de la atencion de mil hombres mas ingeniosos que yo, pero si falta el poder, se alaba á la voluntad y á mi se ha de quedar la gloria eterna de la idea, aunque mis sucesores y los que se elevarán sobre mis hombros me sobresalten en la ejecutacion.

Vienna, August 16, 1873

Dear Friend,

I have been less punctual than usual this time, because I have saddled myself with activities that threaten to swallow up the whole day. ⚘ It is with great admiration that you will hear I am learning

French in the morning and philosophy after lunch, both in Braun's[1] company. But I have teamed up with a very lazy companion who always feigns fatigue whenever we come up against difficult problems, and on other occasions, by contrast, attempts to forge ahead with the most irrational dispatch. This explains why I have not had time to reply to you for four or five days, something that would horrify me were you to do it to me. In philosophy we are on a par, but the angelic (not the English)[2] glances I confessed to yearning for I cannot obtain at home, as you suppose—one does not long for what one possesses but rather I yearn for them because I do not possess them. In worldly matters, you have gained an advantage over me. Your aunt seems to be a woman of great understanding. Now you can rightly say: "I, too, have been a shepherd in Arcadia,"[3] as Schiller put it. Or, if you prefer to read it in another language, "anch' io sono pastore."[4] But I am no shepherd and have not been one all through the holidays, which is curiously noteworthy, yet it is worthy of your confidant.

I beg you to inform me μαλ' ἀτρεκέως[5] whether, as I expect, the game of forfeits has been resumed, of which I have heard it said that you do not always get back what you have forfeited and that you receive a great deal that is not restored to its owners.

I believe that my mother will soon be leaving Roznau and I would like to know when your family will be doing likewise. The "Rivers"[6] with the small brooks and the rest will arrive in Vienna in early September.

I have eaten the cypress samples you sent me with gratitude. They come from two species, but the difference between them is so small that you have to be a seasoned eater of leaves and branches like myself to detect it. If it is not too much to ask, I would beg you to try the taste of a few of these cypresses, of which, according to you, there are supposed to be so many, and to choose for me those with the most particularly bitter taste.

If Mrs. L. asks you to wait for her daughter's coming-of-age before you become her son-in-law, do not reject it out of hand, but keep an eye on the orphan child who, I believe, must be in Roznau as well. If it should scream a great deal and have a good, strong voice, it will turn into a wholesome girl worthy of your attentions. Don't be put off by all the screaming, because in a few years' time you will be calling her voice a silvery one, and the owner of the silvery bell a little angel. ⚘

Yesterday, when I had to suffer an Egyptian darkness for an hour because I could not lay my hands on flint or matches and because, as the Book of Job puts it, I cannot send lightnings to make light for me,[7] I thought up the following conversation in the sphere of light which I shall now impart to you, as far as I can remember it.

Highway of the heavenly host. One star addresses another.

A. Could you kindly direct me to the Little Bear?

B. Ah, the Little Bear, that's quite a long way. I take it you are a stranger. Kindly follow me, it's on my way.

A. Thank you very much, this is my first visit here. (They walk for about three stellar miles.) Do you happen to have a light? The big volcano from which I usually smoke has gone out. Brr, it's terribly cold.

B. You must be from the Equator. If only you had come a millennium earlier—I have just burned out.

A. Burned out! My condolences (shakes his hand). What do you do in a situation like that?

B. (Withdrawing his scorched hand.) Ouch, ouch. As long as you have something to fall back on, you see, you can lead an independent life, but after that it's all up with personal freedom. I went into service, became the Sun's vassal for life, just to keep alive. I, who was renowned as a star of the fourth magnitude, who shone and blazed forth to make the Lord rub his hands with glee.

A. How awful. Is your job easy at least?

B. I'm given no consideration at all. For the past thousand years I have never been allowed to do less than ten stellar miles per second. And to think how slowly I used to be able to amble about when I was my own master! Now I am up at sunrise and must follow my strict mistress, whom I can scarcely see with the naked eye, through the bitterest cold, until it pleases her to go down.

A. Period of revolution?

B. Eighty-one-and-a-half years, and in that short time I have to travel a tremendous distance.

A. Doesn't the Lord take pity on you?

B. What? Him? He's a stickler; I would have given notice, but he had the Archangel Gabriel tell me that I would have to run with the Sun for at least another fifty-four eons before I could leave her service. And it's not at all clear whether I could get a place even then, that luxury is becoming an exceptional privilege— the Sun has 4,563 vassals, Jupiter 8, Venus 3, and the Earth, that poor thing, can't take on more than one. I've been thinking, in any case, of migrating to the other side of the Milky Way. But having a tail stuck on to me like a comet, well, that's a bit much. An honest planet, the Lord says, sticks to his orbit.

A. But how is it that you have the time to chat with me today?

B. Well, you see, the Virgin Mary is coming today,[8] so they all have a holiday and my gracious mistress, the Sun, has given me the day off, too.

A. The Virgin Mary? Do I hear right? Didn't she depart the Earth eighteen hundred years ago?

B. Quite so, but she only arrived today; she's had bad weather and was nearly struck by lightning halfway here. She made the sign of the Cross then, and the lightning struck the Earth instead, setting fire to a church steeple if I remember rightly.

A. What a pity. Isn't that the Earth over there?

B. Yes, but be careful not to get too close, it's dangerous—(the strange star wobbles for a bit, then loses his balance and falls to Earth as a meteor).

B. God in Heaven, that was quick. He was probably shot by some damned stargazer, and I have overstayed my leave. (Runs off with planetary velocity.)

Moral: If that is how stars fare, what right have we to complain?

If you don't like this piece of nonsense, then don't read it again.

For the rest, I assure you of my immutable friendship no less than of my extremely bad mood, and safely leave you to science and gallantry, which vie for your favors as the good and evil spirits do for those of the huntsman. Although I consider myself a cazador by comparison, I do not seriously wish you to meet a cazadora.[9]

Remember me to all those in whose good books I happen to be, and say nothing about me to those who do not think well of me.

Your Sigmund Freud
Cipion

Portion in Spanish

1. Heinrich Braun (1854–1927), one of Freud's classmates; later a prominent social-ist to whom—as well as to Silberstein—Freud owed his knowledge of social demo-cratic politics. Brother-in-law of Viktor Adler, he married Lily von Kretschmann (1865–1916).

2. In German *englisch* means both angelic and English. Tr.

3. From "Resignation": "I, too, was born in Arcadia."

4. After the Italian quotation attributed to various sources: "Anch' io sono pittore" (I, too, am a painter).

5. *Mal atrekeos*, quite truthfully.

6. Allusion to the Fluss family, *Fluss* being German for river.

7. Job 38:35.

8. Reference to Assumption Day, August 15.

9. *Cazador, cazadora:* hunter, huntress. Freud was presumably thinking of the punishment of Actaeon described by Ovid in *Metamorphoses* III. 174ff.

Con mucha admiracion sentirás, que por la mañana aprendo el frances en compañia de Braun y despues de mediodia la filosofia cor el mismo. Pero me he unido con un compañero muy perezoso, el cual siempre simula fatiga, cuando se ha de tomar algo de dificultad y que en trueque otras vezes quiere adelantar con el mas irracional des-pacho. Así ha sucedido, que en cuatro o cinco dias yo no tuve el tiempo de respon-derte, lo que de tu parte me horrorizaría. Cuanto á la filosofia somos iguales, pero las miradas angelicas (no inglesas), las cuales yo confesaba desear, no se pueden coger en casa mia, como tu presumes, porque no se anhela, lo que se tiene, antes bien yo las deseo, por no tenerlas. En las cosas del mundo tu me has ganado la delantera. Tu tia parece ser mujer muy de entendimiento. Ahora puedes decir con mucha razon: "Tam-bien yo he sido pastor en la Arcadia," como dijo Schiller. O, si mas te gusta leerlo en otra lengua "Anch' io sono pastore." Pero yo no soy pastor ni lo he sido jamas en el curso de las vacaciones, cosa muy estraña pero sin embargo digna de tu fiado.

Te ruego que me informes μαλ᾽ ἀτρεκέως si, como ha de ser, han vuelto otras veces los juegos de empeños, de los cuales he oido decir, que no se vuelve siempre, lo que se ha empeñado una vez, y que muchas cosas se reciben, que no vuelven á sus dueños.

Creo que mi madre saldrá luego de Roznau y quiero saber, cuando tu familia hará lo mismo. Los "Rios" con los pequeños arroyos y demas llegarán á Viena en los pri-meros dias del Septiembre.

Las muestras de cipreses, que me has enviado, he comido con sentimientos agra-decidos para contigo. Son dos especies, pero es tan corta la diferencia, que necesita ser un comidor molido de hojas y ramas como yo, para notarla. Si quieres darte esa pena, te ruego, de ensayar el sabor de unos de esos cipresos, como dices, que muchos hay, y me escojas el de la mas intensiva amargura.

Si Señora L. te ofrece esperar la edad de su hija, para ser su yerno, no lo rehuses enteramente; pero observes el niño huerfano, el cual, como creo, debe estar tambien á Roznau. Si mucho grita y tiene buena voz alta será buena moza y digna de tus obsequios. No te parezca feo lo demasiado gritar, que en pocos años podrés llamarla voz de sonido argentino y la dueña de la campanilla de plata un angelito.

Vienna, August 20, 1873

Dear Friend,

I have heard the terrible news of your fall from Frau Lipska's own lips, besides many other things that suited those lips admirably and that brilliantly confirmed the veracity of your own reports. Because I had been "most highly recommended" by Rosa,[1] she commanded my presence two mornings ago, which behest I obeyed at ten o'clock. I did not do so gladly, for—I see no reason why I should keep it a secret from you—my natural good looks had been robbed of their symmetry by the rebellious encroachments of a bedbug. But her reception of me made it clear that she was willing to advance out of the fund of old friendship that which I was unable to acquire anew. I found her almost unchanged, her little face a trifle paler and less composed, and catechised her with the shamelessness of an elderly tutor while she, with the simple artlessness of a doll, responded to my teasing with affectionately told and elaborate stories. "Eduard" replaced the "Herr Sigmund" when the latter wearied of speaking of himself. "Eduard" is cheerful, "Eduard" is enjoying himself—she maintained that she warned "Eduard" just one second before he actually fell, and went on to describe her own fright and that of the others quite enchantingly. I was not particularly surprised to hear of the first coincidence—ya sabes, que el amor es el unico "clairvoyant" [you know that love is the only clairvoyant]. One of her brothers was present but did not bother us or appear to be at all interested: he seems to be troubled water from which I drew but little. I did not come across a sister-in-law, just two gentlemen, in their prime, of inordinate stupidity and with a great deal of local knowledge. I agreed to run a small errand for her and promised to see her to the train and so this bitter cup, too, passed from me!

Your excellent advice, intended to inspire my studies of frances [French], strikes me as making a virtue, something that has nothing to do with "virtus," of necessity. "Frances is the key to the heart," you say, adapting Shakespeare, who said the same of music.[2] "Young ladies are boring, ergo they are a cure for boredom, poison being the best antidote." But if one is healthy to start with, isn't poison just poison, and if one is not bored by oneself, aren't young ladies crystallized poison of boredom and not an antidote against it? It must still be established whether young ladies are boring only if one speaks German to them, or if they continue to be boring if one addresses them in French. In short, young ladies do not come into it at all, and if they do you do wrong to mention them to me. You know, in any case, that I have learned enough frances from you to be able to assure any young lady that, for her brief six years' schooling, she speaks excellent frances, and to acknowledge her return compliment with a humble "Merci Mlle vous êtes bien bonne."

◦⅋ It is very strange that you, member of the Spanish Academy, knowledgeable reader of so many Spanish books or volumes, should not have understood your friend or companion, D. Cipion, when I, dog that I am, wrote one of the least funny jokes that I have ever written. Know, therefore, that when I wrote the expression "englische" glances the first time in German, it was ambiguous. The second time, when I translated it into Spanish, I was forced to say "miradas inglesas ó angelicas" to make my meaning clear. You assumed that there were angels or little angels in my house of whose glances I was speaking, but I replied to you in the greatest haste that your assumption was wrong and that I was simply longing for angelic glances: at home I have none.

My "celestial conversation" does not deserve the praises you have so profusely bestowed upon it, and I hope that you have not been dazzled by the scientific data, which are not correct, the whole thing having been a brainchild of mine, as Caballero[3] would say, or having sprung from the dregs of my brain, as Schiller[4] would put it. But whether good or bad, I can assure you it can in no way be compared to the incomparable biblical imitation that has been lost over the centuries because of the jealousy of the so-called gods.

I used to feel your letters before opening them, and guess whether there might be something thicker inside than a sheet of paper, a photograph perhaps, but I have given up this so-called hope, and also—I trust you to believe me, for otherwise I would tell you nothing—the attachment that bound me to Gisela, that girl whom you know and do not know, whom you have seen and do not remember. Not because another has taken her place; indeed, that place can remain empty. Let us rather say that as nature abhors a vacuum, it has been filled with something other than air. When the hydrographic system which is formed by the Rivers reaches Vienna, I shall absent myself from them many times, and they will not miss me even more often, I am sure. Rosanes has communicated to me in well-chosen words his decision to pine away for them if God so wills it or good fortune decrees! I have grown tired of and been led astray by this overlong game.

For now, farewell, and take care of your body, for, as a famous Spanish poet says,

> Without hands you cannot grasp
> and without a breast you cannot clasp
> and without eyes you cannot see
> and without truth you cannot love!

But this famous poet is neither Cervantes, nor Caballero, nor D. Ramón Mesonero Romanes,[5] but it is D. Cipion, who wrote that quatrain in lyrical mood.

There should have been a festival today at the Exhibition, but because of the rain it has been put off until Friday. It won't be anything much, but whatever it is, you shall learn from my letters, because as you are somewhat indisposed I shall write you two short ones in succession, with no obligation to reply.

Make sure, when you leave for Vienna, to tell me about everyone you encounter on the way, since it is not impossible that you might meet up with those girls and their mother whom we called the "Preraurenses."[6] Almost a whole year has gone by and I have seen and heard nothing of those damsels, so worthy of attention and interest if one has met them. I realize that the hope I place in your journey is slight, but it is said that chance is the tutelary god of those who seek, and I believe that we should let no opportunity go by to discover whatever we can about those mysterious beings.

Get well soon,

> Your most devoted ⚘
> D. Cipion
> Your Sigmund Freud

Regards to your family

Portion in Spanish

1. Freud's sister Rosa (1860–1942). She died at Treblinka.

2. *Twelfth Night:* "If music be the food of love, play on."

3. Fernán Caballero (Cecilia Böhl de Faber, 1796–1877), founder of the school of novelists known as *costumbrismo*.

4. "Die Künstler" (The artists): "And that exalted stranger, Thought / Sprang from the wond'ring brain."

5. Ramón de Mesonero Romanos (1803–1882).

6. Inhabitant of Prerau, a small town in Moravia west of Roznau.

Es cosa muy curiosa que tu miembro de la A.E. ilustrado leidor de tamaños libros ó volúmenes españoles no has comprendido á tu compadre y compinche D. Cipion escribiéndote ese perro, que soy yo, una burla de las menos chistosas que escribió. Sepaste pues, que escribiendo yo en aleman la primera vez la voz "englische" miradas era una ambiguidad. La segunda vez, cuando lo trasladé en español, hube de decir "miradas inglesas ó angelicas" para volver á expresar el mismo sentido cual antes. Tu presumiste que en mi casa hubiera angelos, ó angelitos, de cuyas miradas hablase yo, pero yo con sumo despacho te contesté, que era falsa tu presuncion y que solo desea miradas angelicas; no las tengo en casa.

Mi "conversacion celestial" no merece las alabanzas que tu con tanta profusion le has distribuido; espero que tampoco te han deslumbrado los datos científicos; los que no son verdaderos sino hijos de mi imaginacion, como diría Caballero y que han brotado en el estiercol de mi cerebro, como diría Schiller. Pero que sea bueno ó malo, puedo asegurarte que no puede asemejarse nada en ningun caso á la impar imitacion biblica que se ha perdido en el curso de los siglos por la envidia de los si-dichos dioses.

Antes acostumbraba yo tentar tus cartas antes de abrirlas para ver, si no hubiese allá dentro algo mas grueso que un pliego de papel, quizás un retrato c.d. [?] pero ahora he renunciado á si-dicha esperanza y—si quieres creerme, porque en otro caso no te diría nada—tambien á la inclinacion, que me pegaba á esta niña, Gisela, que conoces y no conoces, has visto y no recuerdas. No es porque otra ha ocupado su lugar, pero el lugar se puede quedar vasio. O como no hay un lugar vacio en la naturaleza, digamos que se ha llenado de otra cosa como de aire. Cuando el sistema hydrografico que forman los Rios llegará á Viena, muchas vezes me ausentaré de ellos y mas vezes creo que no me echarán de menos. Rosanes me ha manifestado en buena lengua su resolucion de abrasarse de ellos [?], si Dios así lo quiere ¡ ó buena ventura así se haga!, el juego demasiado largo me ha cansado y desviado.

Para ahora vivas y cuides de tu cuerpo porque como dice un famoso poeta castellano

> Sin manos no se puede agarrarse (ergreifen)
> y sin pecho no abrazarse
> y sin ojos no mirarse
> y no amarse sin verdad!

Pero ese poeta afamado no es Cervantes ni Caballero ni D. Ramon Mesonero Romanos sino D. Cipion es, quien esa copla ha hecho en un humor lirico.

Para hoy era fijada una fiesta en la Exposicion pero á razon de la mucha lluvia que hacia se ha diferido hasta Viernes. No se hará mucha cosa, pero lo que yo viere luego sabrás por mis cartas, porque estando tu enfermecito dos cartillas recibirás una despues de otra sin deber contestar.

Tengas cuidado, te ruego, cuando partirás para Viena, de advertir todos cuantos en tu viaje encuentres, porque no pudiera ser imposible, que te des con las mozas y su madre, que nosotros hemos nombrado "las Prerauerenses." Casi un año entero ha pasado, sin que yo viese ni oyese algo de aquellas doncellas muy dignas de atencion y curiosidad cuando se ha encontrado á ellas una vez. Sé bien, que la esperanza, que en tu viaje pongo, es muy debil, pero el accidente es dicho un dios protector á los que buscan y creo que cada movil se ha de admitir, para sacar en limpio algo con eses seres enigmas.

Te sanes luego,

tu devotisimo
D. Cipion

Vienna, August 28, 1873

Dear Friend,

I must tell you that a short while ago—two hours ago precisely—my mother, Alexander, Rosa, and Dolfi arrived here, somewhat hot and tired but otherwise in excellent health and good spirits. I am giving you the news immediately because I have learned with pleasure and inner satisfaction how you sped their departure, packing, tying, labeling, and transporting their trunks. You have a thousand small talents, all serving the cause of friendship. I have resolved to sound everybody out about you and to take notice of everything they say about you, but am being kept almost too busy with it, for they decline Eduard in almost every sentence through all six cases: "der Eduard," "des Eduard," "dem Eduard," "o der Eduard," "von dem Eduard."[1] I must thank you cordially for the countless kindnesses you have shown them, so many that they now vie with one another in singing your praises to curious ears, as if touting your worth in the market. I am well aware that all these good deeds were by no means done for my sake, that I am merely a planet that owes the light of your favor to the proximity of a shining sun, but how often have we not been burdened with something we afterward found to be a valuable possession? May you feel that way about me!

This morning, Anna[2] assured me, with the certainty that distinguishes the oracle-pronouncing and oracle-believing half of mankind, that you would be coming along tonight. I can only explain her confidence by assuming that her ears must have burned yesterday, a well-known sign that others are thinking or speaking of us and are willing us to think or speak of them. Incidentally, you must have been playing a leading part—as indeed befits you—in their "closed" society; as far as Alexander is concerned, it is an established fact—and one that he trumpets out loudly enough—that, wait till you hear this, you are in love with Frau Lipska. Children, as everyone knows, always speak the truth. But when two soothsayers contradict each other, which of them should one believe? Your little sister, Mina,[3] is said to have held a different view. I will not allow myself to be swayed, therefore, and propose to adhere to my unofficial opinion until you confirm or reject it once we "take the road" shoulder to shoulder and "bras dessus, bras dessous" [arm in arm].

I am, incidentally, far less happy about your treatment of another young person dear to me. You are alleged to have allowed the said young man, who needs to be treated with indulgence because of his rapid growth, to spend half his days with a somewhat elderly père de famille on the study of dreary subjects; you are said to have restricted the exercise he needs and to have carried matters so far that, in the opinion of all my sisters, who know him well, he really looks quite ill. The smallest physical exertion is said to make him spectacularly wan, which may please the ladies but *me* not in the least, and since his heart is not quite what it should be, anyway, it would seem that the treatment you have meted out to him cannot be justified. I am most anxious to know if all I have heard is true. I shall be seeing you on Sunday for a few minutes at the station, and soon afterward, I think, we shall have a chance to talk to each other properly. I really have to work several hours a day now (four at least), but we shall be able to while the rest of the time away in talking, walking, driving about.[4] Quite apart from the fact that you are my friend of many years, wedded to me by common destiny and the Academia Castellana, I am glad that your company will render superfluous that of the amphibian Rosanes, who has nothing of the student save certificates, nothing of the dreamer save lack of judgment, nothing of the nobleman save indolence, and for the rest has cold blood and a pointed nose.

Before you leave, give my regards once again to all our friends and then come to Vienna, where I await you with longing.

Your Sigmund Freud

P.S.   My wallet pleases me only because I know that its twin sister is in your possession. I bought another Zeplichal yesterday and am ready to make good your loss, but will have to ask you to let me borrow it for two hours a day, as I have acquired a taste for it.

Sigmund Freud

1. Freud has omitted the accusative,"den Eduard." Tr.

2. Freud's sister Anna (1858–1955).

3. The youngest of the Silberstein children.

4. *Versprechen, verlaufen, verfahren:* after Nikolaus Lenau, *Die drei Zigeuner* (The three gypsies): *verraucht, verschläft, vergeigt* (smoking, sleeping, fiddling about).

Vienna, January 22, 1874

Papal Bull: "We cannot" in the presence of the corpse[1]

We cannot, that is to say, I cannot, obtain a ticket for you to attend Brühl's[2] lectures, so you will have to go and get one yourself. The first one, entitled Sea Squirt[3] and Morality, will take place on February 8. Do not be surprised at the unusual heading I have given this Bull, because it had to be written in the dissection hall.

Cipion

In Spanish

1. After *non possumus,* the formula introducing every refusal by the pope to accede to a demand by a temporal power; "in the presence of the corpse" refers to the dissection hall.

2. Carl Brühl (1820–1899), appointed professor of zootomy at Vienna in 1861.

3. *Seescheide; Scheide* is also an anatomical term for the vagina. Tr.

Viena 22/I 1874

Bulla "No podemos" praesente cadavere

No podemos, es decir, no puedo llevarte un billete para las lecturas de Brühl, por eso será menester que vayas mismo por él. El 8 de februario habrá lugar la primera que Seescheide y Moralidad se intitula. No te maravilles del sobre estraño, que he dado á esa bulla porque debria ser escrito en la sala de las secciones.

Cipion

———————

Vienna, August 13, 1874

Dear Friend,

Barely ten minutes have passed since the postman delivered your exotic letter, and here I am already sitting and writing in order to fulfill your request faithfully. I am by no means at a loss for material with which to pad a letter, for I have not seen any friends for a week and have been unable to get anything off my chest. I think it expedient, however, to subdivide the raw material with which I intend to construct this letter into three floors through which you can amble at your leisure one after another. So:

First Floor.[1]

•{ Of literary and friendly correspondence in general and of our own in particular. }•

Had I a dictionary I should very much have liked to write to you in Spanish, but without one I do not quite dare to venture, unarmed against all eventualities, onto Spanish soil. Were you to make the first move—and since all Spanish words follow like soldiers in your train, that would cause you no difficulty—then I should follow suit, attempting to keep my end up with my modest forces.

I am no less hesitant about granting other nations the right to appear in their native dress on the marketplace of our epistolary commerce, for instance in English, Italian, and other sentences and periods—the French, as everyone knows, do not enjoy especial esteem in Europe. But it is up to you, as the more linguistically proficient (i.e., the more widely traveled), to decide to whom our market should be opened or closed. I have tried to set an example in a different field, namely in respect of the form in which a letter should be cast. Just see for yourself how the common man, that misera plebs contribuens[2] for whom it will be our life's work to think, writes his letters. What a mess! The mere fulfillment of the meanest need! No trace of artistry! With all the signs of a difficult birth but quite without its accomplishment! The whole letter might be a postscript, a brief appendage to the salutation of Dear Friend, My Dearest, or Dear Sir, so disorganized is the jostling of news with ideas, the skirmishing of requests and questions, together with reproaches (which every letter requires as seasoning). Now then, I have had a thought that may prove interesting and that I would not wish to keep from you. They (the theologians) have long been puzzled why the good Lord + + + required six days for his work of creation, when he could have completed it in a second. All previously advanced exegeses do not hold up; I alone have the correct explanation. He wanted to show mankind that in any task it is essential to observe a rational order and a logical sequence of steps; had God created everything in a second, this important lesson would have been lost on humanity in its striving toward godliness. The selfsame order must also be reflected in our letters, but it must not be artificial or lifeless, rather that of a work of art, whose parts are not merely distinct, but also closely interrelated. I accordingly present myself as a Freemason who has bricked up the structure of this letter on three floors and, having come to the end of the first floor, I put down my trowel to rest for the construction of the second.

Second Floor.
In which several comments on my deeds and my omissions have taken up residence.

You will deem it a particular advantage of my method of construction that I neglect the stairs completely, so that you can reach one floor from the next without having to draw breath. As you now enter the second floor, and knock discreetly on the door behind which I live, I hear it, get up from my work, and invite you to enter. However, instead of inquiring about your health, etc., courtesy dictates that I converse with you about myself, which I do as follows.

I am one of those human beings who can be found most of the day between two pieces of furniture, one formed vertically, the armchair, and one extending horizontally, the table, and from these, as social historians are agreed, sprang all civilizations, because they have a justified claim to the predicate sessile or "sedentary." Since this position does not involve all parts of the body in equal measure, and the nobler parts protrude above the tabletop to a considerable degree, I am compelled, for the due occupation of both, to engage in two activities: reading and writing. Now, what I write is mathematics, and what I read is paper. For it is thus and not with the sentimental "Words, words" that Hamlet should have answered Polonius when the latter enquired how the prince occupied his time. To be paper is the common property and also the common destiny of all books.

The books which I read deserve this fate so little that they might as well be engraved in bronze, were the hundredweight not too dear. They are Helmholtz's lectures,[3] Carlyle's Sartor Resartus, and Aristotle's Ethica Nicomachaea.

To speak of the first and the last would be superfluous, as I cannot hope to give you any idea of their essence in a few brief words. Carlyle's Sartor Resartus deserves some mention. (For that, I must arrange a separate cabinet in my apartment: read Scherr[4] on Carlyle.) The book is introduced in the manner of Jean Paul[5] and at times shows Jean Paul's sparkle, but for the rest is English and makes fun of us brooding Germans. A German professor, Diogenes Teufelsdröckh,[6] Professor of the Science of Things in General at the University of Weissnichtwo has written a "Philosophy of Clothes" and sent it to the author (Carlyle) with the request that he publish an English translation thereof. The latter complies inasmuch as he translates at least some extracts of this peculiar work, whose author seems to assume every possible guise, being Faust and Mephistopheles in one, satirist and philosopher, and then turns to Hofrat Heuschrecke, a close friend of Teufelsdröckh in Weissnichtwo, for biographical details, which he duly receives and translates as well. Our Diogenes Teufelsdröckh is a foundling, brought up in the small town of *Entepfuhl* by the *Futteral* couple, and, having completed his studies in the *Hinterschlag* Gymnasium, he goes on to attend the university, suffering all the hardships of the future genius, for which Carlyle gives him due credit. Under all these funny names, however, lies a profound wisdom, and the motley scraps of folly cover the open sores of mankind and of the tale's hero. What we are told about the philosophy of clothes is part parody and part witty reflection, which starts from the assumption that clothes are a representation of the manifest and "physical, behind which the spiritual hides in shame." I take it that the metaphysical atmosphere you are getting a whiff of is becoming a bit stifling. You rise, inquire briefly after the health of "my esteemed family," who are very well, and then ascend to the third floor or

Third Floor.
❧ Where Your Honor will find a large gathering of lost people who have poured in from all parts of the world and are now established on the third floor.

Know then, Your Honor, Señor Berganza, that here nothing has been either seen or heard of the museum or of the not long extinct Cretaceous; which is easily explained when one considers that no search has been conducted by myself or by anyone else. Let them sleep in eternal peace! And may the earth rest lightly upon them!

I have not heard anything of Rosanes or of his friend, so it appears that they are well and in need of nothing.

Nor am I able to tell you anything of the others who lived in this town. I am alone, something that has never happened to me before, and yours was the first letter whose answer made claims upon my time.

If you would like me to send you some books that have seen the light of day here and there, such as the continuation of the Shake-speare,[7] you have only to say so. ❧

A large shower of meteors was forecast yesterday and the day before; it may be that the Lord has postponed it until tomorrow because of the bad weather. For the past four days I have been waiting for the chance to take a solitary excursion to the Brühl,[8] but in the early morning I never dare to predict a beautiful day, while later on I regret having missed such glorious weather. I was firmly resolved to venture forth even in dubious weather today, but yesterday thick clouds gathered along the horizon and by this morning the pavement was beneath an ocean. I have just been up in the attic, peering out to see if the much longed-for day will finally arrive tomorrow.

When the builders have finished a house as far as the roof, they fasten pine twigs to boards acclaiming the master builder and the house owner, and usually their children and grandchildren as well. In this case, I am the master builder and you the owner, and from the gable of my newly finished house I call out cordial greetings to you.

Your Cipion

P.S.   The house is not built so meticulously as to ensure that something or other has not been overlooked. The builders then make it good afterwards. La Ac. Esp. requests that you betray less to your new aunt than you did to the old, moreover that you write diligently and very soon and have a good yawn first, so that your letter evinces the youthful vigor and strength of purpose that becomes a finished Gymnasium scholar and future citizen of Academe.

Your Cipion

My respects, and those of my mother, to your parents.

Portions in Spanish, with some Greek and Latin.
   1. Freud gave the names of the floors in English.
   2. The poor taxpayers; a phrase attributed to the Hungarian jurist István Verböczi (*Decretum tripartitum*, 1514).
   3. Perhaps his *Populäre wissenschaftliche Vorträge* (Popular scientific lectures), 1856–1876.
   4. Johannes Scherr, *Geschichte der englischen Literatur* (History of English literature), 1854.
   5. Johann Paul Friedrich Richter (1763–1825), German romantic novelist known for his humorous representations of village life. Tr.
   6. *Teufelsdröckh*, devil's feces; *Weissnichtwo*, who knows where; *Heuschrecke*, grasshopper; *Entepfuhl*, duck puddle; *Futteral*, small box or case; *Hinterschlag*, back of beyond. Tr.
   7. Probably the edition by E. Devrient and O. Devrient, 1873.
   8. A valley south of Vienna.

De correspondencia literaria y amical en general y de nuestra en especial.

En que se han allojado unas noticias de mí y de mis quehaceres y que*no*haceres.

Adonde Vm hallerá grande coleccion de gente perdida, concurrida de todas las partes del mundo, como suelen habitar au troisieme étage.

Sepa Vm, Señor D. Berganza, que ni del museo, ni de la, no largo tiempo ha, estincta formacion de la Greda se ha visto ó oido cosa hasta aquí; lo que facil se puede esplicar, cuando se piensa, que no se [ha] buscado á saber algo, ni de mi parte, ni de otra alguna. ¡Asi duerman en paz eterna! ¡y la tierra les sea ligera!

Οὔποτε τοῦ Ῥωσανοῦς οὔτε τοῦ ἑταίρου αὐτοῦ πέπυσμαι τί, ὥστε εὖ πράττοντες καὶ οὐδένος δεόμενοι δοκοῦσιν.

Nec aliorum, qui in hac urbe manserunt, tibi quidquam referre possum. Solus sum, idquod nunquam antea accidit, et epistola tua prima fuit, quae tempus respondendi mihi abrogavit.

Si quieres, que te envie unos libros, que ahí son dados á la luz, como la continuacion de Shakespeare, no has mas que decir.

Vienna, August 22, 1874

Dear Friend,

When, in your kind letter, you drew my attention to August 18 as the birthday of his Apostolic Majesty, the Emperor Franz Josef I, you probably did not realize that two days later the peoples of Austria would be celebrating the edifying occasion of the majority of our illustrious crown prince.[1] That elevated chick is, his sixteen years notwithstanding, but sparsely covered with feathers and is anxiously being guarded against attempts to fly on his own; nevertheless such days are memorable for drawing attention to the generally overlooked phenomenon that crown princes, too, grow older by one year every 365 days. Some of the newspapers I have read on the occasion of the event have been struck so foolish with surprise that they give voice—whether gratis or for cash down, I know not—to unspeakable balderdash; thus one of them is sorry for him on the grounds that he will have henceforth to forfeit the illusions of golden youth to concentrate his every thought and care on the future reign over a great empire.

As if the most useless things in the world were not arranged in the following order: shirt collars, philosophers, and monarchs. For the rest, one must grant that a measure of surprise at the news under discussion is pardonable; all scions of the House of Hapsburg have the peculiarity of growing up in seclusion, suddenly to emerge in seasoned form. You have only to think of Princess Gisela,[2] who was

generally considered to be a child until one day the newspapers discovered that she was sixteen years old and a bride.

A certain hereditary Grand Duke of Oldenburg[3] gave the first
news of his exalted existence a few days ago—not, mark you, with
a cry uttered at birth but by an act of heroism that bore witness to
considerable maturity. He deigned to be in a bad humor at the Leip-
ziger Station and, in a fit of truly princely condescension, he took
his seat on the counter, spurning a chair. The landlord, who asked
him to abandon his perch (but who did not know him, since otherwise he would surely have offered the noble gentleman a cushion),
was granted a slap in the face as a souvenir, which he, instead of
never again washing his cheek, thus preserving the honor of the exalted contact, returned promptly and with interest, something for
which His Grace was not prepared. The public, too, took sides and
anointed the unrecognized sovereign in spe with fist oil, as the barber did to the godless king in the fable.[4] A policeman finally managed to rescue the prince. Although anyone else might have had to
cool his heels in a cell for twenty-four hours, His Most Serene High-
ness was favored with apologies for not having been recognized.

Who better to place beside such a prince than the Dame aux Camelias?[5] I made her acquaintance two years ago in Freiberg, albeit
in a paltry German plaster cast. I think one cannot but feel compassion, at least while reading the book, even though in several places
one may plainly glimpse the backstage onions intended to squeeze
out our tears. But I would pronounce this work trash no less than
you do. Mind you, I do not hold, as some aesthetes do, that everything immoral according to the letter of the Civil or Mosaic Code
must also be unpoetic: Gottfried's Tristan und Isolde is the most
brilliant refutation of this dictum. Rather, poetry, supported by the
power of our own passions, can go quite some way toward transfig-
uring what is immoral, or, better, what society does not allow. The
immoral in poetry only starts with the foul and the loathsome. This
limit is often crossed in the Dame aux Camelias, and I have as often
thrown the book down, but sometimes the Dame aux Camélias
leads us to idyllic ground and then we must do what every idyll
compels: forget the past and the future and delight in the present as
the story unfolds. That no poet must choose immoral subjects is a
dictate of morality, or if you like of the moral police, rather than a
prohibition nurtured on the ground of poetry itself. Hence the

strange inconsistency of today's public faced with this whole French
concoction of murder, arson, adultery, and political intrigue, and
their manner of rejecting it all time and again and yet noticing, even
acknowledging, it. The line between what is immoral in poetry, and
what is immoral in daily life but permitted in poetry, is generally
difficult to draw. One might put it that, even in poetry, every passion
without adequate motive, without, so to speak, some historical title
to, or natural claim on, the beloved, seems immoral. Second, those
who judge may well deem [im]moral what has had less poetic discrimination bestowed upon it, with the result that, where poetry has
not asserted its exceptional status, morals come into their own. In
Tristan und Isolde, it is the glowing but measured portrayal and the
concurrence of a host of motives with a powerful effect on our emotions that allow poetry to make use of immoral subjects, so that the
very fact that Marke is old and Tristan young, for instance, or that a
love potion has enchained the two, or the fact of Marke's weakness
and inability to allow strict justice to prevail over Isolde, becomes
an excuse for the lovers. In the Dame aux Camélias there is, it is
true, nothing of the kind, nor is there anything about the person of
Marguérite, to permit one's emotion to treat her as an exception.
Dumas, having despaired of moving us with the pure effect of his
poetry, wants to excite us, at least, with the contrast he can create
between other forces and the poetry in us, our imagination. In that
he admittedly succeeds, particularly while the impression is still
fresh. But once it has faded, one can only doubly condemn the paltry
artifice of trying to make his poetic powers appear greater than they
are by engaging them in a struggle in which they are momentarily
victorious, only to be defeated in the end.

Your plan to go to Germany pleases me greatly, only it ought not
to be to dreary Leipzig, where you will lock yourself in a cubbyhole
as you did in Vienna, but to the beautiful *Heidelberg*, celebrated in
song, where Professor Bluntschli[6] teaches, or to merry old Göttingen where you will find Professor Ihering.[7] And what, finally, would
you say to *Berne* or *Zurich*? In my view, a Swiss university combines
both advantages. To consider the cost is absurd since, first, one is
not a student often in one's life and, second, your extra-academic
needs, I am confident, will be confined to the barest necessities
everywhere.

The premature trust you place in my medical skills I cannot, alas, do justice to, since your injury seems to be internal and since even Dr. Schlesinger[8] is unable to cure an internally damaged knee joint on the basis of written information, particularly if it contains such vague symptoms as [your] being prevented from attending a Te Deum. I hope, however, that the injury will have been repaired by the time you receive this letter, obviating the need for further cures. It is, incidentally, hardly likely that you have sprained it, since, in my surgical innocence, I cannot fathom how a knee joint can be sprained.

To broach a subject that should pain you less than your knee, you might perhaps send me a description of your charming aunt, as you now have an excellent pretext for gazing at her attentively the better to portray her.

The Danube has risen very considerably during the past few days and a flood is expected by the hour. Whether she is serious is still uncertain; it looks as if she wants to think it over, and return little by little to her placid attitude in a bed of tranquility.

That all elderly people are adherents of the theory of degeneration is an established fact. Admittedly they have a legitimate complaint when fruit becomes dearer, and you yourself must be sorrowing at the fatherland's decline in this matter. I have an inexpressible longing for the grape season; there is nothing now but monotonous pears. Pears are the crudest, most tasteless, most prosaic fruit in the world.

In my official capacity of M.d.l.A.E. [Member of the Spanish Academy] I must not withhold from you a question of great political significance that has been preoccupying me greatly. At a time when everyone is recognizing the Spanish Republic,[9] the Spanish Academy, an unexcelled model of organization and of such importance to its maternal organism, seems to be turning away from Spain and, unmindful of its origins, granting admittance, or rather exclusive dominion, to barbaric customs and foreign sounds even in its official documents. For how long will one still be able to speak of an *aetas aurea* of the Spanish Academy, rather than having to bemoan an *aetas ahenea* sive *papyracea*,[10] in which the original purity of Spanish manners and customs have become blemished, save for a few traditions? I shudder at the work of the historiographers and cultural historians who will have to paint the picture of this sad decline. I, Don Cipion, a dignitary of the A.E., cannot help thinking that my own disloyal and unpatriotic attitude might be to blame for this degeneration, and though otherwise not conservative, I offer you, Don Berganza, my hand for the reconstruction or renovation of the ruined edifice. An old superstition has it that no building is sound whose foundations have not cost a human sacrifice. To the competence of our A.E. renovada y confirmada [renewed and consolidated] we sacrifice two victims, two princesses or reinas, que antes en nuestro reino han imperado [queens who previously reigned over our realm]. Awaiting your reply to this and everything else and wishing you as much prosperity as can be attained in the familiar 120 years,[11] I remain, yours most faithfully

Don Cipion

With kind regards
Rosa Freud

Cordial greetings from
Anna Freud

1. Rudolph von Hapsburg (1858–1889).

2. Older sister of Rudolph, who married Prince Leopold of Bavaria on April 20, 1873.

3. Friedrich August (1852–1931). The *Neue Freie Presse* reported the incident in its evening editions of August 14 and 21, 1874.

4. Ludwig Bechstein (1801–1860), "Der König im Bade" (The king in the bath).

5. Novel by Alexandre Dumas (*fils*), 1852.

6. Johann Kaspar Bluntschli (1808–1881).

7. Rudolf von Ihering (1818–1892).

8. Dr. Benedict Schlesinger claimed, in a regular series of advertisements, that he could cure 8,700 "private" complaints—that is, conditions normally concealed by the patient—including impotence, premature ejaculation, and all other disturbances of the nervous and reproductive systems.

9. The first, short-lived Spanish Republic, which followed the abdication of Prince Amadeo of Savoy on February 10, 1873.

10. *Aetas aures*, golden age (Ovid); *aetas ahenea sive papyracea*, bronze or paper age.

11. Genesis 6:3: "And the Lord said, My spirit shall not always strive with man, for that he also is flesh; yet his days shall be an hundred and twenty years."

Vienna, September 4, 1874

¡Querido amigo!

Under the fresh impression of the reproaches my illegible hand-writing drew from you, I "hasten," as the saying has it, to submit to you a carefully amended sample of my unruly hand and only beg your pardon if, in the course of this letter, the new virtue should revert to the old vice. With very much pleasure, I gather from your letter that you have included Heidelberg and Göttingen among the candidates for your glorious future academic life. I cannot, for the moment, furnish the required information, but may be able to do so within a few days, and I shall hold this letter until I have gathered reliable news. From what I know of other German universities, they start their enrollment of students on October 15–19. Lectures are usually deferred for another week.

I am sending you the second volume of the Pickwickians,[1] a novel by Bulwer,[2] and our university lecture list at the same time as I post this letter, in order to still your voracious appetite for the robustly monosyllabic English words.[3]

My proposals for the resuscitation of the Spanish Academy have regard, first of all, to the occasion of your going abroad, but can also be applied to the occasion of your staying in Vienna, albeit with less appeal.

The members of the Spanish Academy are among those modern men whose days number more than twelve working hours and whose nights are robbed of dreams by fatigue. As I am in a whirl of duties and tasks that will make my day seem all too brief, and you in the painful predicament of being a newly born academic citizen, we will hardly have the leisure or the inclination to give each other the regular and full reports necessary to make our separation tolerable, unless we turn writing into a duty attached to the sublime name of the Ac. Española and therefore demanding fulfillment at fixed times and with unswerving devotion. Hence my proposal amounts to stipulating that every Sunday each of us, the two sole luminaries of the A.E., send the other a letter that is nothing short of an entire encyclopedia of the past week and that with total veracity reports all our doings, commissions and omissions, and those of all strangers we encounter, in addition to all outstanding thoughts and observations and at least an adumbration, as it were, of the unavoidable emotions. In that way, each of us may come to know the surroundings and condition of his friend most precisely, perhaps more precisely than was possible even at the time when we could meet in the same city. Our letters, which, when the year has passed, may constitute the ornament of the A.E. archives, will then be as diverse as our very lives. In our letters we shall transmute the six prosaic and unrelenting working days of the week into the pure gold of poetry and may perhaps find that there is enough of interest within us, and in what remains and changes around us, if only we learn to pay attention. Moreover, I gladly confess my need to be kept informed of what happens in other faculties and intellectual disciplines lest I run the danger, to which everyone working in his own field is exposed, of becoming set in my ways (e.g., the out-and-out Bohemian, the hidebound physician).

While all these are serious matters, I request, in order to preserve some spirit of romanticism, with which no A.E. can dispense, that every letter be treated as an issue of a weekly journal or periodical of the A.E., appearing as a double edition at two distinct places of publication—or rather writing—and as the only officially accredited organ of the A.E. Indeed, no other form but that of the journal is suited to the inclusion of so varied a content as our letters must possess, according to my plan. The familiar circle of readers, however, for whom the paper is written (consisting, as it does, of but a single person, the recipient) will be spared the disadvantages of the major journals. To what extent we must adhere to the journal form may be the subject of special discussions between us, provided, of course, that you agree to the principle. I would advocate strict observance of the form. An objection one might make to this proposal is that it is too sweeping and that one cannot expect to have, each week at the same time, the mood and skill needed to survey the past six days' life and to give an appealing description of it to a friend. As to the first objection, it can be said that it is truly worth the trouble to sacrifice one or two hours in the week to an end that can establish such lively communication between two people who are separated. And as to the second, I would reply that one should not question in advance one's ability to keep a critical diary and spice it with a bit of humor, and also that such an issue of the Periodico de la A.E. is not a set school composition, but an informal piece and a commu-

nication whose greater or lesser success will naturally depend on
both the material and the occasion.

In any case, I look forward to your counterproposals or additions,
in the hope that both the sense and the nonsense of it all will appeal
to you. However, before the A.E. tackles the task of discussing so
important a creation, I should like to define a fundamental law, one
that has long since been applied in the Spanish Academy. To wit:
that everything in the Republic of the A.E. be decided by unanimous
vote, so that two are needed for acceptance but only one vote for
rejection.

Leipzig, I have seen from the notice, starts on the nineteenth, Heidelberg on the fifteenth of October; I could find nothing from Göttingen University but take it that the date will be similar.

Looking forward to your kind reply
Tu fidelissimo
Cipion

1. Charles Dickens, *The Posthumous Papers of the Pickwick Club*, 1836–1837.

2. Edward George Earle Lytton Bulwer, 1st Baron Lytton (1803–1873), prominent
novelist, dramatist, and statesman.

3. "English words" in English in the original.

Vienna, September 18, 1874

Dear Friend,

Before I accept your thanks for my consignment of books, I must
apologize for making you pay as dearly for the pleasure of borrowing
an English book as the book itself would have cost you. I was firmly
resolved to put stamps on the little parcel if the excess postage came
to more than half a guilder.[1] It now turns out that it far exceeded the
limit I set and I, who am only at home with the lowlands of currency, could not conceive of the altitude of the flight. Really, nothing
can justify the payment of a fine for the effrontery of sending a trifle
to a friend a few miles away, as if, in deciding to disregard the

wooden frontier posts of two countries, one had committed a crimen perduellionis and laesae majestatis [high treason and lèse majesté] and God knows what else.

The list of lectures at Vienna University was missing from the parcel not through negligence but by intent, although I had announced its impending arrival in the letter I wrote first. For—with your predilection for Vienna—I was afraid that your very pleasing intention to spend one year abroad might come to nothing, as happened to several acquaintances of mine, and did not wish, by sending you the list, to rouse your urge to seek out the same nest year after year like a swallow.

Since this reason still holds, I am not sending the list even now. To dispel your anxiety that you might lose a year by staying abroad, I can tell you that you are entitled to spend the first and third years of your law studies wherever you please, since there are no examinations then (unlike the second and fourth years). Indeed, even if you were to dedicate your first year to another, say the philosophical, faculty, it would still be counted toward your legal studies.

Your news that you are diverting yourself in Leipzig by giving private lessons I can take only as confirmation of the paradox that, if he cannot keep them within bounds, man can suffer from his virtues as much as from his vices. Your scruples cause you to take too anxious a view of your parents' attitude. From what I know of him, I believe that your father would not consider it a sacrifice to provide the trifling sums you require for the satisfaction of your student passions, provided he succeeds in getting you to acquire the touch of sophistication for whose sake he is sending you abroad in the first place.

Nor do I grasp in what manner you propose to combine the giving of lessons with a student's life. Being a student means being master of your own time and if you sell your time, spending several hours a day in slavery, you will be left with few opportunities and little desire to enjoy your freedom, the less so as you also want to study and, what is more, without constraint and at your leisure. What then might your student diversions in Leipzig consist of? You are unlikely to spend your time on duels, love affairs, creditors, and dogs, all items that constitute the specific aroma of student life; and association with friends, walks, and a glass of beer, if need be in Auerbach's cellar, are unlikely to prove so costly that they cannot be expected from, or provided by, your parents. No more can I believe that your father would not have allowed for riding and fencing, which you may be including in your expenses, as part of the program for the trip, and that you will have to pay for them. I cannot understand the feverish haste with which you want to escape your youth. Remember that, once grown up and professionally trained, you will be subjected to a thousand demands by your present family and the one you have still to acquire, by domestic and public life, and perhaps by your academic work as well. If you enjoy the pursuit of your studies in the stillness of your own thoughts and feelings and the undisturbed pleasure in yourself that the division of interests and multiplication of cares will never grant you again in later life, then make use of the time set aside for that purpose by your parents and everyone else; for once youth has fled people will tend to begrudge you[2] every moment you devote to your own pursuits. If, however, it is your highest aim to live for others, then remember that everything you now do for yourself will later benefit other people, and grant you the double satisfaction of perfecting yourself while being able to work for them. In any case—use your time for your own good; youth is but the close season in which destiny allows us to gain strength so that we can amuse her by our resistance if she later decides to hunt us down.

I replied to you immediately upon receipt of your "esteemed" letter, as Baiersdorf[3] would put it, because I consider it quite superfluous to sound Braun out on subjects that he can know nothing about. He is not the person to take an interest in things that do not concern him, and I must agree with him if he took the same attitude when he was asked about private lessons. To judge by what happens in Vienna, no mountains of gold can be earned there by private tuition. All the better for you; then you will not be led into temptation.

I laughed heartily at the fire rumpus although it must have seemed more serious to you. I look forward ardently and with great expectations to your proposals for the Periodico d.l.A.E.; though your preliminary remarks lead me to think that you are not greatly in favor of the form, I am still inclined to defend it. One's disappointment is extremely disagreeable when, on tearing open a letter from a distant friend in the hopes of learning his latest news, one is told in a few brief words that he feels bored at the moment and has nothing at all to report. The letter writer thinks far too often that

he has done his duty once he has taken an envelope addressed to us
to the post; he generally cares not a rap whether what is written
inside really recompenses us for his absence or long silence. It is,
however, the unmistakable characteristic of a person distracted in
his own affairs and grown apart from his friends that he should find
letter writing a burden. But someone who is self-possessed and feels
affection for his friends will always find something that engages his
attention sufficiently to be considered worthy of taking up his
friends' time, or that causes him so much doubt as to call for the
support of the friends' reassuring judgment. After all, selfless sympathy with everything that concerns or happens to the other is often
the most valuable, indeed the sole, contribution of a friend. Hence
it is my belief that he who has made himself conversant with this
duty and feels a keen need to correspond with friends has no need
for a special mood to write a satisfactory letter, but can create that
mood at will, the better to relieve his oppression and to cheer himself up. Moreover, a conscientious exchange of letters provides an
inestimable saving in care and worry, which the negligent correspondent can never stave off; I might point out that ears have
stopped burning since the invention of the post. That I have decided
upon a jocular form for our letters is connected with the fact that
since I have ceased keeping a diary I have had no chance during the
six weekdays to deposit anywhere the little humor and good fun one
produces along with everything else in those six weekdays, which
does not mean that I wish to turn my letter into a madhouse. You
yourself have a goodly supply of wit and irony; why should their
expression not benefit a friend who prizes the humor of it, as Pistol[4]
says, above all things? For the rest, the form is immaterial and if our
journal permits the inclusion of a learned treatise or a few thoughts
worthy of Werther, so much the better—there is no duress in the
Spanish Academy.

> Meanwhile accept my sincerest regards and reply soon to
> Your Sigismund
> ó Cipion
> M.d.l.A.E.

Postscriptum. To suggest that I might have overlooked the New
Year[5] is to impute to me a tastelessness of which I know myself to
be completely free. People are wrong to reproach religion for being
of a metaphysical nature and for lacking the certainty of sensory

perceptions. Rather, religion addresses the senses alone, and even the God-denier who is fortunate enough to belong to a tolerably pious family cannot deny the holiday when he puts a New Year's Day morsel to his lips. One might say that religion, consumed in moderation, stimulates the digestion, but that taken in excess it harms it. Even Goethe realized that "nothing harder is to bear than a round of festive fare."[6] And why should that be? Naturally enough, one's stomach is upset. It is most remarkable how certain holidays are distinguished by a very special religious effect on the abdominal organs. Thus the Passover has a constipating effect due to unleavened bread and hardboiled eggs. Yom Kippur is so lugubrious a day not so much through God's wrath as through the plum jam and the evacuation it stimulates. Nonetheless such characteristics do not suffice for distinguishing between all holidays, and an empiricist like myself will on many future occasions continue, as he has done this year, to confuse the New Year with Purim, since nothing specific is consumed on either occasion. Today, however, the death rattle of two fishes and a goose out in the kitchen informs me that the Day of Atonement is at hand. (I am exaggerating for illustrative effect since the beasts were dead when they were brought into the house.) How greatly the alliance between religion and the stomach redounds to the advantage of the former is something that cannot be assessed at first glance. I think the stomach would start a revolution if religion were abolished and what that means is worth pondering; there are people who believe that the stomach can rule the world quite unaided. Perhaps the alliance between alimentation and edification might provide the explanation of why their piety helps clerics to run to fat—but here we become lost in problems of social history that are not really our concern. The truth is that eating is the most stubborn of habits. Our festivals have long since survived our dogmas, as a funeral feast survives the dead. And the question of what the last man on earth will be doing I can answer with what the first man did: he will be eating. Hence we take part in the Sunday and holiday feasts, but with the difference that whereas the pious believe they are doing good works we worldlings are conscious of having eaten a good meal.

1. Freud mistakenly wrote "no more."
2. Freud mistakenly wrote "me."
3. Emil Baiersdorf (b. 1854), a fellow student.

4. Freud must have meant Nym rather than Pistol; see *King Henry V*, II.1, and *The Merry Wives of Windsor*, II.1.

5. Rosh Hashana, the Jewish new year, which usually falls in September.

6. Reference to *Sprichwörtlich:* "Alles in der Welt lässt sich ertragen / Nur nicht eine Reihe von schönen Tagen" (Everything in the world can be borne / Save a round of good days).

Vienna, October 22–23, 1874

¡Querido amigo!

I am setting about answering your two letters in the middle of the night in order to cut short your surprise, if not your concern, about my obdurate silence. Be of good cheer, I am still alive and still breathing—the balmy air of the dissection hall, albeit I barely have time to take cognizance of my breaths. In fact, this is my sole excuse; a letter demands a degree of composure, or artistic calm, a letter is nothing if not an exercise in the so-called liberal arts in which one can take pleasure only when the din of the daily round and cares has been silenced. Despite this, a letter to you was lying ready in my desk when I received your postcard, whereupon I decided to hold it back as it was no longer up-to-date and to replace it with another. As recompense for your long wait I can serve you with an authentic report on the inauguration of our rector which took place yesterday. I have no doubt that you read all about it in the Neue Presse,[1] but since their report, too, was only written by a student and, it would seem, by a fairly inept observer at that, you may like to have my account as a correction and an amplification.

You will remember, from the time you spent here, a proclamation from the Ministry of Education which drew attention to the cutting of lectures by law students and threatened disciplinary action, and another relating to the behavior of professors during examinations. The second incensed the teachers as much as the first did the students. To mark the long-postponed inauguration of the rector, the students had decided to hold a noisy demonstration, meant to remind His Excellency Herr Minister Dr. von Stremayr[2] somewhat emphatically of the meaning of academic freedom. It turned out differently, however, and most unexpectedly so. To our astonishment we discovered that the new rector, Dr. Wahlberg,[3] had saved us the trouble, conducting the demonstration far more effectively than the students themselves could have hoped to do. For a Hofrat and Rector magnificus, such an address was truly outrageous. He stressed the dignity of the premier German university, demanded an administration that cared for individual students' needs in place of the usual bureaucratic one—in other words declared it impossible to restore the university to the role it had played in the Middle Ages when it had served the Church and the State in turn, its present task being to go far beyond the bounds set by concerns of state and nationality—and went on to demand untrammelled freedom of learning and experiment, research and criticism. He reproached the present administration, albeit indirectly, with failing to provide the best academic staff and admonished it not to create discontent but to foster zeal for learning. For the students he demanded some relief from compulsory lectures, so that they would learn less but more thoroughly, and urged them to seek the fulfillment of their ideals in the university if they are to derive any benefit from attending it.

I am setting down the most trenchant of these blunt home truths

The main building of the University of Vienna, endowed by
Empress Maria Theresa; in use until 1884

out of order: these were the ones greeted by minutes of wild applause, by way of tribute to a highly esteemed teacher, in which one could hear the very voice of the university as well as animosity toward Stremayr, who, I was told, sat there uneasily, attempting diplomatic or superior smiles at all the strongly worded passages. When he left the hall, they hissed him, although in moderation; the intermingled applause reported by the newspapers was not meant for him but was a belated salute to the rector. A large part of the student body, myself included, saw no more of the whole affair than his coat and the hats of those beside him; he was left completely in the dark about why those who could see him were hissing, so that the interference of two different collective moods may well have deceived the reporter.

Besides this event from the world at large, I can report several matters from the narrower world and also from the narrowest, namely myself. Of our fellow students, you will not have heard that Wahle,[4] though nominally a philosopher, has nevertheless enrolled for the lectures of a physician of the finest caliber, that Luess has influenced his decision and that he was thus reunited with his inseparable colleague, Rosanes, by a detour. Herzig[5] has remained true to mathematics and is already rhapsodizing about infinite curves and complicated limits, but Herzog[6] has become a philologist, thus sparing me the embarrassment of having to witness his coming to grief. Still, when I think of him I have my doubts whether he is any better placed as a philologist than as a medical man and must take the Lord to task for having created such people, who have no physical or intellectual abilities whatsoever, not even the one that could make up for everything else—I mean outspokenness. For though the teleologists subtly deduced that even the lamb is not all that unhappy when it is slaughtered or the ass when it is beaten, one should remember that patience is neither a narcotic nor an analgesic but simply a sign of weakness. Unfortunately there is no more we can do for Herzog's weakness except leave him to it. Our lectures are thus tending to keep us apart, and only in zoology and in Brentano's[7] classes do we all still meet one another. Brentano is running two courses, selected metaphysical problems on Wednesday and Saturday evenings, and a text by Mill on the utilitarian principle[8] on Fridays, both of which we attend regularly. Mention of Brentano reminds me that you intended to go and hear Fechner,[9] and I do ask you to write and tell me what and how he teaches.

If the fate of my two sisters should still interest you, you will not take it amiss if I tell you that Anna was accepted as a first-year pupil by the Ursulerines[10] after passing her examination, and that Rosa has entered a school of drawing and design newly established for the perfection of feminine handicrafts. I have taken charge of the rest of her education and am sacrificing one of my lectures to that end. The gods cannot possibly have rejoiced at this sacrifice as much as I did.

To give you some idea of my activities I am enclosing my schedule, and, by way of correction, would add that the anatomy classes are not a constant fixture but take place periodically, because they depend entirely upon the amount of available material. In its absence, we have physiology classes or work in the dissection hall. A second enclosure consists of a label I pulled off a professor's chair after the inauguration, and the exalted thought that this shred of paper endured the pressure of a famous physicist's, philologist's, or even philosopher's shoulder for hours will, I hope, make you consider it a particularly precious relic.

I hope most fervently, of course, that you will not follow my example and keep me waiting for your reply, or expect me to mend my own ways by showing greater haste. If you like, I could answer your letters every Sunday or Saturday. It is only the thousand petty duties accompanying the inception of regular work that have held me back on this occasion, much as a machine creaks horribly on starting up. Lest I delay the despatch of this letter even further, I conclude with warm good wishes

Your Sigismund.

P.S.   My thanks to Reitler.[11]

I paid the call on Fluss the day after your departure without too much trouble.

---

1. The *Neue Freie Presse*, founded in 1864. It reported the inauguration on October 22.

2. Karl von Stremayr (1823–1904), Austrian Minister of Education, 1870–1879.

3. Wilhelm Emil Wahlberg (1824–1901), appointed Professor of Criminal Law at Vienna in 1854.

4. Richard Wahle (1857–1935), one of Silberstein's classmates; later Professor of Philosophy at Czernowitz and Vienna.

5. Josef Herzig (1853–1924), one of Silberstein's classmates; later Professor of Chemistry at Vienna.

6. Leopold Herzog (b. 1850 or 1851), a classmate.

7. Franz Brentano (1838–1917), appointed Professor of Philosophy at Vienna in 1874.

8. John Stuart Mill, *Utilitarianism*, 1863.

9. Gustav Theodor Fechner (1801–1887), Professor of Physics at Leipzig, 1834–1839; later taught philosophy of science.

10. Freud meant the Ursulines, an order of nuns devoted to teaching.

11. Anton Reitler (b. 1856), one of Silberstein's classmates.

Vienna, October 26, 1874

Dear Friend,

Your surprise at my silence is not all that unfounded. Though I sent you a fairly long and weary letter yesterday,[1] I am following the first with a second immediately upon receipt of your own, just in case the first be lost and cause us both groundless concern. The mystery, incidentally, is easily solved: I would have had time a thousand times over to tell you in five lines that I am well but, by composing so peculiar a document, I might well have heightened your anxiety and given you a basically false idea of how I apportion my time. I preferred to write a long and detailed letter but had to postpone it from one day to the next and could only finish it yesterday, i.e., Sunday.

So my fourteen days' silence has no graver cause than that. Incidentally, in your place I should have had the same, and worse, fears, for I know perfectly well that he who changes his place of residence is more testy and more subject to worry and unjustified assumptions than he who has stayed put, goes his accustomed way, and has no reason whatsoever to think that anything untoward may have happened.

Still, I do not believe that you will behave toward me as affectionate mothers do toward their children, suffering pangs of despair whenever they see them in danger and thrashing them when they have been rescued; that you will in no way make me atone for the fears you have suffered on my account but will quickly let me know what you are doing in Leipzig, what lectures you attend and which of them you like, and, if you have the time and the inclination, about anything in them you think might be of interest to me. In return, I am at your disposal with all the news you may ask of me. The event of my day is that I made the acquaintance of a Norwegian by the name of Grön,[2] a splendid, slim, fair-haired Teuton who studies medicine in Christiana[3] and has accompanied his father[4] to Vienna, where the latter will be attached to a local hospital for a year or six months. I came upon him in the dissection hall preparing brachial muscles and the sudden thought that the knowledge he has acquired of an arm in Norway has equipped him to cope with the muscle of a Viennese worker vividly reminded me of the unity of the human race, in the face of all the differences of nation and country. In Norway, incidentally, medical studies take six to seven years; physiology, which is here taken first, as the most important of the basic sciences, is studied there simultaneously with pathology, so that its application to pathology goes by the board. To judge by this specimen, medicine must be in a bad way there. Of the Norwegian language he tells me that it strongly resembles Swedish, which is understood throughout Norway; German and French are compulsory subjects at school and English optional. The main stress, however, is laid on the German language. As the Greeks did from Homer, so they learn German from Goethe's Her[r]mann und Dorothea. (I believe much the same thing happens in France.)

Perhaps you will be able to fit in your reply so that mine can follow on Sunday, for I intend henceforth to write every Sunday to avoid similar interruptions.

Your Sigismund Freud

1. Not extant.
2. Kristian Fredrik Grøn, born 1855; visited Vienna in 1874 and 1882.
3. Now Oslo.
4. Andreas Fredrik Grøn (1819–1905).

Vienna, November 8, 1874

Dear Friend,

I write today about a very gloomy week, during which a wintery
mood has descended upon me while my anxiously awaited winter
coat has not yet arrived, thanks to the whim or tardiness of my esteemed tailor. A kind of tremor is passing through the world; the
mortally ill hasten to die, the sickly redouble their coughing and
those still in good health surround themselves with bad conductors
of heat and exhale clouds of fog from their lungs. Fortunately both
of us are among those who have grounds to hope they will see another spring, and I for one have firmly resolved to make better use
of Nature's favors and to take better care of my physical well-being
by going for walks and on brief outings. The soul, as everyone
knows, is immortal and has no need of this; the body, however, is
mortal, and would like to be looked after before it dies. You might
take this to heart as well and get more recreation than your daily
feast of lectures from eight to four o'clock affords. For a lawyer, you
have adopted a schedule so rare that it ought to be pickled in alcohol
and exhibited in a museum. To attend lectures for six hours at a
stretch is something I could no more do than breathe fire or walk a
tightrope for six hours; worse still, your lectures are of a kind to
make all nine Muses take to their heels: public finance, economics,
statistics, and so on. Have you never heard that we only live once?
Even a professor of statistics must have been young in his day and
could not possibly have undertaken as a freshman, the maternal egg-
shell of the Gymnasium still stuck to his back, the arid stuff you
pursue. If there be any refreshing well in that desert, or an angel to
proffer languishing Ishmael[1] a cool source, then do let me know and
I shall cease marveling at your classes. I thank you for your interesting descriptions of the university, beg you to let me have more, and
greatly regret the fact that you have left me in the dark about your
actual work and your more intimate intellectual and daily life. I
should be sorry, for instance, if you, the lawyer, were to neglect philosophy altogether, while I, the godless medical man and empiricist,
am attending two courses in philosophy and reading Feuerbach[2] in
Paneth's[3] company. One of the courses—listen and marvel!—deals
with the existence of God, and Prof. Brentano, who gives the lec-

tures, is a splendid man, a scholar and philosopher, even though he deems it necessary to support this airy existence of God with his own expositions.[4] I shall let you know just as soon as one of his arguments gets to the point (we have not yet progressed beyond the preliminary problems), lest your path to salvation in the faith be cut off. If you should attend Fechner's lectures and pick up any interesting arguments from him, I should be delighted to hear of them and to pass them on to wider circles.

Of these wider circles, which comprise Wahle, Rosanes, Loewy,[5] etc., there is little to report. Wahle and Rosanes are distinguishing themselves neither by their industry nor by their indolence; in Wahle life seems to be falling asleep, in Rosanes to continue its somnolence. I hope that you will refrain from referring to this denunciation in your letters to them. Loewy Theodor[6] is living an unhappy double life, cutting his law lectures in order to take anatomy and zoology, bored by these and yet ashamed of cutting them, too. Herzig is basking in chemical delights, dissolving in infinite series, probably dreaming of differentials and integrals and perhaps also of his niece, who, as I think I told you, is his fiancée, though he makes a secret of it to all and sundry. I saw her a few days ago and grant that she is pretty and looks cheerful. I suspect that it is purely on her account that he has not become a medical student, in order to make his studies as short as possible, and that it pains [him] deeply not to be taller than she is, indeed to be of shorter stature.

I am confident that you, like me, much prefer to be still looking for your future bride than to have her around every day and hour. For the rest, I know of no events great or small that I can report to you. I expect a speedy reply and request plentiful information on your pursuits and undertakings. Wishing you well, your

Sigismund Freud

P.S.   If you write to my sisters they are not likely to be so discourteous as not to reply. You will appreciate, however, that I cannot take on the task of urging them to write themselves. You would greatly please my mother with family news.

Sigismund

Regards to Reitler! What's the young fellow up to?

Please return my piece on Goethe's mouthparts as soon as possible.

1. Hagar gave water to Ishmael in the desert (Genesis 21:19).

2. Ludwig Feuerbach (1804–1872).

3. Joseph Paneth (1857–1890) qualified as a university lecturer in 1886; he is "my friend P." in *The Interpretation of Dreams*, S.E., V, pp. 421–425.

4. Published posthumously in 1929 as *Vom Dasein Gottes* (On the existence of God).

5. Emanuel Löwy (1857–1838), a leading archeologist and one of Freud's intimate friends.

6. There was a classmate of Silberstein's by this name (b. 1855); Freud could also be referring to Emanuel Löwy, as Theodor is the Greek equivalent of Emanuel.

Vienna, December 2, 1874

Dear Friend,

Your prompt reply to my much-enduring[1] letter compels me to emulate your speed, lest you jump to false conclusions about my tardiness, and so that you might hear exactly what happened as soon as possible. The truth is that I reflected on my last letter for five days, and when it had been written I carried it around in my pocket for three days, like a marsupial harboring its young on its body after birth. Next I encapsulated it in an envelope, could not recall your address for a whole day, and when in the end I did remember it, dragged the letter about again—because I was loath to be separated from it—for another whole day as superfluous ballast on my wanderings through the more remote suburbs of Vienna, until finally a yawning abyss in the suburb of Alser[2] received it and carried it the way of all letters, or of those letters that are not misappropriated.

You will realize that after such experiences one is entitled to have a very noticeable physiognomy. If you are surprised that I could forget something so important for so long, then I must rejoin that often, at least twice daily, I recalled my obligation to attend to the letter but never had the time to exploit these impulses of memory. What good were such reminders directly before dozing off, or in the physiology lecture hall, or just as I cut my finger, when each time no post box was handy and the letter was forgotten again as soon as I was out in the street? My absentmindedness, however, seems to me easily accounted for, and I am more surprised that the letter should have left before last Sunday than that it did not leave two weeks ago. A poor troubled medical student is done an injustice if— to put it philosophically—purely per analogiam, he is said to have a will of his own. Rather, he is a drop of liquid pumped by complicated pressure devices from one lecture theater to the next, from one suburb to the next, and forced, by the laws of mechanics, to traverse his path with minimum friction and in the shortest possible time.

Vienna, December 6, 1874

Instead of continuing what I started to write a few days ago, I want to give you, as the event of the day, the news that the second issue of our journal has just appeared and contains a critique of Lipiner's[3] article on the teleological argument autore me [by me], "The foundations of materialist ethics" by Paneth, and On Spinoza's Proof of God's Existence together with an item on definitions by Emanuel Loewy. Of such a wealth of intellectual labor I cannot, unfortunately, give you more than a brief account; it would be impossible to copy it in full. If you should ever come back, you will be able to read it for yourself. A new student fraternity, Austria by name, with V. Schmeidel as Senior, has just been formed. Fleischer,[4] Löw, Conrad, Müller, and Baiersdorf have joined it. I trust that you will never turn up yourself in any colors, which is also my firm intention— albeit I have not had many offers.

For the past few days we have been living under the bitter sway of winter, as poets are wont to say, a malicious old man who empties huge sackfuls of snow on the ground and delights whenever, with the aid of all-powerful water, a mudbath forms in the streets which turns a fifteen-minute trip into an hour-long one. Since, however, as I have just noticed, I have little talent for poetic descriptions, I have no alternative but to leave this gruesome picture unfinished and would inform you that I have obtained old Lichtenberg[5] and am reading him with great pleasure. Instead of continuing to write on matters that must leave you indifferent, I am copying a priceless piece from the first volume of his collected works, namely the famous list of "implements offered for auction at the home of a collector."

1. One knife without blade, handle thereof missing.
2. One double children's spoon for twins

3. One repeating sundial, silver
4. One sundial with screw attachment for traveling carriage
5. One ditto, musical
6. One box of small, finely wrought cartridges filled with gunpowder for blowing up hollow teeth.
7. One chaise per se (probably percée). If one's seat is correctly taken, a flourish of drums and trumpets is heard, which resounds throughout the house. A piece of furniture for the man of substance.
8. An extensive collection of porcelain chamber pots, some of very amusing shapes—
   These last two items may be tested an hour before the auction behind a screen or in an adjoining room.
10. One bedstead in which to travel the room at night.
11. One magnificent imperial bed wherein three Grand Viziers died of the plague.
12). A superb collection of instruments for the conversion of the Jews—They are mostly of polished steel and red morocco leather work. The large whip in particular is a masterpiece of English leathercraft
14). One bottle of water from a block of ice that was found in the street as late as Whitsun in the year 1740. It has the peculiar property, not hitherto remarked by any physicist, of being able, as it were, to recall its freedom and to burst the glass every cold winter that it is placed outdoors. (Complicated nonsense)
17). One astronomer's anaclastic glass; if a friend looks through it and a small screw is turned, it will blow pepper and snuff into his eyes. May also be used for terrestrial work. It is said to have earned the deceased (the collector) a few boxes on the ear.
19). One barometer, displaying constant fine weather. The thermometer next to it indicates a pleasantly temperate heat, year in, year out (an invaluable woodsaver)
20). One complete set of various mourning implements for the superior household (I select a few items only).
   b). One dozen mourning dice, black with white dots
   c) One dozen ditto for half-mourning, violet with black dots
   f). A considerable collection of recipes for the dyeing of most dishes, such as soup, vegetables, or pastry, harmlessly

black, including one for blacking the lemons and rusks next to the corpse.

g). A superb, complete porcelain table service, each piece of which alludes delicately to death. To mention but one, the butter dish forms a death's head, wrought so naturally and artistically that one might think it were alive. The lid or upper part of the cranium is so osteologically perfect, even internally, that if the skull is filled with butter and the lid pressed down properly the butter takes on the exact shape of the brain, which makes a pat that looks gruesomely splendid, especially if the butter is given the right color.

21). A complete wardrobe for a child with two heads, four legs, and four arms, from the cradle to the age of twenty. A veritable masterpeice of the tailor's art. The various items can also be donned by two individuals, causing droll scenes, particularly in mixed company.

25). A most remarkable item! (indeed). One small engine, wrought with indescribable artistry, exemplifying the concubinium (should presumably be either connubium or commercium) animae et corporis.[6] The roller which sets everything in motion has three distinct settings for the three known systems; one for the physical influence, one for occasional causes, and one for the pre-established harmony. Yet the roller has room for another two or three systems; provided only that they comprise a body and a soul, although in case of need the soul could be removed. In this precious mechanism, the body is wrought of much more than semitransparent horn and measures some 4–5 inches. The soul, no bigger than a large ant, is entire, its little wings and everything else are of ivory, with only slight damage to its left leg. The engine is not activated by a crank (which would tear it apart) but by a pair of small windmill sails made of [finest] gold leaf blown upon by a suitable constant-action double bellows (follis infinitus) placed some distance away from the engine, and these sails activate an infinite screw (cochlea infinita) which sets everything in motion.

26) The precise regulations for trying capital crimes set to music by the deceased himself. It is the complete score with timpani and trumpets. In some passages the accompaniment even includes cannon shots.

27) Several molds for making fossils.

30). One team of horses trained by the deceased to eat waste paper. An item for booksellers and publishers.

Please forgive the shoddy manner in which I have written this letter.

The folder has not yet reached me.

Though you have made it fairly clear that you hold me the cause and the perpetrator of Anna's and Rosa's silence, I have in accordance with the biblical saying "For thou shalt heap coals of fire upon his head," Ps. 33.12,[7] done my utmost to persuade the young ladies to write. They were given formal instructions to do so speedily by a family council and you may look forward to receiving a letter, probably next week.

Please let me know before long what book you would like or could best use as a birthday present. You know that I have a completely free hand at Braumüller's[8] and make the fullest use of that freedom, and would like to use it on your behalf as well. In accordance with the statutes of the A.E., no refusal will be accepted.

Your
Cipion ó Sigmund

1. An allusion to *polytlas*, one of Odysseus' epithets.

2. Now the ninth district of Vienna.

3. Siegfried Lipiner (1856–1911), born in Jaroslau, Galicia; a student of philosophy in Vienna at the time, later known as a minor poet and esteemed by Friedrich Nietzsche.

4. Samuel Fleischer (b. 1856), one of Silberstein's classmates.

5. Georg Christoph Lichtenberg (1742–1799), physicist and satirist. Tr.

6. The concubinage (should presumably be either marriage or commerce) of the soul and the body. Tr.

7. Should be Proverbs 25:22 or Romans 12:20.

8. The university bookstore.

Vienna, December 11, 1874

Dear Friend,

Let us hope that the gloomy, one-taler thoughts that left their traces in your last letter have long since relinquished their grip on you; that the melancholy which gazed out at me with little doe-brown eyes from your welcome lines was but a transitory mood; I, for one, would feel unable to join you and sing the second part in Jeremiah's lamentations; I shall gladly impart to you what little I know of the cause of my better humor.

Still, I have your melancholy mood to thank for allowing me to hear once more affectionate words such as I rarely heard from you in Vienna; for we find it easier to express our feelings in deeds than in words, and are ashamed to address sentimental words, even such innocent ones as "dear friend," to those who have long since enjoyed them in our feelings. Writing makes it all easier, and since it does one good to read warm and friendly words addressed to oneself, two friends should always be separated from time to time. For a brief period only, mind you; if you were to be absent for more than two semesters, I, too, should consider the want to which you allude a most painful one. You are right that no correspondence can ever replace conversations; but, precisely because it has so much to make up for, a letter is doubly and trebly precious.

The gap your absence has opened in my social life has remained unfilled, nor have I ever looked for anyone to fill it. I should be unable to muster a dozen friends, although I have enemies by the dozen and of all shapes and sizes—a veritable pattern book. With Wahle alone I have established more cordial relations—his naive idealism endears him to me—and with Paneth I engage in a lively exchange of ideas, fostered by the identity of our studies and the similarity of our aspirations. But Paneth, though otherwise amiable enough, is so intoxicated by his own perfection that it would hardly enter his head to seek his complement in a friend. When you return, therefore, you will find that nothing in my attitude toward you has changed.

I am overjoyed to hear that you are casting off the reins of so-called virtue and beginning to be your own master, the more so as I know that your rule is unlikely to be a brutal one. If, however, you want my opinion on the wearing of ribbons and caps, it is as follows: if you can avoid them then do so, if not then in God's name join one [a fraternity] in Leipzig; but here in Vienna, where the fellows who wear colors are of that supercilious breed who booze and gossip and brood over political drivel instead of pursuing their studies, here please do your friends a favor and remain an honest Fink.[1] If you still can, that is, for a colorful cap, worn at a rakish angle, is said to have strange effects on the brain.

As for my own cheerful mood, it has three causes, the first two of which are unknown to me, while I know a little about the third. That is, I am moderately satisfied because I am spending my time in a way that, while it could be much better, is by no means among the worst. I am referring to my work in the sciences, albeit not the right sort of work. Were I a little more diligent I should be a fairly contented fellow. Moreover, there is in addition the pleasant prospect of every month enlarging my beloved small library, which gives me infinite pleasure. This brings me to your strange refusal to accept the present of a book on the occasion of December 27. Now while it cannot be denied that there is an A.E. article (which forbids the giving of birthday presents), historians of the Spanish Academy recall that the said article was broken not so long ago by a member at present residing in Leipzig, and the logicians and jurists in the A.E. conclude therefrom that the said article is no longer binding on the other member either. Furthermore, it is held that anything decided by the A.E. under certain past circumstances can be revoked, particularly if the time and circumstances should no longer be the same. Nor is the article in question one which has any connection with the fundamental tenets of the A.E., its lack of validity being written all over its face. In short, here is my ultimatum: you can decide to name a book that will prove useful to you while being worthy of a present, or you must run the risk of being sent a book that you do not expect, anonymously and without an inscription. You cannot hope to escape fate any longer. As for the source of my funds, you know very well that the firm of W. Braumüller, the largest bookstore in Vienna, is at my unlimited disposal.

However, since you keep harping on the statutes of the A.E., it would not be an idle task to collate them for once, to subject them to a further revision and then to confirm them. This being an essentially juridic project, I hope you will discharge it with pleasure.

Your pearls are irretrievably lost. Resign yourself to the thought, and stop setting such store by such nonsense. Seidl has none of the talent that goes to make up an utter ass; he is merely clumsy and his pearls, accordingly, are mere trash. The folder has still not reached me. Your aunt cannot find it.

I have had a few glimpses of the letter you will be receiving shortly, perhaps even in the course of this year, from my sisters. They tend to take an excessively tragic view of the matter. I hope that you will temper justice with mercy.

With cordial greetings, your
Don Cipion
m.d.l.A.E., e.d.l.s.n.y.p.

P.S. Don't let your social democrats prejudice you against the Chancellor. Bismarck is a devil of a fellow and a decent man.

---

1. Finch, slang for a student who does not belong to any fraternity.

Vienna, December 20, 1874

¡Querido amigo!

I am answering you in such haste because the matter at issue in our last letters demands a hasty reply. You must not take me for being as ingenuous about legal affairs as the exhilaration of your incipient legal career inclines you to do; on the one hand you have misunderstood me, on the other there is another court of appeal open to me, one that you have not yet considered. Still, I shall drop the matter, pending later, perhaps face to face, discussions—or else you may take me at my word—and formulate my motion as follows: "The useless and irrational law not to treat members of the A.E. on their birthdays shall henceforth be deemed null and void." [1]

I think you can have few objections, but nevertheless give you notice that should you intend to delay the decision by persistent objections beyond the due date, not even that legalistic trick will avail you, as the book would then be despatched to you by illegal means.

But which book? I must confess that, were you interested in Dar-winiana, I would want you to have one of Haeckel's[2] works, but since you would no doubt prefer something historical or legal, you will have to make your own decision and give me the name of the chosen work. And as soon as possible. Needless to say, I should like a reply before you leave for Dresden. If that should take place before the twenty-seventh, then I intend to send you the book as a New Year's present.

For Anna this year I shall probably pick Grube's biographical sketches.[3] I am still unable to value your pearls as you would have me do. Incidentally, Loewy Emanuel is about to send you and Reitler a collection of Aueriana.[4] As you see, I am writing this letter in great haste and must end it here.

Farewell and reply as soon as possible
to your Cipion
m.d.l.A.E.

1. In the original: "La ley inutil y irracional, de no regalarse los miembros de la A.E. á sus dias natales de aquí adelante sea aneantida y abolecida."

2. Ernst Heinrich Haeckel (1834–1919), an early and ardent follower of Darwin; appointed Professor of Zoology at Jena in 1862.

3. August Wilhelm Grube (1816–1884), *Biographische Miniaturbilde*, 1856.

4. Probably a reference to the writings of the social democratic politician Ignaz Auer (1846–1907); less probably, to the works of the typographer and philologist Aloys Auer, Baron von Welsbach (1813–1869), or to the publications of the Imperial and Royal Court and State Printers, of which he was the director.

Vienna, [December 31,] 1874

¡Querido amigo!

Your birthday has passed without my having a chance to allow even a token of my friendly interest to flutter across to Leipzig. So please accept the good wishes that I owe you now, at the turn of the year, at a time when, more than any other, I am reminded of you, and when you, too, in new circumstances and a strange land, may be thinking of me and my family. For we always used to spend Christmas and New Year's Eve together, when you not only dispelled my solitude but also relieved me of tasks to which I was not equal. Today my courage is failing me because I am on my own and am expected this evening, with my own resources, to entertain the youthful company that has gathered for my sister's birthday.[1] Moreover, I curse the invention of postcards, which have been robbing me of a letter from you these past two weeks with their preliminary reports, amplification of which will be deferred for God alone knows how long—I don't. The world grows more prosaic with every new invention; in the end, letters will fall into disuse and be replaced by telegrams. Then we shall be able to correspond with a friend for a decade without so much as catching a glimpse of his handwriting.

Under separate cover, I am sending you the book you have chosen; I know perfectly well that a copy of Don Quixote would be worthier of the spirit of the A.E., but can no longer go back on the preference I have bestowed on a profane work. If you nevertheless wish to own a Don, I would offer you my own, for, alas, I am having less and less time for our noble Spanish. In fact, the only worthy presents to a friend are those books one has perused oneself and relinquishes for the sake of giving the other pleasure. For otherwise a present remains an insignificant object, something one could buy for oneself at small cost. I am seriously considering a proposal to regulate the exchange of presents within the A.E. by statutory means. If one is so certain that one's opposite number is deviously awaiting the opportunity to reciprocate one's present as quickly as possible, then the giving of presents degenerates into a farce from which booksellers alone derive profit. Like, say: you lend me five guilders, then I'll lend you five guilders and we'll be quits. I would propose that, each time, the matter be decided by casting lots, to obviate that scrupulous regularity and punctuality which is the enemy of all surprises. I reserve the right to make further proposals.

The clock has just struck twelve. Mankind is saluting 1875 with cries of Happy New Year.

January 1, 1875

It all passed off fairly well—Gisela and her sister, my uncle,[2] a friend of my father's from Neutitschein[3] were our guests. Only you were needed to make the evening tolerable.

¡Pobre España! "When will a savior arise in this land?"[4]

January 3

At last the book has arrived and I can send this letter off.

A cordial farewell from Your Cipion

P.S.   Why no answer to the letter my sisters wrote to you?

If you should know or come across one Hermann Lippe, a first-year law student at Leipzig, be kind enough to convey the greetings of Heinrich Braun and ask him to write to the latter.

Cipion

Yesterday the court of arbitration expelled Fleischer from the Reading Union[5] for scandalous behavior.

---

1. Anna's sixteenth birthday was on December 31, 1874.

2. Jacob Freud had two brothers, Josef (b. 1825), who lived in Jassy, and Abae (b. after 1815), who lived in Breslau.

3. Jacob Freud's birthplace.

4. Schiller, *Wilhelm Tell*, I. 1.

5. The Reading Union of the German students in Vienna was founded in December 1871 and dissolved in December 1878; it played an important, though not always propitious, role in academic life thanks largely to its pan-Germanic tendencies. See William J. McGrath, *Freud's Discovery of Psychoanalysis: The Politics of Hysteria*, Ithaca and London, 1986.

Vienna, January 17, 1875

Querido Berganza!

I make so bold as to protest vigorously about the unnaturally chivalrous sentiments and emotions your New Year's Eve letter imputes to me. Infinitely more elegant though your construction may be than the sober truth, it has the obvious disadvantage of wronging all those concerned. I am neither in possession of a jewel with the re-

markable properties you mention—and if I were I would make it
over to Prince Bismarck,[1] who seems to be in greater need of it than
I am—nor have I ever heard that frog ponds are inhabited by creatures other than frogs and toads. While my chivalry is thus reduced
to hollow illusions, you must still strip its image of several false-
hoods intended to elevate it to a position beyond anything it might
wish for itself or one you could defend before God or your conscience. Strip it of its lures, its artifices, its serpentine wiles, and its
charms; it is still far from being an Armida.[2]

I find it very arrogant of you to suppose it is in Leipzig ballrooms
alone that you may behold feminine creatures "whose innocence
shines forth from their eyes," and to allow young girls elsewhere to
degenerate into reptiles with venomous fangs, scaly armor, and
Mephistophelean ideas.

About New Year's Eve, incidentally, a postscript for your peace of
mind: authoritative sources have remarked, and told my family, that
I was merrier than normal. But then, a man cannot aspire to everything, and if I am going to continue feeling awkward in the company
of ladies, I am all the more glad that you should feel at your ease
with them.

Your account of the ballroom events reads like a veritable idyll,
albeit a modern French, not a classical one. The classical idyll invariably demands a blue sky, green forest, grazing cattle and sheep,
whereas the modern contents itself with black coats, kid gloves, and
the pleased expressions of young men and girls. All in all, I have
abstracted a prescription for my small psychological medicine chest
from it. If you wish to be in an idyllic mood, then don tails and
white kid gloves. The sun will seem warmer and, though the trees
are bare, the buds will burst open and you will feel like a great big
happy child. But woe unto you if you own neither tails nor kid
gloves, for then you will know nothing but despair, unless you happen to live in the country and can imagine yourself in a classical
idyll.

When I think of your idyllic dances, I forgive all the medieval
qualities you have ascribed to me, for to believe oneself alone in the
love of life and the adoration of women is not very pleasant. Since,
however, I am no Saint Anthony, I shall cut my hectoring short and
merely observe that you are no Homer when you overlook the color
of the eyes and the hair in your description of a person destined to

play the heroine. Be kind enough therefore to make good the omission.

Vienna, January 24, 1875

An event that took place the day I wrote the first part of this letter persuaded me to postpone its conclusion until today. Briefly, that event is that Lady Sun deigned to grant one of her humblest subjects and children a special treat for several minutes, or to put it more precisely, if more tritely, I had myself depicted in her rays, that is, photographed. When I collected the resulting pictures today, I set one aside for you, and enclose it in this letter. You will forgive the little poem on the back and, no doubt, be able to correct it. The likeness, in truth, is of the slightest.

However, do not be too pleased at this enclosure, for, if the old proverb is to be believed, nothing in life is free but death, and I make bold to hope that the pleasure you have in possessing me in effigie will soon cost you your own head in turn. Only one "written in light,"[3] of course. I would, however, greatly prefer to have two specimens—one for personal use and one for the family album.

Although your dancing has no need of encouragement, since by your own admission you cherish that hour of the day above all others, I must tell you nevertheless that, as a dancer, you will be very popular with my sisters, because: it is "proposed," "it is generally mooted," etc., that they, too, are to learn the noble art, needless to say not without the Flusses, for what can possibly take place nowadays without the Flusses! They are the example my lady sisters are endeavoring to emulate now: so if they take dancing lessons, it will be in the company of G. and S. Fluss,[4] and when you come here you will have the pleasure, which cannot be expressed in words, or only feebly and inadequately, of "touching" Gisela, something which I have less motive and occasion to do.

Unfortunately I must add another piece of up-to-the-minute news that threatens to delay our meeting yet again. I have decided, and my father approves—provided those means that are dug out of the earth are in the slightest accord—to spend the 1875–76 winter semester in Berlin, in order to attend the lectures of Dubois-Reymond,[5] Helmholtz, and Virchow.[6] I am as happy as a sandboy at the thought and could not bear the idea of giving up the project. And once I am there for the winter, I cannot guarantee that I shall not want to remain for the summer semester as well. So, advantageous though it may be for members d.l.A.E. to see the "world" in some of its most godforsaken places, it means that the solitary life of the A.E. may have to be extended for one more semester. But all that rests in the lap of the gods.

You still owe me the answers to two questions, whether you know one *Herrman Lippe*, and whether you have received my sisters' letter; kindly make good the omission and accept the cordial regards of your

faithful Cipion

1. The case brought against Count Harry Arnim at the end of 1874 severely injured Bismarck's reputation; it appeared that Bismarck had tried to bribe the Viennese press, using thirty thousand talers from funds set aside to fight the Guelph, or Welf, party (the German-Hanoverian party founded in 1869).

2. Daughter of King Arbilan of Damascus, a character in Tasso's *Gerusalemme Liberata*; the embodiment of temptation.

3. Literal translation of "photograph."

4. Gisela Fluss and her younger sister Sidonia.

5. Emil Du Bois-Reymond (1818–1896), appointed Professor at Berlin in 1855.

6. Rudolf Virchow (1821–1902), appointed Professor at Berlin in 1856.

Vienna, January 30, 1875

Dear Friend,

You guessed right—I did not have my portrait taken voluntarily but on the very highest orders, so as to persuade my relatives in England[1] to commit a similar foul deed. It will not have escaped your notice that I wanted to procure the same thing from you, so bear in mind that I am looking forward to receiving a photograph of you very soon, the better to keep your fondly remembered features before my eyes and to afford me a lasting memento of your stay in Leipzig.

If that should be followed by one or two semesters spent together in the capital of the New German Reich—which, it would seem, need not be considered a complete impossibility—then we should have achieved the ideal, idyllic state of the A.E. we envisaged two years ago on our Styrian tour.

I need not fill in the perfect picture; your imagination is more vivid than mine, as our joint efforts at writing the A.E. novel have revealed. If it should all come about, I should prefer to share lodgings with you rather than with Braun, who also intends to go to Berlin, because his way of life has nothing of the simplicity and Arcadian poetry of the A.E., and because the hustle and bustle of the world at large attract and grip him more than would probably be the case with us; for even in Berlin I should continue to model myself on your thrift and moderation—unless, that is, as hints in your letter suggest, [you] should meanwhile have renounced them. You would have to dig them out again for my sake. True, my day would be sold and bartered away to lectures and laboratories, and half would go to private studies, but the evenings would be ours, and so would one day of the seven in the week, during which we could resume our old study tours and secret walks, perhaps with principles[2]—but let us fix nothing in advance. Alas, nine months still lie between today and this delightful project. —When I was a child, I firmly believed in the envy of the "so-called gods" and would take great care not to speak of the fulfillment of a precious wish lest I invoke the very opposite. But today the world looks brighter and I need not be afraid to consider possible something that, to my greatest joy, promises to come true. With so happy a prospect I may be allowed to mix an obituary; the journal founded by the three, and later four, of us, namely myself, Paneth, Loewy Emanuel, Lipiner, has passed peacefully into the keeping of the Lord.

It was I who delivered the death blow; it had been ailing for a long time and I took pity on its suffering. I gave it life and I have taken its life away, so blessed be my name, for ever and ever, Amen.[3] From now on I shall have to keep my philosophical ideas purely to myself or pass them on unrefined to Paneth. It is a great pity that they are unlikely to please you—no jurist is favorably disposed toward the major cosmic and physiological problems. But no matter.

It may be wrong of me to keep asking about your own pursuits while providing no details or secrets about my activities. That I shall now proceed to do and make you a small general confession whose secrets I know to be safe with a brother confessor. Hear this, then: I am most diligent in theory, and not entirely indolent in practice. Since my way of life is semi-nocturnal, I usually study from ten to two o'clock, quite often over-stretching my energies until four or five and as a result losing a day or two during which I am quite unable to study anything for any length of time. I still like—it [is] a strange habit of mine—to live in accordance with the phases of the moon, and prefer to start a new book, a new subject, or a new method at the beginning of the week, and if possible of the month. From this you will be able to gather that the new year has wrought a complete revolution in my life, what with my not having thought it worth the trouble to do anything sensible in the latter part of December. My course of study is on a fairly large scale; it comprises all the natural sciences, even astronomy, to be done within two year[s]—this one and the next—the biological or organic naturally taking pride of place. For the time being, I am studying anatomy, physiology, zoology, physics, and mathematics, as well as Darwinism, but a host of resolutions crowds round me constantly and impedes the peaceful enjoyment of my work. For nearly all these subjects, of which I must first master the general and basic principles, I have planned study on special topics. Chemistry, geology, and botany are, as it were, knocking at the door, but will have to be patient until my zoology examination, which takes place in April. I have no time for extraneous reading, a little Lessing or Goethe being all I can manage; it is a year since I last read a modern novel or poem. Lichtenberg's works, which I was able to catch up on by chance, are admittedly the exception. As for foreign literature, I grow increasingly estranged from it, though I recently read a chapter of Don Quixote and experienced an idyllic moment. That was at six o'clock and I was sitting alone in my room before a nourishing plateful which I devoured voraciously while reading the magnificent scene in which the noble Doctor Pedro Rescio de Tirteafuera, which must mean something dreadful in Spanish, has the food taken away from under poor Sancho's nose.[4]

Today (February 8) I called on your brother[5] but did not find him in. I shall let you know just as soon as I receive them.[6]

Farewell, and cordial greetings from your
Sigmund

I am sending you the Don Quixote herewith, the familiar copy from which I was reading, of value to me for that reason, in the hope that

you will welcome it more than a new one acquired by a casual sacrifice of money.

1. Freud's half-brothers Emanuel (1833–1914) and Philipp (1836–1911), by his father's first wife, Sally Kanner.
2. Code for girlfriends.
3. After Job 1:21.
4. *Don Quixote*, book II, chap. 47; *tirteafuera*, away with you.
5. Karl.
6. The papers of the Spanish Academy.

Vienna, February 21, 1875

Dear Friend,

Won't you pack your bags around March 15 and come and spend
the next semester in cosy, virtuous old Vienna? Truly, it would be-
token a strength of mind worthy of immortal praise. But what are
you up to, or, better, were you up to before you wrote to me? Seven
or more days have elapsed, and all the saints with the Lord at their
head would like to know what has happened in the meantime. Tell
me, is political economy a form of economics? Two principles, one
"sweet" and the other probably not too bitter either. When the A.E.
was in its heyday, it, too, recognized but two principles, one "ob-
scure" and the other "lucid," but it never discussed matters of taste
discrimination. I might forgive you if the principles had fallen upon
you, like rain upon the cornfield, effortlessly and unexpectedly, but
your actions betray intent. It is quite possible that someone should
learn four Heine verses by heart for no set purpose, but no one learns
a long poem of needless lyrical content by R. Prutz[1] without having
deliberated at length on the profit that might be derived from it. You
seem to be almost like Fritz Marlow in Lindau's "Erfolg," who also
memorized a complete dialogue with quotations in usum delphinarum.[2] I expect some clarification of this whole subject and not by
word of mouth either, for it will be five months or more before we
can meet again. Only in summer does the delight of the principles
come into bloom. I remember a so-called rose garden, a feast of dah-

lias, and I suspect walks, unconscious searching, and undesired yet
hotly desired discovery, and you will hardly be inclined to surrender
all that for a cold water cure in Vienna. Stop, and I mean this more
seriously, at the limits befitting a member of the A.E.; do not become a Tannhäuser in Leipzig. No one today believes in the unbind-
ing power of popes:[3] do not harp on the transitory nature but rather
on the significance of worldly things, and remember that a frivolous
mind will not be compatible with our serious task for long.

The reason why I have not written for so long is my state of health
in the recent past, about which I was loath to tell you for fear of
causing you unnecessary worry. I had been overdoing it, though not
so much with solid work as with a variety of irrelevant tasks, sleeping no more than four hours a day, for a few days living with the
impatience of one who expects this world to end within a fortnight
and whom a professor's chair awaits in the next, growing excessively
nervous, languid, and bored, with the feeling that my limbs had
been glued together and were now coming apart again, and experi-
encing all the painful and shaming sensations of a tomcat[4] (an ani-
mal species that, as everyone knows, is found here as well). For a few
days I kept away from all lectures and laboratory work, roaming instead through the streets of Vienna studying the masses. While in
this state, I received your letter. Fortunately, it all stopped after a
few days' lazing about and a few nights' sleep, so that today I am
able to resume my labors. However, since it is better to live even
this upside-down life than none at all, I intend to shorten the radius
of my circle of studies considerably. Perhaps you will more readily
believe that I was in this condition than why I was, but, truly, no
principle was to blame, rather a certain lack of principle—the old
ones are no good any longer and no new ones have been found—it
is just a time of transition. Today I indulged in a pleasure I have
missed for a long time. I paged through and read the A.E. papers,
which I obtained yesterday from your brother (who has grown into
a strapping young fellow), and reveled in the memory of days gone
by. I wanted to propose an auto-da-fé, but now lack the courage, and
instead confirm that I shall take over the secretariat of the A.E. from
you and accord the archives due care and protection. It is with sorrow that I note the absence from the documents of my scientific
essay on Goethe's mouthparts; I should be extremely grateful if you
could look for it among your papers, or ask your brother to hunt it
down.

Still present are: my "New Mah Nishtanah,"[5] an occasional poem with the appropriate, horrific figure of Christ and the marginal circumscription ABITURIENT.[6]

Several polemical articles by our several hands from that period of romantic revelations, my memorial on the subject of the Cretaceous which led to G.'s dismissal. My awful nocturne in which I vie with Poe, and a hair-raising episode from your novel "Konrad," in which you vie with Balzac. The beginning of my novel "The Journey to Roznau," luckily truncated.

My letter of sympathy when it transpired that you had to go back to Braila, written in pure Castilian. A "Cornelia"[7] referring to our Spanish lessons. My visiting cards when I did not find you in, fashioned in part of highly grotesque characters. The playbills you made for our children's theater. Your extracts from my sisters' diaries. My memorandum drawn up at twelve o'clock on January 13–14, 1873. My vade mecum to be read on board ship with blessings and curses on Mounts Rhadiska and Rhadost.[8] A report of my strange meeting with Ichth.[9] A diary page with a similar entry. My famous treatise "de mediis, quibus in amoribus efficiendis untuntur poetae" [Of the means poets are accustomed to use in matters of love], which alone sufficed to immortalize me as Aristotle's fortunate successor. My precious bankruptcy novel[10] with your most charming interpolations, the reading of which afforded me the merriest hour for half a year. Apart from its ending, which is feeble, the thing is really quite excellent. I need only remind you of the letters between D. Berganza and D. Cipion, of D. Kürschner's willfulness, of D. Möller's grief in love, of his lover's plaint, composed by you, of the scenes in the house of Ichthyosaura, of her bitter monologue, of her biblical lamentation for Roznau, of her relationship to Achilles, Hector, and Briseis and similar foolishness, and finally of Amor and Cazadora. Further, two ideas[11] by my sister Rosa, which undoubtedly betray wit. Your novella Manuela and, last, a letter of congratulation on your birthday written in our noble Spanish.

Other papers which have only been included by accident, such as your petition to the professorial board for the discharge of debts [?], and various letters addressed to you, I shall keep, albeit separately.

My mother has been ill for a few days.

Looking forward to your reply

Your Cipion

P.S.   The treatise on Goethe's mouthparts has turned up.

I would ask you once again for your photograph had I not cause to fear that I might give you occasion to commit an evil deed, namely foisting them onto the principles. I'll take the risk all the same.

1. Robert Prutz (1816–1872); the poem is probably "Nachtstille" (Still of the night).

2. Paul Lindau (1830–1919), "Ein Erfolg" (A success), 1874. In the poem Fritz Marlow tries to impress young women by quoting two lines from Eichendorff's poem "Die Welt ruht still im Hafen" (The world's at peace in harbor).

In usum delphinarum, for the use of immature girls; Freud is playing on *in usum Delphini* (for the use of the Dauphin), which refers to a set of Latin classics edited in France for the benefit of the young Dauphin, son of Louis XIV. Tr.

3. Heinrich Heine, *Tannhäuser:* "Oh, Holy Father, Pope Urban / Who can both bind and free."

4. *Kater,* tomcat, also means hangover. Tr.

5. *Mah nishtana,* Why is this different? The beginning of four questions asked by the youngest participant at the Passover seder.

6. Student about to take the school-leaving examination. Tr.

7. Possibly referring to the two Gracchi, whose mother, Cornelia, brought them up and educated them with special care.

8. Hradisko, mountain near the western border of Moravia; Radhost, mountain near the eastern border, with Roznau at its foot.

9. Could refer to the meeting with Gisela's brother described in the postcard dated March 25, 1872, or to another meeting with Gisela herself.

10. Possibly connected to a projected novel in two parts (*Poverty* and *Riches*) mentioned in Freud's letter to Martha Bernays dated April 15, 1884. *Letters of Sigmund Freud 1873–1939,* London: Hogarth Press, 1970.

11. Freud used the English word. Tr.

Vienna, February 27, 1875

Dearest Friend,

I would very much like to broach a subject that I consider serious but that fills me with painful agitation and embarrassment on your behalf, for which you will soon forgive me. You must know how sincerely I rejoiced at all the qualities you possessed and I lacked, your gift of treating the world with humor and your poetic genius in dealing with life, which gives you the right to consider yourself a poet even though you have never turned your hand to rhyme and verse. You will remember how prominent a part my urgings played in turning your vague plan to attend a German university into a fixed reality. Can you believe that I wanted to keep you far away from me for a year, when in fact I was thinking of the advantages that might accrue to you from the resulting freedom and diversion? This, and our old friendship, may persuade you to grant me the right to pass judgment on your latest affair, and encourages me to say straight out that it is very wrong of you, and causes grave harm to yourself and deep sorrow to me, to encourage the imprudent affection of a sixteen-year old girl and—the inevitable outcome—to take advantage of it. I do not think badly of you and cannot persuade myself that you are being deliberately frivolous; rather I feel that what attracts you is the romantic aspect of the matter, the unconstrained freedom on both sides, the opposition to the sham and sanctimonious stolidity and insipidity of so-called good society. But remember, dear friend, that it is only the initiation of our actions that lies in our hands, i.e., is determined by the admixture of an inner urge, while their course is rarely so determined and their outcome never.

What you start with innocent intent, or perhaps no intent at all, may have the same effect as something that you pursue with dishonorable intentions from the very beginning. Yet, I confess, I attach lesser weight to this consideration than I do to another, which I hope will impress you still more. For a man, in my view, may try and taste many things, may injure himself and cause himself unhappiness for a time, and yet do far less harm to himself, on the whole, than a woman or girl would in similar circumstances. A man seems capable of tasting passions, of losing himself in wild sentiments, even of relaxing the reins of morality, for he retains within himself the principle of his actions, the consciousness of what is good and what bad. A thinking man is his own legislator, confessor, and absolver. But a woman, let alone a girl, has no inherent ethical standard; she can act correctly only if she keeps within the bounds of convention, observing what society deems to be proper. She is never forgiven if she rebels against convention—perhaps rightly so; all her dignity and worth rest in general on one point, whereas a man may regain the respect he has lost through work. Therefore do not become the

cause of the first transgression of a young girl—one who has barely
outgrown childhood—against a justified moral precept, by arranging
meetings and exchanging letters against her parents' wishes. For
what else can you write or tell her but that you love her, etc., and
what purpose will it serve when you lie yourself into a passion and
she dreams herself into one? Even assuming that you are too honorable to act in that way, you have nevertheless taken the first step
along a path that cannot possibly add to her dignity, you have taught
her to anticipate a dangerous and wanton freedom which she can
exercise to her detriment, if not now, then at some future time. Is
that not too great a price to exact for the satisfaction of a romantic
whim? I should be overjoyed if instead of laughing at my sermoniz-
ing—which, alas, I cannot avoid—you were to heed my advice and
eschew both rendezvous and secret correspondence. And if you feel
you are too weak, then hasten back to Vienna; there you can exchange the normal civilities instead, or swagger about like any student—or do you think you are too good for that?

On your general approach to girls, dear friend, I also cannot refrain
from commenting adversely. You have heard time and again how
deleterious an effect flattery has on people, especially on those who
are unstable, incapable of grasping their own unimportance and
whom nature has, moreover, inclined to be vain, a combination especially found in girls. Every man is, as it were, an educator of all
those he meets: by his example, by his behavior toward them. But
you do harm to the poor things when you accustom them to flattery
and gallantries that they quickly come to consider as necessities,
expecting them as their daily bread and no longer as delicacies. How
often have I not complained of the miserable education of girls, de-
ploring their ineptitude for life's serious tasks. What is a poor
woman to make of the exertions demanded of her as a wife and
mother when she thinks back on the flatteries with which she was
treated and spoiled as a girl? I cannot absolve even you from also
being a little vain; how could [you] derive even the slightest satisfaction from the fact that a sixteen-year old girl is not indifferent to
you? Does she have judgment, reason enough to distinguish the
solid citizen from the fop? She cannot even have enjoyed a proper
education—which is not so much a virtue in itself as a bastion of
virtue—if she could so easily promise you what you have mentioned. Why then, my friend, play so dangerous a game with that

girl? How ashamed I would be if you returned to Vienna and I had to keep an episode of your life in Leipzig from our friends and my parents.

So much in sober vein. You will appreciate my request and my anxieties, the rest I must leave to you.

I replied to you immediately on receipt of your letter; please do likewise. My next letter will contain reports and news from here that are sure to interest you.

My mother is suffering from a protracted illness admitting of no quick improvement: infiltration of the lungs; she is bedridden and weak, and will be going to Roznau at the beginning of May. You would make her happy if you added some news of your mother. Braun sends his thanks for the information you supplied and asks you, if possible, to obtain further details, and also the name of the person who told you about H. Lippe. Should he be a fellow student, Braun would like his address so that he can write to him.

> Reply soon, and accept the most cordial greetings,
> of your
> Sigmund

Vienna, March 7, 1875

¡Querido Berganza!

As I am writing this letter late at night, you will have to forgive the unusual format. But do not be afraid, it is not about to turn into a treatise, for it is one o'clock and my feet are freezing. Tomorrow I dare not miss a single lecture, for tomorrow they certify attendance at lectures and tomorrow the last week of the semester begins. These university semesters are wont to come to strange endings, expiring not at a stroke but with a slow death rattle—one limb dies off at a time and one is tempted to finish off those that go on twitching, the sooner to enjoy the freedom of the vacation. Zoology takes her leave on Tuesday, physics on Wednesday, physiology on Friday; only our philosopher, Prof. Brentano, continues to lecture until Saturday, and on every day, no less, to make good the lacunae caused by his illness. The two of us (Paneth and I) have established closer contact with him; we sent him a letter containing some objections and he invited us to his home, refuted them, and seemed to take some interest in us, asked Wahle about us, when he had had the good fortune of being the only student at a lecture announced at the last minute, and now that we have sent him a second letter of objections, has summoned us again. When you and I meet, I shall tell you more about this remarkable man (a believer, a teleologist (!) and a Darwinian and a damned clever fellow, a genius in fact), who is, in many respects, an ideal human being. For now, just the news that under Brentano's fruitful influence I have arrived at the decision to take my Ph.D. in philosophy and zoology; further negotiations about my admission to the philosophical faculty either next term or next year are in progress. My Berlin plan has accordingly received an important modification. I shall be spending the next winter semester here to prepare for my Rigorosum,[1] and next summer semester 1876 and winter semester 1876–77 will see me in Berlin (triumph!!). I was very pleased to hear that your mother is going to Roznau, which gives me hope of having you with me in Vienna for a longer stay, though our prospects of seeing Roznau, that first promised land of our friendship (Styria being the second and Berlin the third, if, as we hope, it comes about), must be considered slight.

As for your love affair, I am so glad that you take the matter no less seriously—at least in theory, which, one hopes, practice cannot resist—than I do, though you reproach me with seeing things, because of the great distance involved, through the blue spectacles of fantasy and unclearly. For all that, I cannot absolve you from the charge of being a little vain—rather I accuse you of not even trying to recognize and refute that charge. For the behavior of the mother, which ruined it all for you, I would proffer a different explanation, one that brings less shame on the poor, silly woman, albeit not much credit either. I mean her attempt to capture you, an eighteen-year-old, for her little sixteen-year-old daughter; such boldness strikes me as much too southern and calculated for anyone to try in German lands; the following is a much more likely explanation. —The old girl is a shrewd woman, or thinks that she is; she knows that beauty and youth alone cannot support her daughter, but that a wealth of coquetry is needed to vaunt these advantages and to captivate men with social graces. Her daughter may have shown few signs of this so far, which is why she sends her to dancing school, makes sure that she is in male company, and does her utmost to bring out the innate but latent coquetry of the sixteen-year-old daughter of Eve. In that she quickly succeeds, the child takes to the game, and with obvious pleasure that you are taking notice of her small attentions, and this explains the apparent collusion of mother and daughter. In short, your part in the whole business was that of a dressmaker's dummy masculini generis, that is, of a tailor's dummy. If there is anything to console your injured self-esteem for this discovery, it can only be the realization that she has been playing no nobler part in your eyes. You were plainly rehearsing the role of the tragic lover that you intend to enact one day. So much for my opinion. Quite honestly, I would like you the better were you to shed the last remnant of your "Sturm und Drang." No doubt you will do that soon without greatly missing it later.

Karl Grün, whose essay on Börne[2] you enjoyed so much, is known to me as well. A few weeks ago I attended a lecture he gave for the benefit of the German Students' Reading Union on the three ages of the human spirit, which culminated in a glorification of modern science and of our most modern saints such as Darwin and Haeckel, promising the students blessing upon blessing. Since he has, moreover, published a biography of *Feuerbach*[3] which does special justice to the importance of one whom I revere and admire above all other philosophers, I respect the man and am happy to salute so steadfast a champion of "our" truths. I am unable, however, to say anything about his intellectual status. I have not read his cultural history of the sixteenth century,[4] nor any of his other works, though I intend to make good the first omission forthwith. It is typical of our student body that they dismissed the man as a fraud because he dared to *speak* with enthusiasm of matters one cannot help *thinking* about with enthusiasm, which did not please them, of course, since a miserable, shallow, urbane and frivolous skepticism, rather than the genuine critical sort which sooner or later leads to a rigorously substantiated conviction, rules the little minds of our fellow students and future world leaders.

As far as politics are concerned, I have reached a low point where I can scarcely lay claim to a political opinion. True, I am a republican, but only inasmuch as I consider a republic as the only sensible,

indeed self-evident, system. Hay gran trecho [it is a long way], however, from there to the practical attempt to introduce the republic. I
should be very interested to hear whether your social democrats are
revolutionary in the philosophical and religious spheres as well; I
believe one can tell more readily from this relationship than any
other whether they are truly radical in character.

Do me the favor, therefore, of letting me know whatever you can
discover in this matter. I am not, incidentally, averse to socialist
aspirations, though I am unfamiliar with the forms they assume today. There is truly much that is rotten in this "prison" we call the
world, which might be improved by humane measures in education,
the distribution of property, the form of the struggle for existence,[5]
etc. All these are Mill-ian ideas to which I hope to devote myself
with zeal in the near future.

&ℓ *Official section.* Business of the Spanish or Castilian Academy.

Because Don Berganza, sole member of the Spanish Academy
with the exception of Don Cipion, writer of the above, has complained more than five times to the above-mentioned Don Cipion
about the loss of his notes, the "pearls or marguerites,"[6] Don Cipion
replies that these "pearls" have not been discovered despite inten-
sive searches, nor are they, in Don Cipion's view, worth seeking or
bemoaning, so worthless and devoid of talent are they. It would seem
that Don Berganza remembers them with the greater warmth and
zeal because they are a reminder of, and a glimpse into, his days at
the Gymnasium than for any other reason; but Señor Don Berganza
would do well to reflect that there are enough other things to serve
him as reminders of those days and that it is advisable to allow the
pearls to sink into the ocean of oblivion. That is all I have to say in
reply to your ultimatum.

Another point is that Don Cipion hereby proposes the incorpora-
tion of the following terms into the official style of the Spanish
Academy, which terms are not new, but old and well known and
worth being brought out for use by members of the Spanish Academy. Members of the Spanish Academy shall refer to themselves as
"dogs," which is the greatest title they enjoy or are ever likely to
enjoy. They will refer to the world in which they live as "Seville"
and to their country of residence, that is, Germany, as the hospital
of Seville. Lastly, they will refer to their lodgings as the "mountain"

(or if there is another word meaning "thickness"[7] and which the famous Cervantes, in the passage well known to you, has used, it shall be that other word). Thus members of the Spanish Academy must never say that somebody "has died," but rather that he has departed from Seville, must never say that someone has left Germany, but that he has moved from the hospital of Seville, must never say that he has traveled in Germany from Vienna to Berlin but that he has changed his thickness. Vienna shall be called by another name, and so shall Berlin, but I do not wish to make any specific suggestions for these names and leave the matter to Your Honor, may you live for twelve hundred years

and be preserved for two thousand years
as is the wish of your Don Cipion 🙰

Portion in Spanish

1. Oral examination for the doctorate. Tr.

2. Karl Grün was the pseudonym of Ernst von der Haide (1817–1887), a champion of socialism and deputy of the 1848 Prussian National Assembly; for his essay on the writer Ludwig Börne, see "Bausteine" (Building blocks), Darmstadt, 1844, pp. 19ff.

3. *Ludwig Feuerbach in seinem Briefwechsel und Nachlasse sowie in seiner philosophischen Charakterentwicklung dargestellt* (Ludwig Feuerbach presented through his correspondence and unpublished works as well as the development of his philosophical character), 1874.

4. *Culturgeschichte des sechzehnten Jahrhunderts*, 1872.

5. Freud used the English phrase, which occurs in Darwin's works but was not coined by him.

6. The Spanish *margarita* means pearl.

7. In Cervantes' play *El trato de Argel* there is a reference to *el Cerro Gordo* (the fat or thick mountain). Freud mixed up the gender and the meaning of the two words in recalling this phrase; *cerro* means mountain.

Parte oficial. Cosas de la Academia Española ó Castellana.

Como mas de cinco veces Don Berganza, miembro único de la A.E. con escepcion de D. Cipion, que eso escribe, á dicho D. Cipion se ha quejado de la pérdida de sus noticias llamadas "perlas ó margueritas," se le responde del lado de D. Cipion, que esas "perlas" ni se han hallado hasta ahora á despecho de mucho buscar ni merecen, segun D. Cipion cree, ser buscadas, ni quejadas, por su poco valor y el escaso ingenio, que tienen. Parecese, que Don Berganza con mayor calor y zelo se recuerda [de] de ellas por ser recordanza y momento de se sus tiempos gimnasticos, que por otra cosa; pero piense Señor D. Berganza, que hay otras cosas asaz que le sirvan de acuerdo de esos tiempos y que se conviene dejarse las perlas mergidas en la mar del olvidado— Eso cuanto he que responder á su Ultimatum.

Otro punto es, que propone D. Cipion la introduccion de siguientos terminos en el estilo oficial de la A.E., cuales términos no son nuevos, pero viejos y bien conocidos y merecen ser sacados en limpio para el uso de los miembros de la A.E. Llamanse los miemb. d.l.A.E. "perros," que es su mayor titulo, que tienen ni tendrán, llamese "Sevilla" el mundo, en que están y el hospital de Sevilla el pais en que viven, es decir la Alemania. Llamese en fin el paradero, en que están, la "cerra" (ó si otra palabra es, que quiere decir "Dicke" y que el famoso Cervantes en el lugar, que V. conoce, ha usado, sea esa otra palabra). Así los m.d.l.A.E. jamás digan de alguien "ha muerto," sino ha salido de Sevilla, jamas digan, ha dejado la Alemania sino ha quitado el hospital de Sevilla y jamas digan, ha viajado en Alemania, de Viena á Berlin, sino digan, ha mudado de cerra. Viena llamese con otro nombre y asi tambien Berlin, pero los nombres no quiero proponer, sino dejo á Vm de proponerlos, que viva mil y docientos años

y sea dos mil años mantenido
como desea Su D. Cipion

Vienna, March 13, 1875

¡Querido Berganza!

I am most surprised that you should have preferred a stay in Cadiz to a visit to Madrid.[1] As you see, I accept your terms and congratulate you on your ingenious amendment of my proposal. Am I perhaps to conclude that it is for the sake of your principio? Or have you merely deferred your intention to foot it to Madrid? If that should be the case and you really do reach the capital de España, tierra prometida de la A.E. [capital of Spain, promised land of the Spanish Academy], then please send me a "Cartel des hospital," meaning a list of university lectures, so that I can see what delights await us there.

The equanimity with which you mention the first kiss you exchanged with your principle strikes me as an evil omen in two respects, first that you accept kisses so easily and second that you take kisses so lightly. It is my duty to draw your attention to a calculation by the famous statistician Malthus,[2] who proved that kisses tend to multiply in proportions that increase with such unusual speed that, soon after the beginning of the series, the facial area no longer suffices and [they] are then forced to migrate. For these reasons, Mal-

Nationale.

Vor- und Zuname des Studirenden:	_Sigismund Freud_
Vaterland und Geburtsort:	_Freiberg in Mähren_
Muttersprache, Alter:	_Deutsch. geb. 6 Mai 1856_
Religion, welchen Ritus oder Confession:	_israel._
Wohnung des Studirenden:	_IX. Kaiserjosephstrasse 3, 2tr 10_
Vorname, Stand und Wohnort seines Vaters:	_Jacob Freud Kaufmann ds._
Name, Stand und Wohnort seines Vormundes:	—
Bezeichnung der Lehranstalt, an welcher der Studirende das letzte Semester zugebracht:	_Universität Wien_
Genießt ein Stipendium (Stiftung) im Betrage von fl. kr.	
verliehen von unter dem 18 3.	
Anführung der Grundlage, auf welcher der Studirende die Immatriculation oder Inscription anspricht:	—

Verzeichniß der Vorlesungen, welche der Studirende zu hören beabsichtigt.

Gegenstand der Vorlesung	Wöchentliche Stundenzahl derselben	Name des Docenten	Eigenhändige Unterschrift des Studirenden
Physiologie	5	Prof. Brücke	Sig Freud
Physiol. Übungen	6	Prof. Brücke	Sig Freud
Anatomie i. Vertebraten	5	Prof. Claus	Sig Freud
Anatomie Vertebraten Methode	2	Prof. Claus	Sig Freud
Zoolog. Practicum für Anfäng	3	Prof. Claus	Sig Freud
Logik	4	Prof. Brentano	Sig Freud
Philosoph. Lesungen	1	Brentano	Sig Freud
Optik	3	Stefan	Sig Freud
Theorie der Wärmebildung	2	Stefan	Sig Freud

Kostet 2 Neukreuzer.

Record of lectures attended by Freud during
the 1875 summer semester

thus is a staunch opponent of kisses and a young political economist ought to heed his authority.

But seriously, if her mother is truly cruel enough to wish ruin upon the poor child by turning her from a decorous china doll into an indecorous flirt, *then do not be party to her plan.* What of your promise, given freely in your last letter, "otherwise to act as you have suggested"?

My report that I intended to change over to the philosophical faculty must be amended inasmuch as it was my original plan to combine attendance at two faculties and to take both doctorates in three to four years. This, however, is impossible, at least the first part; I shall have to make closer inquiries about the second. In any case, I am free to take zoology, my main subject, in the philosophical faculty and to attend philosophy lectures whenever I please, which is what will happen next semester. Naturally, a Ph.D. examination remains a possibility and tomorrow I and Paneth, who is involved in these plans, will be seeking Brentano's advice.

To give you a clearer idea of the course of my studies, I am setting down the schedule for the summer semester, as I intend to follow it with few if any changes.

7–8	M, Tu, W, Th, F	Vertebrate Anatomy
7–9	Saturday	Mollusc anatomy
9–11	M, Tu, W	Optics (theoretical and experimental)
9–11	Th, Friday	Physiology laboratory
11–12	M, Tu, W, Th, F	Physiology
9–12	Saturday	Zoology practicum
12–1	M, Tu, W, Th, F	Organic chemistry
1:30–4	three times a week	Physiology laboratory
1:30–6	twice a week	Physiology laboratory
4–6	twice a week	Logic (with Brentano)
6–7	Saturday	Philosophy lecture by Brentano

As you can see, I am not short of courses, almost all of them stimulating, and if I manage to do everything as I have set it out, the semester will be a model of how to spend one's time. And there is still time left over to loll about in the bath for an hour before taking supper at the Hirsch, for there is no study at night, except for lectures, though I do plan to read various things on philosophy and natural history.

"And thus we live, thus fortune guides our steps," though Fried. Nietzsche took David Strauss to task in Strasbourg for this philistine dictum in 1873.[3] Of my relationship with Brentano, which you may be imagining as closer than it really is, and of the philosophical outlook I have derived from it, I shall write to you tomorrow, when our visit to him, at ten o'clock, is over.

Monday, March 15

Below, an account of that visit, given at length, the better to convey an idea of the man and our relationship to him. The beginning of the conversation was about the weather and an accident Paneth had witnessed; next, he brought out our letter and wanted to refute our objections, which was still necessary only in one case, however. Then he made a few quite favorable remarks about our endeavors, saying he was glad that we were so keen to acquire greater knowledge and that, though of the opposite opinion to him, we did not allow prejudice to stand in our way (he knows perfectly well that we are materialists). He complained that philosophy was in absolute chaos here, whereupon Paneth, who had attended Zimmermann's lectures, made some highly disparaging remarks about the latter, thus forcing Brentano to pronounce on Herbart.[4] He utterly condemned his a priori constructions in psychology, thought it unforgivable that Herbart had never deigned to consult experience or experiment to check whether these agreed with his arbitrary assumptions, declared himself unreservedly a follower of the empiricist school which applies the method of science to philosophy and to psychology in particular (in fact, this is the main advantage of his philosophy, which alone renders it tolerable for me), and mentioned a few remarkable psychological observations that demonstrate the untenability of Herbart's speculations. There was much greater need for thorough research into individual questions, the better to arrive at reliable individual conclusions, than for attempts to tie up the whole of philosophy, which was futile because philosophy and psychology were but young sciences and could expect no support from physiology in particular. When we asked for personal advice, he told us that it was quite feasible and a good idea for us to attempt a doctorate in philosophy as well as in medicine, and that this was not unprecedented—Lotze[5] had done just that and had then opted for philosophy. We would do well to specialize in a philosophical subject; the Minister had enjoined him to train lecturers in philosophy. (Though we are unlikely to take him up on this.) From among philosophical writers he selected some he advised us to read and took the rest to task mercilessly. We ought to start with Descartes, and study all his writings because he had given philosophy a new impetus. Of his successors, Geulinx, Malebranche, and Spinoza,[6] none was worth reading. All of them had picked up the wrong end of Descartes' philosophy, his complete separation of body and soul. Spinoza indulged in pure sophisms; he was to be trusted least of all. *Locke* and *Leibnitz*, by contrast, were indispensable, the first being a most brilliant thinker, the second not fully satisfactory only because he tended to dissipate his strength. These two were succeeded by the popular philosophers, who were of purely cultural and historical, not philosophical, interest. By contrast, two figures from the skeptical period, *Hume* and Kant, were indispensable, *Hume* being the most precise thinker and most perfect writer of all philosophers.

Kant, for his part, did not at all deserve the great reputation he

Franz Brentano

enjoys; he was full of sophisms and was an intolerable pedant, child-
ishly delighted whenever he could divide anything into three or four
parts, which explains the inventions and fictions in his schemata;
what people praise in him Brentano was ready to credit to *Hume*,
what is entirely Kant's own he rejected as harmful and untrue. In
short, Kant comes off very badly in Brentano's eyes; what makes
Kant important is his successors, Schelling, Fichte, and Hegel,
whom Brentano dismisses as swindlers (you can see how close he
comes to the materialists in this regard); he told us how discouraged
he felt in his youth, when he started to read philosophers, how he
nearly despaired of his philosophical talent until he was made aware
of his abilities by [?] an older philosopher.

"And so you want to let us off without reading them?" I asked.
More than that, I want to warn you against reading them; do not set
out on these slippery paths of reason—you might fare like doctors
at insane asylums, who start out thinking people there are quite
mad but later get used to it and not infrequently pick up a bit of
dottiness themselves. Of the most recent philosophers, he then recommended Auguste Comte, whose life he described to us, and he
was about to go on to the English philosophers when Prof. Simony[7]
turned up and we were packed off, with permission to call again
during the "vacation" and to fetch him for a walk.

So far, so good, and you might flatter yourself on having a friend
thought worthy of the company of so excellent a man, were it not
that thousands of others have been invited to his home or to converse with him, which greatly detracts from our distinction. He
came here to found a school and to gain disciples, and hence proffers
his friendship and time to all who need it. For all that, I have not
escaped from his influence—I am not capable of refuting a simple
theistic argument that constitutes the crown of his deliberations.
His great distinction is that he abhors all glib phrases, all emotion-
ality, and all intolerance of other views. He demonstrates the existence of God with as little bias and as much precision as another
might argue the advantage of the wave over the emission theory.[8]

Needless to say, I am only a theist by necessity, and am honest
enough to confess my helplessness in the face of his argument; however, I have no intention of surrendering so quickly or completely.
Over the next few semesters, I intend to make a thorough study of
his philosophy, and meanwhile reserve judgment and the choice between theism and materialism. For the time being, I have ceased to

be a materialist and am not yet a theist. Though he upholds man's
descent from the animals, he opposes Darwinism and has shattered
my own belief in it, not so much with his own arguments as with
the report that the computations of Thomson[9] in London have dem-
onstrated that the organic history of the earth could not be put at
more than one hundred million years; but even if Darwinism stands
up, as I hope it does, it does not conflict with his teleology or with
his God.

My mother rose from her bed today. She thanks you warmly for
your regards and hopes to meet your mother in Roznau.[10] I take it
you will not be going home but will be spending the summer in
Roznau.

Your Cipion
p.e.e.h.d.S.[11]
M.d.l.A.E.

Send me your portrait.

1. Madrid stands for Berlin, Cadiz probably for the "harbor" of Braila.

2. Thomas Malthus (1766–1834), in *An Essay on the Principle of Population*
(1798), theorized that populations have the tendency to increase faster than their
means of subsistence.

3. The quotation is from Goethe, *Zueignung* (Dedication). David Friedrich Strauss
(1808–1874), in *Das Leben Jesu, kritisch bearbeitet* (The life of Jesus, considered crit-
ically), presented the Gospels as the unconscious product of the primitive Christian
communal spirit. Nietzsche (who worked in Basel, not Strasbourg), commented on
this view in *Untimely Meditations*, I.4.

4. Johann Friedrich Herbart (1776–1841), best known as the father of scientific
pedagogy based on psychology. Tr. Robert Zimmermann (1824–1898), appointed Professor of Philosophy at Vienna in 1861, was a leading Herbartian.

5. Rudolph Hermann Lotze (1817–1881), appointed Professor of Philosophy at Leipzig in 1842 and at Göttingen in 1844, described his philosophy as "teleological idealism."

6. Arnold Geulincx (1625–1669) developed the doctrine of occasionalism; as a meta-
physician, Nicolas Malebranche (1638–1715) stands between Descartes and Spinoza.

7. Friedrich Simony (1813–1896), appointed Professor of Geography at Vienna in
1851.

8. Theories of light by Huygens and Newton, respectively.

9. William Thomson, Lord Kelvin (1824–1907) taught in Glasgow, not London.

10. Crossed out: I don't quite understand one passage in your letter. What do you
mean, my prospects for the third semester, etc. . . .

11. *Perro en el hospital de Sevilla*, dog at the hospital of Seville.

Vienna, March 27, 1875

Dear Friend,

Received your kind letter with the disagreeable news that the devil arranged a minor illness for you in a foreign land. I hope your rebellious foot will capitulate in time to allow you to go to Berlin. I take it that your lectures, too, do not start before the twelfth.

Our alma mater, of course, considers it beneath her dignity to publish a list of lectures at this early date; hence it is quite possible that actual work here will not start until later. You will find Herzig in Berlin; he intends to spend three semesters there. He is a bright fellow and I am glad he managed to escape from his barbarous Sanok.[1] His young niece and fiancée will meanwhile be able to perfect the romantic role of yearning heroine. But don't mention any of this to him. He is keeping it a secret even from me; I learned it from another source.

For the homoeopathic papers you sent me, many thanks! Previously I had read but little and I have now found that my expectation of being served up utter nonsense was not fulfilled; yet it is no great achievement to remain on the well-trodden path of common sense for ten pages. So far, I can conclude only that these gentlemen are great metaphysicians, and Kantians in particular, which is most laudable but perhaps unhealthy. We shall see. They say Leipzig is the main center of homoeopathy.[2]

I can hardly convey to you how greatly my faith in what is generally held to be correct has been shaken and how much my secret leaning toward minority views has grown. Ever since Brentano adduced such ridiculously simple arguments in favor of his God, I have been afraid that one fine day I will be taken in by the scientific proofs of the validity of spiritualism, homoeopathy, by Louise Lateau,[3] etc. In short, I have been too little of the dogmatist, adhering to all I believed in out of logical conviction alone.

Your appreciation of Brentano is uncommonly good and you may accept my compliments for assessing the main features of my relationship to him so accurately. Indeed, his God is a mere logical principle and I have accepted it as such. He repudiates any direct intervention by God on the grounds that it would be dysteleological. How far he allows regard for God to affect life is still unclear, though as far as I remember he once hinted at something like that in ethics. And I still have to find out what he thinks of ritual and a thousand other things that are more important in practice than his empty God concept. Unfortunately, when we allow the God concept we start down a slippery path. We shall have to wait and see how far we fall. His God is a most peculiar one. Since he claims that man knows very little of the world, perhaps stopping short at the Dubois-Reymond limits of cognition,[4] he may be forgiven for crediting God with even less knowledge. Man lacks a proper conception of God and can approach it only by analogy; it.cannot be reached by human calculation. Confusing though it all seems, it is nevertheless closely reasoned, and madly methodical. In short, Brentano cannot possibly be refuted before one has heard and studied him and plundered his stores of knowledge. So sharp a dialectician requires one to hone one's own wits on his before challenging him.

I am gradually making up for my lack of knowledge of modern literature through our Union library. Thus I have read one volume of Freitag's[5] Die Ahnen, as I think I have already told you, and recently I devoured half a dozen tragedies by Friedrich Hebbel,[6] whom you will do well to cultivate if you do not know him already. His is a harsh and revolutionary nature, full of bitter criticism. There is little trace of the kind of plot in which, although the hero who has fought for a good cause may be bested, his cause is triumphant, or the writer can at least promise it victory. When it comes to murder, he is a veritable Shakespeare—he is most keen on ruination paved by passion, all his heroes are stubborn and given to cracking open each other's skulls, and he invariably paints passions as so large that it is worth the writer's trouble to examine them and perhaps, if I understand Hebbel rightly, to excuse them. I particularly like his Judith, which poses a sexual problem: an excessively strong woman stands up to an excessively powerful man and revenges herself upon him for the inferiority her sex has imposed on her. To you especially, old admirer that you are of Penthesilea, I recommend Judith warmly. Holofernes is a boor—imagine Gargantua or Pantagruel as a bandit chief issued with letters patent and endowed with exclusive privileges by His Assyrian Majesty and you have Holofernes. You will readily grant that the Jewish characters are wonderfully drawn, given Hebbel's talent for describing the headstrong. By the way, Hebbel himself characterizes his heroes in a few prefatory lines much better than I can hope to do here. "Mariamne" is good as well, but less stirring; I do not really like the play, for the intricate and dangerous psychological experiments it portrays have something improbable about them. Incidentally, I see with astonishment what magnificently tragic material is contained in the despised history of the Jews. If only eternal Jehovah were not so monotonous. "Agnes Bernauer" first bored and then vexed, indeed infuriated, me. Not only the emotions but logic too can muster weighty arguments against its ending. A masterpiece, by contrast, is "Maria Magdalena," a thesis play like no other; a deeply moving tragedy achieved by the simplest means. "Genofeva," too, has poetic beauty—the story is well known, the passion of the unfaithful Golo is steeped in all the incandescent hues of hell, as you can imagine. The "Ring des Gyges" takes up a sexual problem again, often quite charmingly. If you add the Nibelungen trilogy with its heroine Chriemhild, then you will realize that all of Hebbel's heroes are women and that the great majority of the plays were named after women. His intention was not, however, to depict women from different points of view or to glorify them politically; rather, he prefers women as the poetically more warm-blooded animals because, in addition to the obstinacy they share with men, they can also have glowing emotions.

At present, I am reading Freitag's Bilder aus der deutschen Vergangenheit.

There is little to report of my family. My mother is convalescent. Anna, and perhaps Rosa as well, will enclose a letter.

> Keep well, and accept the
> kind regards
> of your Cipion
> p.e.e.h.d.S.

1. Herzig's birthplace in Galicia, southwest of Przmyśl.

2. Leipzig had a homeopathic hospital and was the seat of the Central Association of German Homeopaths.

3. Louise Lateau (1850–1883), daughter of a Belgian railway worker, allegedly manifested the stigmata in 1868.

4. Refers to a lecture delivered in Leipzig in 1872 entitled "Über die Grenzen des Naturerkennens" (On the limits of our understanding of nature).

5. Gustav Freytag (1816–1895), Die Ahnen (The ancestors), 1872–1881; Bilder aus der deutschen Vergangenheit (Pictures from the German past), 1859–1867.

6. Christian Friedrich Hebbel (1813–1863), dramatist, poet, and short-story writer. Tr.

Vienna, April 11, 1875

Dear Friend,

So as not to delay a much delayed letter even further, I am today using ordinary paper instead of the writing paper which alone is socially acceptable but which I cannot fetch from the adjoining room because my father is asleep. You will understand why I am in such a hurry to reply to you when I tell you that I started writing two letters but had to put each aside uncompleted, being interrupted each time by some business or other. For we are on the threshold of the second semester, of a new life in which I shall appear for the first time as philosopher and zoologist, attending psychology, logic, and two zoology courses. Never before have I enjoyed that pleasant sensation which may be called academic happiness, and which mostly derives from the realization that one is close to the source from which science springs at its purest and from which one will be taking a good long drink. The dark side of my present good fortune is something I shall try to portray on another occasion.

With you, too, signs and wonders never seem to cease. You seem to be waging a struggle with yourself, one, that is, of a much more serious nature than were your previous Werther and Lotte conflicts. You are searching for truth in life with the same urgency as I try to seek [it] in science. The big question you must be asking yourself daily is, Third or Fourth Estate? Republican or Social Democrat— for me it is theist or materialist, causality or skepticism. Still, you must find it more pleasant than I do; you are about to become a neophyte while I am almost a convert.

For the time being, I have to confess that I badly mistook the basic questions that agitate me, and that I was completely lacking in philosophical insight. The rueful confession of a former swashbuckling, stubborn materialist! But even in my new coat I feel anything but comfortable, and have thought it best to defer a final decision until such time as I may be more versed in philosophy and more mature in science. Perhaps you will find my example worth emulating. It would seem that contact with the social democrat[s], from which you did not at first expect any effect on your convictions, nevertheless made a fairly marked impression on you. In any case, you are wrong to think that social problems and your approach to them or your contacts with the Leipzig crowd leave me indifferent; they interest me most keenly, and I hope you will let me have regular and detailed reports on the matter. The fact that they have turned their views into dogma, and permit no discussion of it, seems to be no recommendation for them, and certainly not the right way to attract adherents from the learned estate. The unshakability of their convictions, which you praise, is the worst possible proof of their validity, for all their claims and hopes are based on these very theories.

I have read the A.B.C. des Denkens für Wissende[1] with interest and would like to make a few comments on it, on the assumption that you have read it as well.

I can be brief, and cite Dr. Douay himself as admitting it was legitimate to assume that God exists. "Nothing is true," we read, "but what can be proven by the evidence of one's senses or rests on previously proven propositions." In the second part of the sentence lies the proof of God's existence. Were the proven propositions of science, the law of causality, to demand the existence of God, then, Dr. Douay concedes, he could not object. But Kant, the most levelheaded of all philosophers, is supposed to have presented four proofs a hundred years ago refuting most incisively the possibility that a God exists.[2] This seems to be clearly wrong; Kant did refute the three or four proofs of God's existence, but he adduced only *one* refutation of all possible proofs, which is connected with the fundamental assumption of his system, namely of synthetic a priori judgments. Now, it is not very nice of Dr. Douay to use philosophy as a scarecrow when it suits him, and otherwise in a purely speculative question to silence her. Perhaps he has read Kant's Critique of Practical Reason and discovered that the most thoughtful of all philosophers cannot dispense with a God, even though he cannot prove His existence. Nor is it correct that Kant's proof has gone unchallenged; his proof rests on the assumption of synthetic a priori judgments and stands or falls with them. Now, a large and truly scientific school, that of the English empiricists, decisively rejects the possibility of such judgments. "All our knowledge not only begins with, but also springs from, experience,"[3] they claim, which sounds materialistic enough, and is in any case more scientific than the idea of innate forms of understanding. If, therefore, the social democrats are so keen on Kant's irrefutable proof, then let them stand up and champion the existence of a priori synthetic judgments and establish whether the nature of causality is analytic or synthetic. For let them not be deceived, the existence of God cannot be settled by union debates, parliamentary speeches, or speculation, but only by logical and psychological studies, for which not everyone has a taste, no more so than for astronomical computations. Hence it is just as wrong to think everyone is competent to pronounce on the existence of God as on the existence of Neptune.[4] Once logical analyses have led to a certain conclusion, the existence or nonexistence of God will be as firmly established as that of Neptune, and will have to be accepted as unreservedly by all who do not happen to be philosophers or mathematicians. However, the analyses will have to show whether the nature of the object and of the arguments admit of such certainty in the first place.

The other popular arguments against God have been mustered with great incisiveness and I am indeed most curious to discover how the theist, Brentano, will deal with them. Inasmuch as he considers God a logically necessary scientific hypothesis, he may perhaps skirt the issue, saying: we do not know much about God, our conclusions lead us as far as Him but no further, so that all the evil in the world, whose full range we do not comprehend either, cannot be used to refute Him. More of that later.

The bad part of it, especially for me, lies in the fact that science of all things seems to demand the existence of God (I say seems, for the result of this analysis is partly dependent on logical analyses). The principle of the conservation of energy, of the interaction of natural forces, which we consider as the best fruits of scientific research, seem to involve the end no less than the beginning of the world. According to a verbal report by Brentano, Prof. Fick (physiologist) of Würzburg not only granted this fact but also emphasized it in his lectures on the above laws.[5] We are completely powerless in the face of attacks from that quarter.

But let us cut our philosophical deliberations short. I cannot promise that I shall still be holding these views next week. You may not perhaps attach enough importance to the whole matter to justify so lengthy an account in a friendly letter.

Of more intimate matters I do not, alas, have much to report. If the past still interests you, you might like to hear that Gisela Fluss was in Italy (though only as far as Verona) and that she has been treating my sisters to accounts of her travels ever since. Rosa seems to be very indignant that you wrote a mere five lines in reply to her no doubt pages-long letter; I leave it to you to reflect whether you really want to fall out with a young lady. You may want to authorize me to make your apologies. If you come to Vienna, don't fail to make the acquaintance of Bertha Speier, a striking female genius of the type that you seem to have met recently. I myself know her only from the accounts of my sister Anna, who never tires of admiring and criticizing her. Do not, for heaven's sake, forget to report the result of your meeting with the lady you mentioned (bluestocking, political martyr, and social democrat), her experiences and her works; there is no need, however, to send me her works, which, doubtless, she will be presenting to you. I, for my part, am able to send you something that is closely connected with our public life here. Our Readers' Union is strong on patriotic politics and reform; when the notorious Ofenheim[6] was acquitted, they decided to petition the arbitration court to remove his name from the list of members (which petition, incidentally, I signed). For that reason, the Deutsche Zeitung[7] and several provincial papers decided to make a hero of him, while the Neue Presse ignored the whole affair. Ofenheim, as I know from a reliable source, is said to have offended that paper badly. Now a philosopher, a Dr. Volkelt, has delivered an attack on the whole Ofenheim clique in the debating chamber of our Union, in a speech that was clear, elegant, appropriately rude and entirely justified.[8] He quoted the venerable Kant, whose categorical imperative—but you will be able to see for yourself, for I am sending you the address, which has been printed by the Union publishing house. Pass it on to your social democrats and let me have your own opinion of it.

Keep well and accept the cordial greetings
of your Sigismund

P.S. Ceterum censeo,[9] it is high time you sent me your photograph. I have quite forgotten what the man for whom social democrats and the republic are vying really looks like.—Homoeopathic journal received.

1. Adolf Douai (1819–1888), ABC of knowledge for thinking people, Leipzig, 1874. Douai, a schoolteacher, published *Volkskatechismus der Altenburger Republikaner* (Popular catechism of the Altenburg Republicans) in 1848; following a year's imprisonment, he emigrated to the United States, where he worked as an editor and teacher.

2. Douai wrote: "Kant, the most thoughtful of philosophers, proved incisively, almost a hundred years ago, that there could be no valid proof for the existence of God."

3. John Locke, *An Essay concerning Human Understanding*, II.1.2: "In that [i.e., experience] all our knowledge is founded and from that it ultimately derives itself."

4. The existence of the planet Neptune was postulated in 1823 by Friedrich Wilhelm Bessel (1784–1846); the planet itself was not sighted until 1846.

5. Adolf Fick (1829–1901), *Die Naturkräfte in ihrer Wechselbeziehung* (The interaction of natural forces), 1869.

6. Victor Ofenheim (1820–1886), a railway magnate, was made the scapegoat for the stock exchange collapse of 1873, in particular by Austrian anti-Semites. His trial in 1875 ended in acquittal.

7. A national-liberal Viennese daily, it carried reports on the Ofenheim trial from January 3 to February 28, and from March 10 to April 11, 1875.

8. Johannes Immanuel Volkelt (1848–1930), *Kants kategorischer Imperativ und die Gegenwart* (Kant's categorical imperative and the present), 1875. The lecture was delivered on March 10.

9. For the rest it is my opinion; from Cato's dictum *Ceterum censeo Carthaginem esse delenda* (For the rest it is my opinion that Carthage must be destroyed). Tr.

Vienna, April 28, 1875

Querido Berganza!

I am exceedingly sorry not to have replied sooner to your much appreciated letter, the more so as I do not wish to set you an example of how to neglect a friend. On the contrary, I think of you more than ever and am glad that next winter I shall be speaking to you, and above all seeing you, at least once every two weeks. Leipzig, although it contains enough original characters to enable a legion of novelists to fill an Alexandrian lending library (vide: the homeopaths, sailors, social democrats, emancipated poetesses, and foolish virgins in your letters), appears nevertheless to lack a decent photographer, seeing that the procurement of your likeness is meeting with such remarkable difficulties. You know that this is my ceterum censeo. Perhaps you will recall that an opportunity for granting me a pleasant surprise like that is about to occur.[1] As I do not like being negative, I shall defer my criticism of your new acquaintance to a more suitable moment, when we shall [be] peacefully united in the Prater[2] or the City Park in the land of milk and honey, and be able to settle this along with other questions. I cannot, however, refrain from enquiring about your heroic principle, though I should perhaps have waited for you to give me further news of it unprompted.

Our city chronicle is devoid of interesting news; in any case, you see the Viennese papers. You will know that the old Danube has leaped into her new bed.[3] I went to see for myself a few days later: quite an impressive body of water. Our family chronicle, it is true, was marked by a tragic event: last night a stone flew through the window, leaving a nice round hole—nothing else. Anyone with imagination could easily picture the pleasure of being a minister or professor in bad times and possessing a few more windows. Our spring is rather reluctant, one warm day is followed by several that are horribly cold and dull and I, like so many mortals, am nursing a well-developed cold, so that if I had to speak rather than write to you, you would find it difficult to understand my amiable address.

But let us take solace: everything is but a passage, as was once inscribed on a bridge, "passage," although to what no one can tell. So it is best to put up with the passage to spring. It is well known that our universe is approaching the enviable state of an evenly distributed and pleasant temperature,[4] from which there is no redemption: no more winters, but, alas, no more blossoming or greening in the summer. How glad would one be on doomsday to have one's face slapped by a neighbor; but, alas, the neighbor will lack the "living force"[5] needed for this labor of love. When we experience that happy time, we will all of us have turned into Dutchmen—nothing will be capable of disturbing our sweet peace, neither war nor murder, no new discovery nor cravings for women's emancipation, for no trace of any of these things will exist. The most beautiful women will not take the trouble to please, and even if they should want to, would find it hard. And all that for a little bit of warmth, for the promise of freedom from cold! You may work, study to become a German sage, deliver speeches, whip up the masses or look after your physical well-being and live it up—you will still remain a killer of yourself and the whole universe: you are transforming living force into heat and cannot change it back. You are at your most dangerous, however, when you are happy, when there is a glow in your heart, for then you are swallowing up the world by the spoonful, and guaranteeing an early demise for you and yours. For the moment, I have forgotten the mathematical formula from which this elegiac[6] state is derived; I shall add it to my next letter.

Old Gellert, who wrote a treatise "On the Dangers of Knowing One's Fate,"[7] certainly never imagined that harmless mathematics would bring about this unpleasant situation in the highest degree by predicting the fate of us all. Naturally, this infinitely augments my respect for higher analysis, to which we owe all this information, and I do not believe that your emancipated Dionysian tormentress[8] will have the fortitude to grapple with the spheres of "higher" optics and acoustics governed by it. This phenomenon, incidentally, is not uncommon, and I have been told that D. Nussbaumer, Brühl's assistant, whom you may remember, has used it to good scientific effect.

For the rest, however, farewell and accept the cordial

greetings of your
D. Cipion
m.d.l.A.E.p.e.e.h.d.S.

1. Freud's birthday was May 6.
2. The large recreation and amusement park in Vienna. Tr.
3. From 1873 to 1875 the Danube was being regulated in its course through Vienna.
4. Reference to the thermodynamic theory of Clausius and Thomson. Tr.
5. Impetus, the force that sets a body in motion, as opposed to "dead force," which does not.
6. Freud wrote *eligisch* instead of *elegisch*.
7. Christian Fürchtegott Gellert (1715–1769), "Warum es nicht gut sei, sein Schicksal vorher zu wissen" (Why it is not good to know one's fate in advance).
8. A maenad; a frenzied woman.

Vienna, May 17, 1875

Dear Berganza,

How can it be, Señor Don Berganza, that for nearly a month you have not written to me nor replied to my previous letter—supposing you are alive, in good health and have become neither a Christian nor a socialist, in which case, as with every conversion, you would be expected to consign your old friends and acquaintances to hell with a spate of curses? But in your case one may hope that you would never agree to such conditions.

I was very concerned about your well-being, imagining that you might have been killed in a duel or the like, until I heard from your brother Carlos a few days ago that nothing is wrong with you and that you write regularly to your parents. So I beg you "to break your silence forthwith," as they say in novels, and give me news of yourself, your intentions, your doings and adventures, as well as of the whither and the quibus auxiliis[1] of your holidays, and you will find me, I assure you,

entirely yours
Don Cipion
member of the Spanish Academy

In Spanish
1. With whose help; one of the questions (quis, quid, ubi, quibus auxiliis, cur, quomodo, quando) in the rhetorical exercise known as the *chreia*.

Viena, el 17 d[e] Mayo 1875

¡Querido Berganza!

¡Como puede ser, Señor Don Berganza, que ya desde casi un mes no me habeis escrito nada, ni respondido á mi carta anterior, puesto que estais vivo, en buena salud y aun no os habeis hecho ni cristiano, ni socialista, en qué casos, como en cada convertimiento, fuera menester, dar al infierno con las mayores maldicciones á vuestros viejos amigos y conocidos? Pero de vosotros se puede esperar, que á tales condicciones nunca jamas consentiréis.

Mucho he curado acerca de vuestro bienestar, imaginando, que os han matado en duelle ó otra cosa hasta que, unos dias antes oí de vuestro hermano Carlos, que nada os falta y que escribís muy en regla á vuestros padres. Así os ruego, de "romper luego ese silencio," como dicen en los romances y de darme noticias de vuestra persona, intentos, hechos y aventuras, como tambien de vuestro adonde y quibus auxiliis en las vacanzas y hallaréis en mi, os aseguro

todo el vuestro
Don Cipion
m.d.l.A.E.

Vienna, June 13, 1875

¡Querido Berganza!

Preparatory studies for the zoology examination (which take up more of my time than the actual studies), and which I only finished yesterday, just in time to tackle the subject itself tomorrow and to take the examination on July 15, have prevented me from replying to your kind letter as speedily as its contents merit.

If you think that I can be of use to Klamper,[1] then I shall be glad to call on him and to cultivate his companionship. Since, however, I still lack a reason for doing so, and cannot possibly appear before him with your letter and say that I am soliciting his friendship as appointed visiting nurse, I must ask you to take the first step from Leipzig, perhaps by informing him that I have asked for his address (which, forgetful fellow that I am, I do not have in fact), so that he may have a reason for calling on me and I am given the chance of influencing him in the way you think desirable. For the rest of this year (until July 15, since the student calendar contradicts the astronomical one), I shall not be able to see much of him during the week; however, thereafter I shall, of course, be able to fulfill your request more adequately.

I should naturally make every effort to find time for Klamper, were I to share your view of his condition. Ever since Werther and Faust, every decent "German man" has experienced a melancholy period of being weary of life without really sharing these heroes' fate. Otherwise, suicide and insanity would be much more prevalent than in fact they are in our half-rational world (homo semisapiens L.).[2] Klamper will survive this passing dark mood just as everyone else does, particularly when the causes of his present state (that the lack of suitable friends should be the *main reason* is hard to believe) eventually lose their oppressive grip on him.

Moreover, your view of his low spirits overlooks the fact that if a person has grounds for complaint at all, then he also feels the need to unburden himself, and he will be most likely to do this to his best friend. And so Klamper pours out his heart to you every week or two with bitter complaints, all the while keeping you in ignorance of what may have pleased or amused him during that period.

I would also ask you to remember that I do not yet enjoy his confidence, and to help me out a little so that in his contacts with me he will feel free to speak of what oppresses him.

De me pauca[3]—I shall spend the vacation in Vienna. A small microscope and a small chemical laboratory will enable me to study histology and zoology on my own. A pile of books lies waiting to be read in my small library.

With you, politics seems to have ousted science completely. At least, you replied to my physiological questionnaire by originating a political correspondence. Take care lest you capitulate to the social democrats body and soul. Youthful impressions are hard to obliterate.

Your mother, I believe, did not leave until yesterday.

If you can lay your hands on a secondhand and cheap but still readable copy of *Helmholtz's* physiological optics,[4] please buy it for me—I shall send you the money for it before the end of the month (maximum ten guilders). But for heaven's sake don't make me a present of it, otherwise I shall never again be able to tell you that I need this book or that.

Awaiting your early reply\
Your Cipion

P.S.   It would seem that you, Señor Don Berganza, do not know your own name, as you signed your letter of June second Cipion, thus misappropriating my name. However, if you would like us to change names, as Jean Paul has Siebenkäs and Leibgeber do,[5] I agree and await your decision.

One who has hitherto called himself\
Cipion

Portion in Spanish

1. Sigmund Klamper (b. 1855), a schoolmate of Freud and Silberstein.
2. In the Linnaean system.
3. A little about myself.
4. *Handbuch der physiologischen Optik*, 1856–1866.
5. In vol. 1, chap. 1 of *Blumen-, Frucht- und Dornstücke, oder Ehestand, Tod und Hochzeit des Armenadvokaten Fr. S. Siebenkäs*, 1796 (English edition, *Flower, Fruit and Thorn Pieces*, 1845).

P.S.   Parece, que no sabeis, Señor Don Berganza, como os habeis de llamar, pues que á vuestra carta del 2. Junio subscribís Cipion, lo que es usurpacion de mi nombre.

Pero si quereis, que mudemos de nombre, como Jean Paul dice, que Siebenkäs y Leibgeber hicieron, consiento y espero vuestro arbitrio.

El que hasta allí
se llama
Cipion

———————

Vienna, June 15, 1875

Dear Friend,

I forgot to add that Helmholtz's physiological optics costs ten talers new and you must add the forwarding costs when deciding whether the price is right. I shall send you the money by postal order; please convert the talers at the prevailing rate of exchange, which will be to my advantage (the local booksellers convert at 1.80 guilders). In any case, let me know if you discover a (serviceable and cheap) copy before you buy it.

Thanking you very much in advance for your trouble, and looking forward to your kind answer to my last letter

Your Cipion

Postcard

———————

Vienna, June 28, 1875

¡Querido Berganza!

Please accept my hearty congratulations on your first public address, which I was particularly pleased to see was given, not in favor of the social democrats, but in honor of stenography, which does so much credit to the century of steam. I would never dream of trying to impose restraints on you where I would have you let yourself go most unreservedly: in a letter to a friend. Moreover, I can read your shorthand script quite comfortably, much better than my own, which is so atrocious that in my correspondence with you I am com-

pelled to cling to the old cursive script which your triumphant address has as good as rendered obsolete. I do not know whether, in
your address, you also discussed the changes that the use of stenography will provoke in society, which, I think, would be interesting
to do and which you might well attempt in a second address. Just
think, it would no longer be considered mere flattery if one wrote to
someone: the few, but richly informative, lines I received from your
esteemed hand, etc. One might, of course, use writing paper narrower by two thirds, thus compensating for the alteration. I also [?]
hope that the frequency of your letters will be influenced by stenography, also the style, etc., and I have particularly great expectations
of the inevitable transition period before stenography has succeeded
in coming into general use. At that point, written insults will lose
much of their sting, for who will still be able to be righteously incensed at what it takes him half an hour to read?

For official documents only, you should, in my opinion, allow the
cursive script to prevail, for, first: officialdom has in general a perfect
right to lag 50–100 years behind the rest of mankind; second, it behooves an official document to be written voluminously and at
length; and, third, officials would otherwise produce so frightful a
scrawl that it would become impossible to tell a servant's reference
from a doctor's diploma. What distress would that not cause to all
and sundry!

My Helmholtz is proving a nuisance. I am not insensitive to the
reproach that I divide my modest forces among a host of heteroge-
neous subjects and, at present, I am less inclined than I was earlier
to study physical optics during the vacation. Since, however, a weak-
kneed character like myself likes to leave decisions to God's judgment (chance is the little finger of God's hand, I read recently in a
novel), I shall agree to the following: if, on receipt of this letter, you
have already placed the advertisement, so be it—if not, then please
desist. In the first case, please let me know your expenses in full; it
would be wrong to allow your purse, no doubt depleted by your contributions to the social democrats' secret war chest, to suffer from
my whims. In any case, buy the book only if it really merits the
transaction (in good condition and very cheap) and let me know as
soon as possible. I doubt that the book has appeared in more than
one edition.[1] It is a specialist work and expensive. You can see that
I still hanker after it, even though for the time being it would have
to remain an ornament in my library.

Klamper's address was missing from your letter. May I ask you, lest you forget all about it, to let me have it in your next letter—not in the mainstream but on a river bank. Rosanes and Wahle are unlikely to be of any use to Klamper; moreover, the first will be spending his whole vacation in Pistian, and Wahle is already in Mödling.[2]

I am studying for the zoology examination, but the devil is bound to ensure that I shan't be able to take it before October.

It does not precisely redound to the honor of homeopathy that it should be flourishing in Spain.[3] A few days ago I made the acquaintance of a poor scholar who speaks Hebrew, French, English, and Italian and understands Spanish, has written several papers of a literary nature (I am, for instance, about to receive the one on Nathan) and is now working on a geography of Palestine. He is undoubtedly brilliant, but unfortunately a Polish Jew.[4]

Please reply *soon* and accept as many regards from me as the social democrats have wishes. I, III, III . . .

Your
Sigmund

1. The second edition appeared in 1896.

2. Pistyán, a health resort on the Waag River; Mödling, a holiday resort south of Vienna.

3. At the time some three hundred homeopathic doctors were practicing in Spain.

4. The only person to whom this description might possibly apply is Nachum Sokolow, born 1859 or 1861 in Wyszogrod (near Plock), died 1936; author of *Geographie von Palästina* (Geography of Palestine), Warsaw, 1885. See Simcha Kling, *Nachum Sokolow*, New York, 1960, and *Nachum Sokolow: A Miracle among Men*, New York, 1971.

Vienna, July 2, 1875

Dearest Berganza,

The good spirit has triumphed. Forget about the Helmholtz. I am very grateful for your trouble.

Yours
Cipion

Postcard; in Spanish

¡Queridisimo Berganza!   Wien, 2. Juli 1875

El bueno espiritu ha vencido. Dejad lo del Helmholtz. Vuestra cura mucho os agra-
dezco.

El vuestro
Cipion

Vienna, July 15, 1875

Dear Eduard,

I am leaving on Friday at 7:30, will be arriving in Leipzig at 5:30
p.m. on Saturday, and hope to see you at the station and to spend
1–2 days at your place. My final destination is Manchester.

Your Cipion

Postcard

Hamburg, July 20, 1875

Dear Friend,

I am sailing at midnight on the Huddersfield for Grimsby, from
where, without delay, I shall proceed to Manchester. Hamburg is a
very interesting city. That business with the money no longer both-
ers me, and I certainly hope that I shall not touch your three talers.

Remember me to my friends and accept the regards of
Cipion

I have just circumnavigated the port of Hamburg.

Postcard; in Spanish

Hamburg, 20.7.1875

Teurer Freund!

Á medianoche iré con el Huddersfield á Grimsby & sin perder tiempo de aquí pasaré á Manchester.—Hamburg es ciudad muy interesante. Lo del dinero no mas me inquieta, espero por seguro, que no tocaré a tus 3 taleros.

Saludes los amigos de mí y seas saludado de
Cipion

Vengo de circumnavigar el puerto de Hamburg.

---

12 Green Street, Ardwick, Manchester, August 3, 1875

Dear Berganza,

Were you not the celebrated Don Berganza and were I not Don Cipion, the two of us the sole members of the Spanish Academy, what would you think of him who, having dispossessed you of part of your money, then [did not] write to you, as if he had been swallowed up by the waves of the Germanic sea? But that is not what happened, I am well, on that blessed island which they call England, and I have not written to you because all my time is taken up with talking, walking, eating, and drinking. I am staying with my older brother and his family, my nephews and beautiful nieces, and sometimes I see my younger brother, who three years ago took an intelligent and lovable wife;[1] I look at the streets, the places of entertainment, the buildings and the people of this city, which, having six hundred thousand inhabitants, is bigger than Vienna and could be divided into fifteen Leipzigs.[2] What with so much that is new to me, and with my innate laziness, you will forgive me for not having written to you and for being unable to write to any other of our friends. Please do me the favor, when you talk or write to any of them, of telling them quite frankly and emphatically not to expect a letter from me, because I have better things to do. However, I make an exception of you, and trust that you will not leave this short letter unanswered, but give me the opportunity to write again by telling me of any changes of address and the date of your departure from home, which must be imminent now. I am not short of money here. To make sure I lack for "nothing" in his home, my brother provided me with "an allowance"[3] of five shillings the first time, and six shillings the second time. But neither of these sums amounts to three talers, and so I beg you to wait until later this week when I shall probably be sent some money from home, some of which will go to you. Tell me as well what English products you would like me to bring you, because I know that when I am on the point of departure I will not be short of "sovereigns" and "guineas." Finally, you should know that the Castilian written herein is no more than the ruins of the building the two of us constructed in days gone by.

> Farewell and write without delay
> to your
> Cipion
> dog on the island of England

My address: Mr. E. Freud
    for S. F.
    Thomas Street 69
    Manchester
Thomas Street 69 is my brother's business address; Green Street, where I am writing from, his residence.
My nephew John[4] speaks and understands a little Spanish.

In Spanish
   1. Philipp Freud married Matilda Bloome Frankel (1839–1925) on January 15, 1873.
   2. Manchester (with Salford) had 496,342 inhabitants in 1876; Leipzig (without its suburbs) 127,387 in 1875; and Vienna 673,865 in 1875 (1,020,770 including its suburbs).
   3. Freud used the English phrase. Tr.
   4. John Freud (b. 1855); untraceable.

212 Greenstreet, Ardwick
Manchester, Aug 3, 1875

Querido Berganza!

   ¡Si tu no fueras el celebrado Don Berganza y yo no fuera D. Cipion, ambos los unicos miembros de la A.E., qué pudieras presumir acerca de mí, quien habiendote despojado de una parte de tus dineros asi te escribió, como si le hubiesen engullido las olas de la mar germanica? Peró no se ha acontecido así, sino estoy bien sobre esa isla benedita, que llaman Inglatierra y no te escribí, porqué el hablar, el pasearme, el comer y el beber no me han dejado el tiempo. Vivo en casa de mi hermano mayor en compañia de sus niños, mis sobrinos y hermosas sobrinas, voy á ver á vezes á mi hermano minor, que tres años ha se ha llevado una mujer, muy cuerda y amable, miro las calles, los lugares de placer, los edificios y la gente de esa ciudad, que con tener seiscientos miles de habitantes es mas larga de Viena y puede ser divisa en 15 Leipzigs. Con todo eso, que me es nuevo y con la nati[v]a pereza, que me es propria, bien te puedes escusar que no te escribo, ni estoy en estado de escribir á otro de nuestros amigos. Hagame, te ruego, el servicio, cuando hablas á uno de ellos, ó le escribís, de decirle franca y espresamente, que no se ha de esperar una carta mia, porqué tengo mejores cosas que hacer. Sin embargo á tí escepto y confido que no dejes sin respuesta esa cartilla mia y me des occasion, de escribirte mas, señalandome el cambio de paradero ó la salida á casa, que has de hacer en esos projimos dias. No mi falta aquí el dinero. Para procurarme el "nada," que pudiera faltarme en casa he recibido de mi hermano "an allowance" de cinco shillings la primera y seis la segunda vez. Pero ninguna de esas sumas alca[n]za á tres taleres y por eso te dejo esperar hasta que me enviesen dineros de casa, de los cuales tu parte habrás, creo en las dias de esa semana. Escribame tambien que cosa querrias, que de los productos de la Inglatierra yo te llevase. Porqué sé, que al tiempo de mi salida los "soberanes" y los "guineas" no me harán falta. En fin sabes que el Castellano que aquí escribo, no es mas que la ruina de un edificio, que ambos en dias pasados hemos edificado.

Vale y Escribas imediatamente
á tu
Cipion
perro en la isla de Ingl.

Mi adresa: Mr E. Freud
pro S.F.
Thomasstreet 69
Manchester
Thomasstreet 69 es el lugar de negocio de mi hermano, Greenstreet, de donde escribo, su residencia.
Mi sobrino Juan habla y entiende un poco el Español.

Vienna, September 9, 1875

¡Querido Berganza!

Two mornings ago I returned to dear old Vienna after my seven-and-a-half weeks' travels, have made use of the first two days to wean myself from English habits, and now that my little room looks

comfortable once again, all my treasures have been stowed away and
my mind is settled, I am sitting by the light of a miserable, eye-
destroying paraffin lamp (in England, evey beggar uses gas) in order
to reply to your letter, which reached me in Manchester while I was
in the middle of preparations for my return home. The reason why I
am not writing in Spanish is because of a resolution I have made.
Since I am heartily ashamed of not owning a diccionario, I have decided to purchase one. Once I have one, things will be much easier
and I shall write frequently in Spanish—therefore, why write in
Spanish today when I have not yet acquired the dictionary? As you
can see, this is sound idler's logic. I am delighted that you recently
had occasion to use the noble lengua castellana [Spanish language]
and once again managed to exercise your verbal skills at some
length, and I am longing for the hours and walks next year during
which, after a twelve months' separation interrupted by a three days'
meeting, we shall be able to exchange words for words and, God
willing, thoughts for thoughts as well: I really believe that we shall
never be rid of each other; though we became friends from free
choice, we are as attached to one another as if nature had put [us] on
this earth as blood relations; I believe that we have come so far that
the one loves the very person of the other and not, as before, merely
his good qualities, and I am afraid that were you, by an unworthy
act, to prove quite different tomorrow from the image I keep of you,
I could still not cease to wish you well. That is a weakness, and I
have taken myself to task for it several times.

You will, no doubt, wish to know about my relatives in England
and about my attitude toward them. I don't think I've ever told you
much about them. There are two brothers on my father's side, from
my father's first marriage, twenty and twenty-two years older than
I, the older, Emanuel, having married in early youth, the younger,
Philipp, two and a half years ago. They used to live with us in Freiberg, where my elder brother's three oldest children were born.[1] The
unfavorable turn their business took there caused them to move to
England, which they have not left since 1859. I can say that they
now hold a generally respected position, not because of their wealth,
for they are not rich, but because of their personal character.

They are shopkeepers, i.e., merchants who have a shop, the elder
selling cloth and the younger jewellery,[2] in the sense that word
seems to have in England. My two sisters-in-law[3] are good and jolly

women, one of them an Englishwoman, which made my conversations with her extremely agreeable. Of those persons in our family whose uncle I may call myself, you are already acquainted with John; he is an Englishman in every respect, with a knowledge of languages and technical matters well beyond the usual business education. Unknown to you, and until recently, to me, are two charming nieces, Pauline, who is nineteen, and Bertha, who is seventeen, and a fifteen-year-old boy by the name of Samuel—which I believe has been fashionable in England ever since Pickwick[4]—and who is generally considered to be a "sharp and deep"[5] young fellow. In the case of all my relatives I would find less to criticize than to praise, and much to praise warmly, if I were not disqualified by my biased position of brother and uncle, and by the cordial reception I was accorded, from occupying the judge's and critic's bench. As for England itself, I need not observe such niceties and can say straight out that I would sooner live there than here, rain, fog, drunkenness, and conservatism notwithstanding. Many peculiarities of the English character and country that other Continentals might find intolerable agree very well with my own makeup. Who knows, dear friend, but that after I have completed my studies a favorable wind might not blow me across to England for practical work. Let me confess to you: I now have more than one ideal, a practical one having been added to the theoretical one of earlier years. Had I been asked last year what was my dearest wish, I would have replied: a laboratory and free time, or a ship on the ocean with all the instruments a scientist needs; now I waver about whether I should not rather say: a large hospital and plenty of money in order to reduce or wipe out some of the ills that afflict our body. That is to say, if I wished to influence a large number of people instead of a small number of readers or fellow scientists, England would be just the place for that purpose. A respected man, supported by the press and the rich, could do wonders in alleviating physical ills, if only he were enough of an explorer to strike out on new therapeutic paths. All these are still vague ideas, and I must stop here.

I saw nothing of London, Sheffield, Birmingham, Oxford, and so on, all of which someone who travels for pleasure is expected to visit; I have been flattered with the hope that I might see England again next year or the year after.

To move the poet in you as well, just think: I have seen the sea, sacred thalatta,[6] following the waves of the high tide as they retreated thunderously from the shore, and have caught crab and starfish on the beach!

I have brought back only a few books, but the acquaintance with English scientific books I made over there will always ensure that in my own studies I shall always be on the side of the Englishmen in whose favor I am now highly prejudiced: Tyndall, Huxley, Lyell, Darwin, Thomson, Lockyer, et al.[7]

I am more suspicious than ever of philosophy, but you will probably prefer to learn that I have a fine penknife and a good razor for you, for about nine shillings = three taler. And you will believe me when I say that I am waiting impatiently for the day when I shall see you again. Tell me the date and time of your arrival; I am a devotee of waiting-at-the-station. Warm regards

from your Cipion

P.S.   My mother asks you to remember her to your mother and to let her know whether her health is as good as all of us wish it to be.

---

1. John, Pauline (1856–1944), and Bertha (b. 1859).

2. Freud used the English words "shopkeepers" and "jewellery." Tr.

3. English in the original. Maria Rokach, born 1834 or 1836 in Milov (Russia), died 1923, married Emanuel Freud 1852?; and Matilda Bloome Frankel.

4. Samuel Freud (1860–1945); the first name of both the founder of the Pickwick Club and of his servant Weller was Samuel.

5. English in the original. Tr.

6. Ocean; reference to Xenophon, *Anabasis* 4.7, or to Heine, "Meergruss" (Salute to the sea).

7. John Tyndall (1820–1893); Thomas Huxley (1825–1895); Charles Lyell (1797–1875); Joseph Norman Lockyer (1836–1920).

Vienna, September 19, 1875

Dearest Berganza,

You are right in thinking that I shall share with you my thoughts on my travels, but if by the exclamation mark [?] you placed in your

note before the word Erinnerungsschwelgerei[e]n[1] (I beg your for-
giveness for using so common and popular an expression) you meant
to imply that these memories are mixed up with matters of love, I
believe you are mistaken and far off target. I sent the list of lectures
you asked for yesterday, and I am sorry that it will be several weeks
before you come to Vienna, because next semester I shall have much
to do; no less than eight examinations are waiting for me and I have
done no, or practically no, studying so far. The philosopher Brentano, whom you know from my letters, will lecture on ethics or
practical philosophy from eight to nine in the morning, and it would
do you good to attend, as he is a man of integrity and imagination,
although people say he is a Jesuit,[2] which I cannot believe, trusting
my own judgment rather than rumors spread by Mr. So-and-So.—
You owe me a photograph; just a reminder.

You will see by the inconsistencies in the lines I have written,
which are all over the map, as they say, that there is little to write
about, and that all are well whom you wish to be well. And that is
the reason I do not write at greater length, in the hope that you will
reply before you leave for Vienna, telling me the day and the time to
meet you at the railway station.

With all possible salutations
your faithful and very affectionate
Cipion
not a Roman emperor, but a dog at the
hospital of Seville God besser's.[3] Amen.

Here is something else that comes to mind to write to you! Are there
any Veronicas[4] in Braila with whom you can dance? I've been telling
everyone that you're a wild dancer, so that males cross themselves
at the mention of your name and females are dying with longing to
meet you. I hope I have not embarrassed you with this assignment,
because it would certainly provide a lot of fun for me.

Cipion
the same dog at the hospital of Seville that I was.

In Spanish

   1. Wallowing in nostalgia. Tr.

   2. Silberstein did attend this lecture; Brentano was not only no Jesuit, but left the
Church in 1873.

   3. Yiddish: May God change it for the better.

4. Because the German name for the flower whose genus is *Veronica* is *Ehrenpreis* (price of honor), the term is applied to girls of easy virtue.

Sevilla, Set. 19.1875

¡Queridisimo Berganza!

Justo eres en creer, que yo te haré compartidor de mis recuerdos de viaje, pero, si por medio del apóstrofo, que en tu letrilla has puesto antes de la palabra "Erinnerungsschwelgerein" (Perdones, te ruego, que de la lengua comun y popular me sirvo) has intendido ostender, que se habrán mezclado cosas de amor en esos recuerdos, creo que yerras y tiras lejos del blanco. El catalogo, que deseaste ayer, te he enviado y mucho me duele, que no llegarás á Viena antes de unas semanas, porque el año projimo mucho habré que hacer; no menos de ocho examinaciones me atienden y nada ó casi nada hasta aquí he bufelado.—El filosofo Brentano, que de mis cartas conoces, leerá Etica ó filosofia pratica de las 8 á las 9 de la mañana y será bueno, que tu vayas á escucharle, pues es hombre de entidad y ingenio, aunque dice la gente, que es jesuita, lo que no puedo creer, confiando en mi juicio proprio en lugar de los rumores del Señor noséquien—Tu me debes una fotografia; basta que te recuerdo.

Ya ves de mi poca constancia en los reglones, que he escrito, saltando del numero primo á cien y mil, como dicen, que es muy escasa la materia de escribir y que se hallan bien todos los cuales tu podrias haber interés de hallarse bien. Y esa es la razon, porqué no te escribo mas, esperando que me respondrás, antes que salgas por Viena comunicando me el dia y la hora, cuando te podré hallar en el camino de hierro.

Con todas las saludaciones posibles
tu fiél y muy affeccionado
Cipion
no imperador romano, mas perro en el
hospital de Sevilla God besser's. Amen.

¡He aquí, que me ocurre otra cosa de escribirte! ¡Ha Veronicas a Braila, con las cuales puedes danzar? En toda parte he dicho de tí, que eres danzador furioso, así que los machos hacen la cruz sobre de tu nombre y las hembras se mueren de deseo, de verte. Espero, que no te he embarazado con esa tacha, porque mucho me reiría.

Cipion
el mismo p.e.l.h.d.S. que fuí.

Written a quarter of an hour after receipt

⁓⁋ Vienna, October 2, 1875

Dear Berganza,

Do not worry about your brother's effects; there is a gentleman here from Freiberg who owns a boarding house, and since he is a friend of my parents, they thought of commending you and your brother to him so that you could live in his house. My father used a ruse to invite your brother on a inspection and to explain that he had some effects, etc. None of it has anything to do with Klamper. As far as the above-mentioned house is concerned, it seems to me to be well situated for your brother, but it is less suitable for you, being in Wieden, quite a long way from the University.

I agree with all you say about the lectures in our alma mater and, like you, I am very sorry it should be that way. Even the theoretical lectures in medicine are worthless and open to criticism because they do not change from year to year and contain no more than the official parts of the official disciplines. But don't voice this opinion when you come to Vienna, because people might easily think you are boasting that you have been in the "Reich."

I have heard nothing from Klamper. I wrote to him when I left for England, but have had no time to write since my return. Seeing your anxiety, however, I shall write today (provided I can find his address) and ask him to come and see me. I don't think there is much cause to worry about him. If he has carried out the plan he once made he will have been a soldier since yesterday.

Other news that will weigh heavily on you I cannot keep back; Wahle's father[1] died suddenly without being able to take his leave of his family, having lost consciousness on the stairs of his own home. He had a heart attack and died of a stroke. The poor wife is beside herself with grief, the children are more composed.

Braun is looking forward to your arrival as he is anxious to hear about conditions at your University of Leipzig. He asked Herzig how things were in Berlin and received a very unfavorable report on that great city.

I am very pleased with your photograph; I expect to receive those of my nieces in Manchester in a few days. Enclosed with this letter you will find a piece of paper covered with verses that people con-

Eduard Silberstein as a university student
(presumably the photograph sent to Freud)

versant with the classics call hexameters. You can imagine that only
a most extraordinary occasion could have inspired me to such poetic
heights, and what that occasion is you will learn when you read it.
True, not all the verses are hexameters, and you will find some with
either five or seven feet, but consider these exceptions to the rule.
To tell the truth, I cannot see why all the verses should be restricted
to the number six, and why they should not have one more or less
if by that addition or subtraction they can run faster and the poem
is beautiful, which mine will not fail to be.

With heartfelt greetings
I am your
Cipion
dog at the hospital of Seville, fifth semester 🐾

Vienna, October 1, 1875

Hochzeitscarmen
von einem Homeriden der Ac. Esp.

Singe mir Muse, den Ruhm der Ichthyosaura communis
vormals mächtig im Lias und anderen Formationen,
die ein leuchtendes Vorbild gewesen der Academía,
so daß ein Preis auf ihre Erscheinung von ihnen gesetzt war.
—Doch sie erdrückte die Wucht der nach ihr folgenden Kreide,
bis auch diese zerbröckelt—denn nichts auf Erden ist ewig.
Solche Erinnerung pflege mir Muse und freu' Dich der Nachricht,
die Du soeben brühwarm vom Freunde begeistert vernommen.
Doch wie fang' ich es an, unkundig der lesbischen Laute
jene zu preisen, Helena an Schönheit, die unwiderstehlich
Herzen der Männer erobert, sie selbst dem Geseufze dahingab?
Nicht allzu groß war ihre Gestalt, sie glich nicht der Pappel,
welche untadligen Wuchses gradaus zum Himmel emporstrebt,
noch der Fichte und Tanne, dem Schmuck der nordischen Wälder,
noch des Libanons Zeder, dem klassischen Baume der Juden
sondern der Formen höchste, das Ideal der Gestalten,—
kugelartig erschien sie und herrlich voll abgerundet,
rund das Gesicht mit den geistvolle Funken sprühenden Augen,
rund des Leibes Umfassung und wenn dem Dichter vergönnt ist,

schauenden Aug's zu dringen in was dem gewöhnlichen Blicke
     verhüllt ist,
zweifelt er nicht, daß die Rundung Prinzip sich bewähre der
     Formen,
welche dem glücklichen Manne enthüllt der selige Abend.
Neider behaupten und Hasser, daß alle Ichthyosauri,
—welche Linné so benannt und Jussieu der Gelehrte—
kürbisartigen Hauptes versehen bewandeln die Erde,
aber kein sterbliches Auge ersah an Ichthyosaura den Mangel,
—außer vielleicht der Friseur—denn glänzend fiel ihr vom
     Scheitel
und von den Schläfen herab des Haupthaares wogendes Flutmeer,
bald zu Zöpfen geschlichtet, bald frei sich bewegend im Winde,
bald mit dem Glanze der Sonnen, bald matt wie Strohfarb'
     erscheinend,
herrliche Zierde der Schönen, in Madrid und Sevilla beneidet.
Aber o Muse, betraure den reißenden Hingang der Zeiten,
und die eilende Post, die nicht zu säumen vergönnet,
nicht zu beschreiben der Äuglein Glanz und innere Farbe,
welche ob grau, ob grün, kein sterbliches Urteil entscheidet,
nicht die Formung der Nase, des Kinns und der Ohren Gestaltung,
sondern mit flüchtigem Blick Dich heißt überglänzen die Jungfrau
prangend, die jetzt sich vereint mit dem Manne, um Hausfrau zu
     werden,
aber *den* Zweifel noch löse mir Muse, denn drückend erscheint er.
Spötter, Lächler und Gottesverächter, unkundig der Schonung,
Momusse, Kritiker auch, die das Kind im Leibe der Mutter
schon bekritteln, bevor es ein Auge der Menschen gesehen,
sagen zumeist—es verderbe sie Zeus, der Rächer des Bösen—
daß in dem sonnigen Leib nur dumpf der Geist sich bewege,
unansehnlich und machtlos im schmalen Gehirn die Vernunft
     thront,
eingeengt durch der Bänder und Schleifen und Zöpfe Besitztum,
daß der feineren Bildung Strahl nie aufgefangen das Auge,
nie geglänzt im Verständnis der geistig waltenden Kräfte,
nie mit wunderndem Blick geschaut in die Tiefen des Wissens,
nie zu schauen begehrt, wie des Maulwurfs Auge beim Wühlen.
Minerva und Juno, die Göttinnen zwei, nie schmückten sie,
     welche
einzig der Liebling gewesen der lächelnden Aphrodite,

Löse mir Muse den Zweifel. Du weißt es besser als jene,
sahst in die Schule sie gehen, belauschtest ihre Gedanken,
hörtest des Galliers Sprache sie murmeln, stolzschwellenden
    Mundes,
und die Wissenschaft sämtlich—soweit sie frommet dem
    Mädchen
und wird gelehrt im Pensionat—die weißt Du, besitzt sie.
Auch an Kunstfertigkeit nicht findest Du ihr gleich die andere.
Rasch entwächst ihren Händen der Strumpf bei der Nadeln
    Geklapper,
emsig führt sie das Werkzeug, das Löcher bessert in Kleidern,
allwo die Gähnung der Poren der Luft das Besitztum erlaubt hat.
Schicklich teilt sie dem Häring den Leib und wäscht ihn mit
    Wasser,
scheidet die Milch von dem Fleische und bringt die Speise zu
    Tische.
Schmackhaft ist ihr Gebäck, des Salzs nicht ermangelnd und
    Zuckers,
nicht der Würze die Brühen, so reich ist ihre Gewandtheit.
Also nicht darf sie sich schämen, die Hand zu reichen dem
    Jüngling,
welcher in Deutschland studiert die Kunst das Geld zu erwerben,
Rosenzweig' genannt, weil auf ihm als Zweig sie blühet als Rose.
Glücklich seien sie beide und reich sei gesegnet ihr Brautbett
—beide untadligen Stamms, an Schönheit prangend und
    Reichtum—.
Segen erfülle ihr Haus, nie raste am Herde der Braten,
nie sei leer des Papiers die eiserngefestete Kassa,
und so mögen sie beide das Los vollenden des Lebens
gleich den Insekten und Würmern, die unsere Erde bevölkern,
ungestörter Atmung begabt und Nahrungsaufnahme,
nie von dem *Geiste* berührt, das wünscht die *Academía*.

Epithalamium
by a Homerian of the Academía Española

Sing me, oh Muse, the praises of Ichthyosaura communis,
Once great in the Lias and other Formations,

To the Academía so bright an example,
That for her presence they offered a prize.
—Yet she crushed the Chalk that ensued in her wake,
Until this too turned to dust—for nothing on earth is eternal.
Such memories cherish, oh Muse, and rejoice in the tidings,
The latest of news received from a friend with delight.
But how should I, unversed in the Sapphic lute, even begin
To praise, Helen's equal in beauty, she who irresistibly
Conquered men's hearts and left them lovesick?
Not too large was her stature, unlike the poplar's,
Which pierces the sky in an impeccable line,
Nor like the fir and the pine, the pride of the northern forest,
Nor like the Cedar of Lebanon, the classical tree of the Jews,
But rather like the noblest of forms, the ideal of shapes,—
Spherical she appeared and gloriously rounded,
Rounded her face, wittily sparkling her eyes,
Rounded her girth, and if the poet be free
To probe with a curious eye what is normally hidden from view,
He will find the sphere's principle pervading the forms
Blessed night reveals to the fortunate groom.
Envious tongues and detractors claim all Ichthyosauri,
—So named by Linnaeus and by Jussieu[2] the learned—
Walk the earth with a pumpkin-like head,
But no mortal in Ichthyosaura has espied that defect,
—Unless perhaps her hairdresser—for glossy fell from the crown,
From the temples, the surging flood of her locks,
Now tamed by plaits, now blowing free in the wind,
Now lit by the Sun's rays, now dull and the color of straw,
her crowning glory, envy of Madrid and Seville.
But, oh Muse, lament the furious passing of time,
And the hastening mail that lets me not linger,
To describe her eyes' luster and fine inner hue,
Which, whether gray, whether green, no mortal can tell,
Nor the shape of the nose, of the chin or the ear's conformation,
But commands one, with fleeting glance, to survey the whole
    maid,
Resplendent now, who, at one with her groom, a housewife
    becomes,
But of *one* qualm relieve me, oh Muse, for large does it loom.

Mockers, cynics, and contemnors of God, untutored in charity,
Momuses,[3] critics, who find fault with the child in the mother's
    womb,
Belittling ere any man's eye has beheld its form,
And generally say—may Zeus, the avenger of evil, destroy them—
That the spirit but dully moves in the sunny flesh,
That reason's sway in the tiny brain is but frail,
And confined by the ribbons, the bows, and the plaits,
That the eye was not pierced by learning's sharp rays,
Ne'er aglow with the light of the intellect's force,
Ne'er curiously probing of wisdom the depths,
Ne'er keen to behold like the eye of the burrowing mole.
Minerva and Juno, goddesses two, never adorned her
Upon whom Aphrodite alone bestowed all her smiles.
Relieve me, oh Muse, of my qualm. Far better than they can you
    tell,
You who saw her at school, fathomed her thoughts,
Heard her stammer the tongue of the Gauls through proudly full
    lips,
And the sciences all—as much as young ladies may need,
And in finishing school are taught—those, you know, she
    commands.
In handicrafts, too, you will not find her surpassed,
To the clicking of needles the stocking soon grows in her hands,
Busily she handles the tools to mend holes in those garments
Where the gaping of pores has granted air sway.
Nimbly she cuts through the herring and laves it in water,
Separates the milk from the meat[4] to serve it at table.
Tasty her pastry, not lacking in sugar or salt,
Nor is her soup wanting spice, so deft is her skill.
No demur need she feel in joining her hand to that youth's,
Who in Germany studies the art of acquiring money,
Rosenzweig[5] is his name, a twig fit for a rose in full bloom.
Happy be both, softly ensconced on their nuptial couch
—Both of impeccable stock, resplendent with beauty and wealth—.
May blessings abound in their house, the roast never rest on their
    stove,
May their ironclad safe be filled to the brim at all times,
And so may they both live out their allotted span,

Like the insects and worms that inhabit the earth,
Blesséd with splendid digestion and lungs,
Never plagued by the *spirit*, such is the *Academía's* wish.

October 1 and 2, 1875

P.S.   So rare an event as the marriage of a principle deserves a special effort indeed. We practiced such moderation that we could swear an oath to write a similar poem on every such occasion and our leisure would still not be disrupted more than once a year. Herewith this Formation comes to an end. I now bury the magic wand[6] that aided her education, and may a new age begin without forces working in secret, that has no need of poetry and fantasy! Let no one seek a principle save in the present, not in the alluvium or diluvium, nowhere save among the children of man, not in the gruesome primeval past when wild creatures could consume the oxygen of the atmosphere unpunished by man—

So may this letter, a mixture of sadness and jest, speed on its way, and find you in happy spirits.

Cipion

Portion in Spanish
    1. Adolf (Abraham) Wahle, a businessman, died on September 29 at the age of forty-nine.
    2. Bernard de Jussieu (1699–1776), botanist and taxonomist, often referred to as the French Linnaeus.
    3. Momus, the Greek god of blame and mockery.
    4. One of the laws of kosher cooking. Tr.
    5. The German word means rose twig. For a discussion of the bride and groom's identities, see the Introduction. Tr.
    6. *Zauberstab*, magic staff; perhaps a reference to Prospero's words in *The Tempest*, V.1: "I'll break my staff . . . "

Viena, 2 Octubre 1875
¡Querido Berganza!

    Lo de los efectos de tu hermano no te inquiete; hay aquí un señor de Freiberg, que tiene un pensionado y siendo amigo de mis padres le quisiéron entregar á ti y tu hermano para vivir en su casa. Se sirvia mi padre de un ruso, para convidar á una vista tu hermano y le hizo saber, que tenia efectos etc. No hay nada que hacer con Klamper.

Cuanto á la mansion dicha, me parece, que es situada muy á propos para tu hermano, pero menos apta para tí, siendo en la Wieden, lejos de la Universidad.

Todo cuanto dices de las lecciones de nuestra alma mater puedo confirmar y como tu mucho me duele que sea así. Aun las lecciones theoreticas [?] de la Medicina no valen nada siendo abrido al vituperio, porque no se cambian año por año y no contienen mas que las partes oficiales de las disciplinas oficiales. Pero si vendrás á Viena no digas esa nuestra opinion á voces, porque la gente facilmente creiria, que te vas vanagloriandote, de haber estado en el "Reich."

De Klamper nada sé, cuando partí por Inglatierra la escribí, desde que he llegado aquí, no podía hacerlo, mi tiempo siendo muy escasso. Pero hoy como veo tu mucha inquietud le escribiré (supuesto, que hallo su paradero) y le rogaré de venir á verme. Creo, que no hay mucha razon de temer para él. Si ha cumplido con el plan, que antes hizo, ha de ser soldado desde ayer.

Otras nuevas, que mucho peso te causarán, no puedo retener; el padre de Wahle ha muerto repentemente y sin podiendo congediarse de su familia, habiendo perdido la inteligencia en la escalera de su misma casa. Tenia un fallo de corazon y moría de una apoplexia. La pobre señora es fuera de sí, los jóvenes son mas compuestos.

Braun atiende tu llegada para inquirir en el estado de tu universidad Leipzig. Ha preguntado á Herzig, como están las cosas en Berlin y recibido respuesta muy desfavorecida á esa grande ciudad.

Soy muy satisfecho de tu fotografía; espero en pocas dias de recibir las de mis sobrinas de Manchester. En adiccion á esa carta hallerás un papel cobrido de versos, que la gente vertida en los clásicos llama héxametros. Puedos imaginar, que solamente ocasion muy extraordinaria podia inspirarme á tanto alcance de poesia y cual esa ocasion es, en la lectura sabrás. Es verdad, que no sean todos hexametros, pero se hallan tambien unos versos con cinco ó siete piés, pero esos has de considerar como excepciones, que á la regla no tocan. Á decir la verdad no veo, porqué todos los versos se han de restringir al numero seis y porque no han de tener un mas ó menos, si con esa addicion ó disminuacion corren mas pronto y es hermoso el poema, lo que el mío no faltará de ser.

Saludandote de todo corazon
estoy tu
Cipion
p.e.l.h.d.S. V Sem

Vienna, October 2, 1875

Dear Berganza,

I have already written once today, but having seen Rosanes and having been charged with a small commission I am writing a second time. Wahle, who as you know from my last note has lost his father (the funeral takes place tomorrow), wants to know from you whether you would like to live with them; they will be moving.[1] We can take it that they will not ask too much—Frau Wahle is an honorable woman, as you know—and so I would beg you to consider their offer.

But, my friend, do not allow yourself to be carried away by your feelings of compassion, but think of yourself as well, because it is, so to speak, your duty to live in a manner that will not impede your studies, and if you prefer living alone to boarding with others, do as you wish and everyone will agree with you.

It must not be a sacrifice. This I beg of you, because I know that you are only too ready to sacrifice your own interests out of consideration for others.

Your Cipion

In Spanish
1. Silberstein did move in with the Wahle family soon afterward and lived with them for some time at 19 Weintraubengasse.

Viena, 2. Octubre 1875

Querido Berganza!

Hoy ya te he escribido una vez, pero como he visto á Rosanes y he recibido una cargilla, te escribo otra vez. Wahle, quien, como sabes de mi letrilla anterior ha perdido á su padre, (mañana estará el entierro), te ruega, si quieres vivir en su casa; mudarán de habitacion. Es de presumir que no pedirán demasiado, sabes que Señora Wahle es mujer honorable y así te ruego, de observar á su propuesto.

Pero amigo, no te dejes abandonado á tus sentimientos de compasion, pero pienses tambien en tí, siendo casi tu oficio y deber de vivir en modo de no empecharte en el estudio y si crees mejor, vivir solo que en pension hagas segun tu voluntad y cada uno te dará razon.

No sea sacrificio alguno. Eso te ruego instantemente, porque sé, que eres muy pronto á sacrificar tus intereses á los respetos, que debes á otro.

Tu Cipion

Trieste, March 28, 1876

Dear Berganza,

Here I am in Tergeste. Believe me, Your Honor, writing would be by far the silliest thing I could do. I shall tell you all about it by word of mouth. I would like to read some brief lines from you, but do not ask for any from me. Know then, that Trieste is a very beautiful city and that the beasts are very beautiful beasts.

With which observation
I am your
Cipion

My address
Herr S. Freud
Member of the Imperial and Royal Zoological Station *Trieste*
Passeggio di S. Andrea
The paper in Trieste is very poor.

In Spanish

Triest, 28. März 1876

Querido Berganza

Hé me aquí a Tergeste. Creame Vm, que escribir seria lo mas estupido, que hacer podría. Todo le contaré a V. bocalmente. Leir quiero á sus cartillas, pero no me pida V. de las mias. Sepa, que Triest es muy bella ciudad y que las bestias son muy bellas bestias.

Con cual observacion
soy su
Cipion

Mi Paradero
Herrn S. Freud
M der k.k. Zoologischen Station *Triest*
Passeggio di S. Andrea
El papel es muy malo á Triest.

Trieste, April 5, 1876

Dear Berganza,

Today is a day for writing letters; all parties will have to be satisfied today, for yesterday is gone and the day before yesterday I left my writing things at the Station, and what tomorrow will bring, I cannot tell. The theater, no doubt, since there are posters on all the street corners of this great seaport announcing that on Giovedi, 6 Aprile, Francesca da Rimini[1] will be given in this theater, Otello in that, each play being staged by popular demand and with the famous tragedian whose name we Philistines will probably be hearing for the first time tomorrow, for a prophet is without honor—even outside his own country. What is left to him then, I wonder? We shan't talk about that, however, rather about Trieste and its fauna. I shan't write separately to you about how I eat, drink, and spend my day; ask my family to show you my letter when next you go to see them. I would much rather report to you on what I have been able to see of bella Italia, and how I serve the beast-killing (ζωόκτονος)[2] science. When, at 6:30 in the evening, hands stained with the white and red blood of marine animals, cell detritus swimming before my eyes, which disturbs me even in my dreams, in my thoughts nothing but the great problems connected with the words ducts, testicles, and ovaries, world-renowned words—when, that is, I go for an evening stroll after my work, I see precious little of the physiology of the natives of Trieste. Most of what I know I gathered on my first day, when everything was new to me and I found it worthwhile to pay heed to it. I am a person with the unfortunate tendency of finding everything ordinary and becoming used to everything quickly; when I, a landlubber for eighteen years, am transplanted suddenly to the shores of one of the most beautiful seas, I feel as nonchalant by the second day as if I had been born on a fishing smack. And the Adriatic is beautiful indeed. Trieste, as you know, lies within a small bay[3] [fig. 1] or, to put it more soberly, Trieste has a so-called harbor, which is called the Harbor of Trieste, and I prefer to leave the ruling on whether Trieste was named after the harbor or the harbor after Trieste to philologists, archaeologists, and metaphysicians (a fine crew). I need only tell you, therefore, to give you a clearer picture, that the sea, which may be seen at all times from my window,[4] is usually as smooth as glass. Actually, it looks even better in a good

Fig 1.

Fig 2.

Fig 3.

Fig 4.

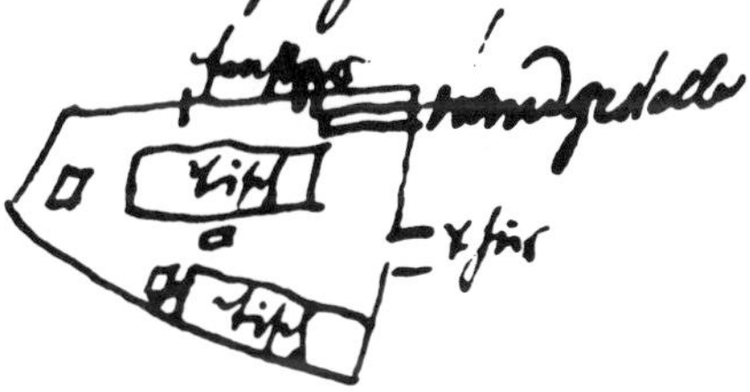

Fig 5.

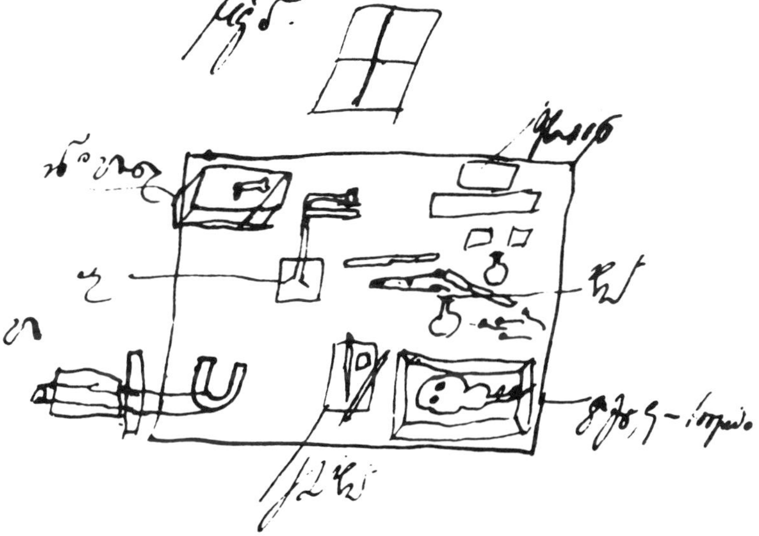

wind, as there is today. Then, viewed from afar, it is covered in a
mass of white flecks, which is a beautiful embellishment for the
deep-blue sea. For the rest, the sea deserves a better oceanographer
and seafarer than I am; last Sunday was wet, cold, and vile, indeed
perfidious, since the entire week before was splendid. I take this for
a kind of anticlerical demonstration by the Adriatic, which, as perhaps behooves a true Italian, hates the Pope, priests, and Sundays.
But, dear Adriatic, please do not throw the bathwater out with the
baby, for even heretics look forward to Sundays, which they must
otherwise spend indoors. Like the sea, the people and the street
names too are Italian. As far as the latter are concerned they are
called after all the saints; you often come across a properly Catholic
name, like that of my street, Via SS Martiri, or a gloriously romantic
one, like Via Madonna del Mare. History has not yet been plundered
for street corners. The people, finally, are very ugly, with few exceptions. (By "people," I refer to all living beings who live and work in
Trieste.) The horses and oxen are the same as anywhere else, as are
the men, although if anything the latter are worse—short, fat, and
with an overabundance of whiskers. Donkeys may be seen here and
there in the streets around the port; they are real, honest-to-
goodness donkeys [fig. 2]. One cannot expect them to be cleverer
than elsewhere—I do not know whether they speak Italian. The cats
are beautiful and friendly, but the women are especially distinctive.
Most of them are true characters in your Leipzig sense, and often
have the typical Italian figure, slim, tall, slender-faced, with a lon-
gish nose, dark eyebrows, and small raised upper lip. So much for
the anatomical features. Physiologically, all that I know about them
is that they like to go for walks. They speak the language, which
sounds exceedingly ugly in the mouths of the men, so prettily that
their a's and o's, clearly and openly enunciated, ring out over and
over again. Unfortunately they are not beautiful in our German
sense, but I remember that on my first day I discovered lovely specimens among the new type which I have not encountered since. For
the rest, they are paler than they should be, and have, or rather wear,
fine heads of hair. Some of them adorn themselves by permitting a
lock of hair to hang down their foreheads over one eye [fig. 3]. I believe that the extreme forms of this asymmetrical fashion extend to
the more dubious classes of society. It is a sort of masonic identifi-
cation sign.

fig 6.

fig 7

fig 8.

fig 9.

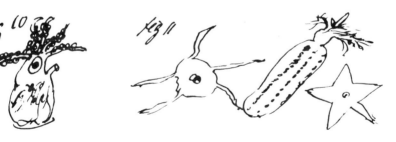

fig 10

fig 11

Few small children appear on the streets. Those I have seen look very precocious, and already temper their beauty with face powder. Since it is not allowed to dissect human beings, I really have nothing to do with them.

Another topic. Our institute bears the *German* name of Zoologische Station, is five seconds from the seashore, or rather is on the seashore, five seconds from the last Adriatic wave. It is a lovely little house, with a garden and arbor, is on three floors, of which the first is occupied by the superintendent, Dr. Graeffe,[5] the second by the zoologists, and the third is now being prepared for them. This reckoning, however, is correct only if the ground floor is counted as one, as I have done; by every other count the house has two floors. My little room has an odd floor plan, one window, in front of which is my worktable, with a great number of drawers and a large top, a second table for books and ancillary implements, three chairs, and several shelves holding some twenty test tubes. Last but not least,[6] there is also a sizable door, which, if you follow its lead, takes you outside [fig. 4]. On the left side of the table, in the corner, stands the microscope, in the right corner the dissection dish, in the center four pencils next to a sheet of paper (my drawings are therefore cartoons, and not without value), in front stands a series of glass vessels, pans, bowls, troughs containing small beasts or bits of larger ones in seawater. In between stand or lie test tubes, instruments, needles, cover slips, microscope slides, so that when I am busy working there is not a spot left on which I can rest my hand [fig. 5].

I sit at this table from eight to twelve and from one to six, working quite diligently, assidue[7] [fig. 6].

Once a day I am startled by the cry: the fishing fleet is in. Then I throw everything down, rush into the courtyard where the fishermen, veritable Beelzebubs from top to toe, have stood their baskets with the catch for the Institute. Then the inspection starts. There is enough material to keep an army of zoologists busy. We share it out fairly. I take the fishes [fig. 7].

My colleague Grobben[8] (whom Rosanes knows) gets the worms and the crabs [fig. 8]; my second colleague[9] abducts the ascidians, which he searches for fleas: copepods, small crustaceans, that live on them as parasites [fig. 9].

Molluscs have found no takers so far, and the most beautiful cuttlefish, too, which keep changing color when you annoy them, are

Fig 12

Fig 13

Fig 14

Fig 15

Fig 16

Fig 17

Facsimile of two pages from Freud's letter of April 5, 1876

still without collectors [fig. 10]. Recently, I have taken up echino-
derms as well [fig. 11].

What these fishermen mostly come up with, however, is small fry.
Each morning, besides, a consignment of fish for me and of crustaceans for the others reaches us from the fish market and keeps us
busy all day. So every day I get sharks, rays, eels, and other beasts,
which I subject to a general anatomical investigation and then examine in respect of one particular point. That point is the following.
You know the eel [fig. 12]. For a long time, only the females of this
beast were known; even Aristotle did not know where they obtained
their males and hence argued that eels sprang from the mud.
Throughout the Middle Ages and in modern times, too, there was a
veritable hunt for male eels. In zoology, where there are no birth
certificates and where creatures—according to Paneth's ideal—act
without having studied first, we cannot tell which is male and
which female, if the animals have no external sex distinctions. That
certain of their characteristics are in fact sex distinctions is something that has first to be proved, and this only the anatomist can do
(seeing that eels keep no diaries from whose orthography one can
make inferences as to their sex); he dissects them and discovers
either testicles or ovaries [figs. 13 and 14]. The difference between
the two organs is this: the testicles can be seen under the microscope to contain spermatozoa, the ovaries reveal their ova even to
the naked eye [figs. 15 and 16].

Recently a Trieste zoologist[10] claimed to have discovered testicles,
and hence the male eel, but since he apparently doesn't know what
a microscope is, he failed to provide an accurate description of them.
I have been tormenting myself and the eels in a vain effort to redis-
cover his male eels, but all the eels I cut open are of the gentler sex
[fig. 17]. That's all I have to tell you for now . . . Farewell, reply soon,
and give my regards to Rosanes, Wahle, and Paneth (Herzig if you
should see him); I have no time to write to them, and hope they will
forgive me. I'll talk to them all they want, and present each of them
with a shark.

Your Cipion

1. Tragedy by Silvio Pellico (1789–1854).
2. *Zooktonos*, animal-killing.

3. Freud used the word *Busen*, which also means bosom or breast. Tr.

4. In his work room at the Institute; Freud lived three blocks from the harbor.

5. Eduard Graeffe (1833–1916), founder and first director (1874–1899) of the Zoological Station.

6. English in the original. Tr.

7. Should be *adsidue*, continuously.

8. Karl Anton Matthias Grobben (1854–1945), appointed Professor of Zoology at Vienna in 1884.

9. A student named Johann Roscher (b. 1853).

10. The Polish zoologist Szymon Syrski (1829–1882), in his "Über die Reproduktionsorgane der Aale" (On the reproductive organs of eels), 1874. He was director of the Trieste Natural History Museum from 1866 to 1875.

Trieste, April 23, 1876

¡Querido amigo!

Your letter pleased me all the more as it gives me a chance of penning a reply and as it is most desirable to be able to write letters from time to time. Don't be surprised at this "sudden" change in attitude: that I earlier[1] tried to shed the burden of replying, but now long for it. A natural law that holds for me is responsible for the complete transformation of my mood. I cannot stick to any place or subject to the bitter end, regularly skip a lecture when the course is in its final stages (the earlier stages are not under discussion here) and am almost eaten up with impatience whenever my stay anywhere is nearing its end. This is precisely what has been happening to me in Trieste. The lovely days in Aranjuez[2] have also turned out to be far from lovely. I believe that I wrote to you once before that the weather, out of a mistaken sense of liberalism, is wont to turn vile on Sundays and holidays; well, ever since Easter Tuesday,[3] this force of nature has been behaving so abominably that we have all been hankering after the old tradition of a beautiful Sunday. It rains every day, sometimes drizzling, sometimes pouring; the sky, normally a glorious blue, and at night blue, red, green, orange, and violet (perhaps in the early mornings as well, but I tend to sleep through the dawn), has been shrouded, as the novelists put it, in a uniform gray, and people have been doing the best they could—they got soaked and greeted one another with the wise but simple observation: terrible weather we're having, or, what really terrible weather we're having, or, when we were alone: what damned filthy weather. And though a different wind is to blame each day, the scirocco this time, the bora or something or other the next, etc.—since the one brings rain and the other brings rain as well, the distinction leaves us cold. Suffice it to say that it rained and that the streets have witnessed the formation of a substance which has so much in common with protoplasm that the Italians refer to it as I know not what, but we Germans in strong language as Drecco.[4] Such weather offends man, robs his eyes of light and his hands of zoological specimens, for on such days the fishermen do not put out, hence catch nothing, and the fish market is as bare as it is in the Schanzer[5] at home on Sundays, Mondays, Tuesdays, Wednesdays, Thursdays, and Saturdays, in short, on all days of the week except Fridays, as the lecture list would put it. For the fishes and other beasts, too, simply do not go out in bad weather. The sharks and rays stay in their cubbyholes at the bottom of the sea, perhaps talking politics or cursing the facchini [porters] and the perils of the straits, the less highly organized bony fish drink coffee at home or play cards, while all the maritime rabble, whose sole purpose is normally to be devoured or caught, all the pelagic matter that sports itself on the waves of the Adriatic, exerts its every hydrostatic skill to sink out of sight so as to survive until a better day. When—inadvertently—half a good day actually did manage to insinuate itself, the barometer took fright, the meteorological station prophesied storms, and the fishermen thus stayed at home. True, the storms did not materialize, it merely rained, and enlightened heads could not but wonder whether it would not be better to hire frogs with free room and board as predictors of the weather than to maintain a meteorological station.

On Saturday, at long last, the sky cleared. On Sunday morning we made great plans for the afternoon, by noon it was coming down again, sometimes more, sometimes less, but sufficient at any rate to dilute the salt content of the sea by several degrees. One of our trio was otherwise occupied, the other two of us defied the wet and the soft among the four elements and took the steamer to Muccia, a tiny place magnificently sited in a nearby bay. I must tell you more about that excursion, because I was strangely affected by several things.

To instill in you some respect for the town of Muccia, I shall go straight in medias res: a house in Muccia's main square—as large as my room—is fronted by a weatherbeaten beast hewn in stone, which, in my conjecture, was a lion, beneath it the date 1444 and next to it a mysterious inscription that I prefer to present in the original rather than in my own interpretation. Qui duce Judaeos Veneto migrare senatu praetor et omne procul abire nefas iussit ac (a given name which I have forgotten) nobis monumenta reliquit Andreas ipse meritis suis clarior vir 15xx. My translation goes as follows: To this place the praetor ordered the Jews to emigrate under the command of Venetus and forbade them to depart from here, the memory of which has been preserved [for us] by XYZ Andreas, a man of great merit.[6] With Wahle's help, you will no doubt be able to decipher more. Enough; you can see this is antiquity. Nor is that all. The foundations of the town are an ancient wall, here and there containing the ruins of buildings, the remains of gates, etc., into which remains the homes of present-day Muggians (that is the correct spelling) have been fitted in the most remarkable fashion. The wall itself is the remains of an old fortress; the buildings were part of a monastery that the French knocked to pieces at some time or another;[7] the Muggians all live uncomfortably close to and on top of one another in frightful burrows and blind, purblind, lame, deaf, and tottering houses. The town, however, has a harbor where the ship plying between it and Trieste can put in: a molo (jetty) right round. The harbor is scarcely deep enough to wash one's hands comfortably, and it sends an offshoot right into the center of the town where the fishing boats of the exclusively seafaring community repose. This canal is so filthy that its depth cannot be gauged. We ambled curiously through the streets, discovered three cafés, four or five inns, and a barber, but what made the most impression on me were three massive signboards with beautifully flowing letters and the full names of levatrices approvatas [approved midwives], a striking number for so small a place, especially when one considers our very cursory survey of the streets. The mystery was solved soon afterward: bambini of all ages loitered through the streets, ragazzi played and scuffled, there was no lack of donne, and there was an ample number of facchini. When we went first into an inn, and later into a café, we discovered that the levatrices had work and earnings enough; in the two establishments we had chosen at random both the landladies were pregnant, which, according to Brentano's probability computations, raises even higher expectations of other landladies and women. I did not bother to check whether the local women, perhaps influenced by the marine fauna, bear fruit the whole year round, or whether they only do so at certain times and all together, and whether, in the latter case, the number of levatrices increases periodically—questions that must be left to future biologists. It was nevertheless interesting and gratifying to find that the girls and children in the ancient ruins were assai belle [pretty enough], half of them rustic beauties, and that even the women were pleasing to behold, whereas the corresponding class of population in Trieste, which ought by rights to be beautiful, is brutta, brutta [ugly].

True, on my first day in Trieste, I felt that the city was inhabited by none but Italian goddesses, and I was filled with apprehension, but when I stepped expectantly into the streets on the second day, I could discover no more of these, and ever since a beautiful donna has been one of the rarest things to encounter in the street. In Muggia, however, the women, as I said, are more attractive, mostly blonde, oddly enough, which accords with neither Italian nor Jewish descent; the locals are not Slavs either, and do not even speak that tongue.

Now let me tell you how we came to the inn and what happened there. In Trieste, Carlini's had been recommended to us, and so we asked, at a certain point in our walk, I in Italian and my colleague[8] in Slovene, where Carlini's was. Oh, Carlini, è qui, we were told, ma è chiuso, non è piu, and a flood of words poured over us. Further enquiries as to where we might find a buona osteria were met with the reply, si trovan pertutto,[9] but the best was al Monte Muggiano over there. We eventually succeeded in tracking down the osteria; it was gloomy and rather bare and my prosaic colleague looked down in the mouth. The best table next to the window was covered with spilled wine, and we had to have it wiped before we sat down. I soon discovered that the inn was decent enough. The wine was a local Muggiano of acceptable quality, the bread tolerable, the cheese excellent—what more could anyone ask? The landlady was a fine figure of a woman, her two pretty children ran about among the cus-

tomers as keen observers, and the company was colorful indeed. A
Triestino peasant, versed in all three languages, sat down at our table
with a buon appetito and con permesso, a little further away sat several soldiers, and the center of the room was held by a drunk at
whom the landlord, the landlady, and the waiters kept poking fun.
He had run out of money but wanted more to drink; they held out a
bottle of wine, handed it to him, but as he began to pour they demanded payment. He claimed that he had paid already, they said
that had been for an earlier bottle, then the poor devil grumbled
about how wicked people were and went on to lament the loss of
his purse. When he had calmed down, they asked him again if he
wanted a drink, etc. Meanwhile, the little children insulted him and
opened the door as if to throw him out. While we sat there, the place
became more and more crowded. Three pullets, a dim-witted dog,
and a magnificent white cat with yellow-brown spots and stripes
started to scrounge for scraps. Next an old man came in and begged,
then an ancient woman came in and begged, and then the open door
admitted two professional entertainers at once, a small boy with a
concertina and a woman carrying a guitar in a coarse sack. The boy
was tiny; he sat huddled up on a bench and provided most of the
noise. The poor woman, presumably his mother, had such pale features and sunken eyes, and so pointed a nose, looked so wretched
and scraped away at her instrument so desperately, coughing all the
while, that we were inclined to believe theirs was genuine misery,
of which, after all, there is plenty in the world. We satisfied all our
scroungers, except for the chickens, which our table companion
chased away remorselessly. When we stepped out into the street
again, it was raining so hard that my companion urged that we take
shelter in a café and play chess. In that café we again encountered a
landlady with two golden-haired children, one of them a piccolo
bambino, and a third in the offing. One of the customers teased the
little girl, complimenting her on being so big and beautiful for ses-
santa anni; the little one objected to the imputation, shouting "no,
cinquanta," and was apparently proud to have shed ten years of her
age. The little imp was actually barely five. Here, too, there was a
drunk, a weedy fellow who in his cups made out that he was a man
of great intelligence. He delivered political speeches and sang political jingles. "Roma, Venezia", he began, but could not go on. Then

he walked up to a customer and addressed him as follows: Voi siete un dei piu grandi uomini del nostro tempo. Garibaldi—ecco![10] The man so honored made a bow and thanked him for the compliment. Every now and then the landlady would seize hold of the fellow and spin him about his own axis, for which he would reward her with a few well-chosen words, unfortunately incomprehensible to me, but no doubt conveying his thanks. We played scacchi and dama [chess and checkers] until seven o'clock, then hurried to the boat that lay waiting in Muggia harbor. The local beauties were out promenading on the molo, inspecting and laughing at the strangers. A beautiful woman with a lovely boy who had been visiting his uncle in Muggia and had been given a present of a chick, yellow all over, tied up in a fazzoletto [handkerchief] and squawking pitifully whenever it was squeezed, kept us company during our crossing. I gave the boy a few shells I had picked up on the seashore, and parted from him with a kiss as befits a zio, an office which has been bestowed on me again in the last few days in Manchester.[11]

In all probability we shall be leaving here on Thursday night. I hope to be back in Vienna on Friday, at six or seven o'clock.

With cordial greetings
Your Sigmund

Please remember me to Wahle and to his Mama. For two jurists busy with examinations, both of you seem to have preserved quite a "feeling for nature."

1. Freud wrote *ferner* (further) instead of *früher* (earlier).

2. Schiller, *Don Carlos*, I.1: "Die schönen Tage in Aranjuez / Sind nun zu Ende" (The lovely days in Aranjuez / Are ended now).

3. April 18.

4. From *Dreck*, filth. Twenty years later, Freud mentioned "Dreckology" in a crucial context; see letters to Fliess dated December 29, 1897, and January 4, 1898.

5. The Schanzel, a large food and fish market on the Danube Canal.

6. The inscription is on the town hall, in two distichs:

QUI DUCE IUDAEOS VENETO MIGRARE SENATU
PRAETOR ET OMNE PROCUL IUSSIT ABIRE NEFAS
HAEC BONDUMERUS NOBIS MONUMENTA RELIQUIT
ANDREAS MERITIS CLARIOR IPSE SUIS
ANNO DNI MDXXXII

Andreas Bondumerus, the praetor [mayor], who at the request of the Venetian Senate had the Jews expelled and all vileness removed, and who through his own merits is more famous still, has left us this monument. In the year of our Lord 1532.

7. In 1511 Maximilian I bombarded Muggia.

8. Probably Johann Roscher.

9. Oh, Carlini is here . . . but it's closed, it's not there any more . . . you'll find them everywhere.

10. You are one of the greatest men of our time. Behold, Garibaldi!

11. *Zio,* uncle; Morris Freud was born to Freud's half-brother Philipp and his wife Matilda on April 2, 1876. Tr.

Vienna, August 2, 1876

Dear Berganza,

I am very surprised to gather from the fact that your letter is dated "Vienna" that your whereabouts have not changed.[1] Write to me soon, I am waiting to hear from you. We shall be writing to my mother this week. I could not carry out your very strange little commission concerning "re data, re non secuta"[2] as I did not know where to look for Wahle. Nothing new has happened since you left; if there were no water or bath in Vienna I should perish from the heat.

I am as always
your faithful
Cipion

Postcard; in Spanish

1. Silberstein was actually in Roznau, as was Freud's mother.

2. A provision of Roman property law, according to which a thing handed over is not made over.

Viena Aug. 2. 1876

Querido Berganza.

Mucho soy sorprendido, que no habeis mudado de paradero, fechada vuestra letrilla de "Viena." Escribidme luego, que estoy esperando, de oir de vosotros. Á mi madre en esa semana escribiremos. Tu cargilla muy estraña sobre "re data, re non secuta" no pude executar no sabiendo, adonde hallar Wahle. Nuevas no se han pasado, desde que partístes; si no hubiese agua y un baño á Viena, me perecería de calor.

Soy como siempre
su fidel
Cipion

Vienna, August 13, 1876

Dear Berganza,

So you've become a martyr? Perhaps you would like to be canonized after this life, which would not be all that difficult, considering that the great Christopher Columbus is going to be canonized one of these days,[1] and all he did was to discover another more beautiful and happier land, which the Pope and the Church finished off? And you, who have sacrificed your health on the altar of canon law the better to discover and proclaim in public how bishops used to dress and the reasons they gave to discard their unwanted "nieces," would you not have greater expectations than Columbus? But I am hopeful that it will be a long time yet before the proverb de mortuis nil nisi bene[2] applies to you—and hence repeat what I have said many times before to you, namely that you have studied without rhyme or reason and that you deserve some kind of punishment, severe enough to be felt and remembered. It is thus right that fate, a very severe taskmaster, should make you copy out "Constantinquelle" a thousand times. But enough of your punishment because we must speak of other things.

In the first place [you will not yet have heard] of the death of Fernan Caballero, or Cecilia Böhl de Faber, who was a woman, our author, and the daughter of a German businessman, and who spent the first twelve years of her childhood in Germany.[3] (interrupted)

A grand design rules this letter, which I have been writing for three days without being able [to finish].

My mother and my sisters have recently arrived, speaking marvels of you . . .

The Freud family in 1876. *Left to right, standing:* Paula, Anna, an unidentified girl, Sigmund, Emanuel, Rosa, Marie (Mitzi), Simon Nathanson (cousin of Freud's mother); *seated:* Adolfine, Amalie, Alexander, an unidentified boy, Jacob

Another interruption: just now I spilled half a glass of water over this wretched letter. Perhaps, to crown it all, it won't even reach you and you would then think that I have forgotten your existence and the obligations of friendship. Perhaps that is what you already believe, because I have not sent you the bow for the small fiddle, as you asked in your letter. But know that this cursed instrument of torture is at this very moment staring at me, and that tomorrow, for certain, you shall have it, but please use it in moderation—bearing in mind your frail health, and also out of respect for me because every time you play the violin my left ear starts ringing.

Behold new misfortune right now in the form of an oval and pointed inkblot, which has so upset me that I must conclude, promising you another, more sensible, letter in the *next few* days, which does not mean to say that your reply should not follow as quickly as possible.

With a thousand regards, your
Cipion, who shall not be going to Trieste[4]

Regards to your mother and aunt. Your sister is already in possession of the books.

In Spanish

1. In 1873, Ferdinand Donnet, Archbishop of Bordeaux (1795–1882), proposed the canonization of Columbus. The congregation of sacred rites turned down the application in October 1877.

2. *De mortuis nil nisi bonum*, let nothing but good be said of the dead.

3. Nicholas Böhl von Faber (1770–1836) was a well-known Hispanicist as well as a businessman; his daughter moved with him to Cadiz in 1813. She did not die until April 7, 1877.

4. Freud did pay a second visit to Trieste, from September 2 to October 1.

Sevilla el 13 de Ag. 1876

Querido Berganza

¿Así os habeis vuelto martiro? ¿Acaso queréis ser canonizado despues de esa vida, lo que no sería cosa muy dificil, considerando, que van canonizando hoy días al gran Cristoforo Colon, el que no hizo otra cosa sino descubrir otra tierra, mas hermosa y mas dichosa, en la cual se acabó con el Papa y la iglesia? Y vosotros, quien immoló su salud en el áltar del derecho cánonigo, para saber y hacer público al mundo, el como vestian los obispos y con cuales razones podian deshacerse de sus "sobrinas" usadas, no tendríais vosotros mas esperanza de Colon? Pero soy lleno de esperanza que tengáis todavía lejos de ser sujeto al refran: De mortuis nil nisi bene—y por esa razon vuelvo á deciros como dice muchas vezes antes, que habeis estudiado muy á tontas y locas y que mereceis algun castigo y que sea grave bastante, para ser sentido y recordado. Así era con derecho, que la suerte os dió que copiar mil vezes "Constantinquelle," que es maestro de escuela muy cuerdo. Pero quedese V. aquí con sus castigos, que hemos de hablar de otra cosa.

En primer lugar no [several words deleted] muerto Fernan Caballero, o Cecilia Böhl de Faber, que era mujer [?] nuestro autor y hija de un mercadero aleman, pasaba los primeros doce años de su niñez en Alemanía. (interrumpido)

Gran dicha que tiene esa letrilla, [deleted] de tres dias soy escribiendola sin pode [rest of line missing]

En esos dias han llegado mi madre y hermanas [rest of line missing] han referido maravillas de V . . .

otra interrupcion; en ese momento acabo de echar medio vaso de agua sobre esa pobre carta. Quizás para coronar la obra, no llegará, y entonces creerá V. que yo he olvidado su existencia y mis deberes de amistad. Puede ser que ya lo cree ahora, porque yo no he enviado arco de geigolina, como V. pedía en su carta. Ha de saber V. que en ese momento está delante de mis ojos el maldito instrumento de tortura y que mañana por cierto V. lo tendrá, pero le ruego de usarle con moderacion alguna, considerando su salud endeble y tambien de mi parte hay un respeto porque cada vez, que V. suena el geigolino, á mi me suena la oreja izquierda.

Vease otra maldicha en ese momento, que ha de figurar un klecks oval, puntado, cosa que tal me desconcierta, que voy á acabar, prometiendole otra carta mas racional en los *projimos* dias, lo que no quiere decir que su respuesta no ha de ser cuan mas pronta.

Con mil respetos su
Cipion, el cual nó irá a Triest

Respetos á su madre y tía. Su hermana ya goza de la posesión de los libros.

Vienna, August 25[?], 1876

Dear Eduard,

Your advice about the umbrella case was very sensible and I am only annoyed that I did not hit upon this expedient earlier, for the object had truly begun to become an instrumento de tortura to me. A case that was long enough was unobtainable (I admittedly did not ask in the bigger city stores, but I did establish that a case of that length comes with a disproportionately large and expensive depth and width). I hope that you will receive the object at the same time as this letter so that you will be able to play the fiddle to your heart's content and delight the whole world. There is probably not enough time left for you to give concerts on your instrument, and this impossibility redounds to my—however modest—credit.

I should like to add a few words about your little sister, feeling sure that I shall not be making matters worse, since I am saying it to you alone, and perhaps saying only what you know already. She is far from being an inscrutable character, but is rather the model of a thoroughly healthy, talented child, though precocious and unbridled as well. Such children are natural rebels against the procedures that make up our education, much as peasant lads who have spent their time climbing trees and scrapping with their playmates rebel against the school bench. I am convinced that all she lacks in her boarding school is freedom; if she tries to insinuate that she cannot stay on for some other reason, then it is only to scheme with a will and skill that are rare in one of her age. Her stay in the boarding school has done nothing to impair her health; I observed her carefully during her last visit here and when I took her back, and felt certain that she looks as well and behaves as boisterously as ever she did before. I believe that the attempt to curb her by institutional discipline is fully justified, and think it would be quite wrong to give in to her by boarding [her] with a family. But you mother is right in not wishing to exert continuous pressure, which could only have a deleterious effect on a child so constituted, and in not wanting [to break] a will that springs from the irreproachable youthful conviction that freedom is better than the classroom. In the circumstances, it would be best not to give up the attempt to accustom her to boarding-school life, and, if she should show an invincible aversion to this particular one, to put her in another. Perhaps her willfulness will be satisfied by having achieved a minor [?] success. She might be told that there is no chance of her being released from the second boarding school and be promised that, if her conduct is irreproachable, she will enjoy a good time in the holidays. It is perfectly possible that, elsewhere, she may even come across a teacher and some girlfriends who will make her enforced stay a pleasant experience. Your mother may still find, perhaps, that she longs to break loose from the boarding school and wants to come home. But if she refuses to conform for a whole year as resolutely as she has done over these past three months, then it would be unjustified not to give the girl her head. I think that on this point my view differs from your own, that you want to keep her in an incubator for refined young ladies come what may, because it seems to be the more sensible thing for her. But education must always be considered a boon by the pupil and may be enforced only while there is still hope that he may come to acknowledge it as a boon. Please forgive these lines brought about by your letter to my mother. Do write me something less businesslike from Braila soon.

Your
Cipion ó Sigmund Freud

My prisons [Vienna], October 17, 1876[1]

Dear Berganza,

I know that you've been in this city since Monday, I called on you yesterday afternoon but did not find you in, and since I cannot meet you except at night, I would ask you to come to my house at any time after six o'clock in the evening that suits you best.

I am longing to see you
Yours, Cipion

Postcard; in Spanish
1. The title of an autobiographical novel by Silvio Pellico, 1832. The card was sent from Alsergrund, where the Institute of Pathology and Anatomy was situated.

Le mie prigioni 17. Octubre 1876
Querido Berganza.

Se que desde Lunes estás en esa ciudad, iba a verte ayer por la tarde, pero no te hallé y no pudiendo hallarte, sino de noche, te ruego de venir á casa mia cuando mas quieres despues de las 6 de la tarde.

Soy deseos de verte
el tuyo. Cipion

Vienna, December 18, 1876

Dear Berganza,

Please wait for me until half past five at the meeting of the German asses,[1] because I have a lecture that does not end until five.

Always yours
Cipion

Postcard; in Spanish
1. Probably a meeting of the German Students' Reading Union. *Esel,* "ass," in school and university slang refers to pupils or students.

Viena, 18/12 1876

Querido Berganza!

Me esperes, te ruego, hoy hasta las 5 y media en la Junta de los asnos alemanes, porqué se me dura una lectura hasta las 5.

Siempre el tuyo
Cipion

Vienna, August 15, 1877

Querido Berganza

Your letter from Zborov[1] brought me the reassuring news that your circumstances are idyllic. I wonder whether at this moment you find yourself on the very ground of the great martial epic[2], or are you perhaps on the tragic soil of Siberia? I hope that the former is the case, and am therefore addressing this letter to your hometown. For if you were in Irkutsk, my letter would have no hope. An official, imperial and royal Russian letter-filcher would read it and discover so much that is incomprehensible, and among what is comprehensible and legible so much that is unorthodox, that he would feel justified in placing himself as an obstacle between our godless exchange of ideas. Here it is so inhumanly hot that all the juices of pious thought[3] have curdled(!) in me and all the bilious and poisonous constituents of my Self have begun to seethe. This very letter is a kind of crisis intended to rid me of morbid matter. I wish for all the rabble found on this earth to be struck down by heavenly thunder and the world to become so depopulated that one would encounter just one human being every three miles. If this wish remains unfulfilled, posterity will rue the day. A certain number of scoundrels is quite acceptable, for it helps people to grow hot under the collar, but too many are unhealthy.

Right now, the flower of mankind is assembling in your home territory; I hope you will let me know exactly how the spectacle looks from your father's house. I have nothing against the Russians, a priori I even like them; they impress me from a distance, and for the rest I know nothing about them; but I am referring only to the people; as for the ruling circles and above all the Romanovs, those insane rulers, bad citizens, and incompetent soldiers—those apes of the victorious corporal in Berlin[4]—I have not enough hate to express my feelings and only console myself with the knowledge that they are digging their own graves. In times like these one is tempted to turn into a petroleur.[5]

What do I do when I am not getting annoyed? I make all sorts of diffident attempts to pursue my studies, incerto marte [with the uncertainty of war], I read what is at hand and await what lies in store. Do procure the Tageblatt of August 14 and 15; you will find the translation of a new sketch by Bret Harte[6] in it which is well worth reading. Your Macaulay contains an essay on Lord Bacon which could not be more perfect. On a few occasions I have risen early. I hear nothing at all from other members of our circle. Your sister Mina came to visit us last Sunday and we all went to the Prater. She looks very well, seems to be growing quickly, and, during the first half of her stay here, was more unruly than ever. Later she calmed down. Among other things, she drew up a list of books in my room of which you may make her a present.

Andreas's fairy tales, Auerbach's Auf der Höh'.[7]—A very strange creature. Still, it seems a characteristic of your family to suffer from a surfeit of energy until you are fifteen, and, all in all, that is not a bad sign.

My sister Dolfi is better. All of us have stayed at home.

Let me know what you see, hear, and do, and when you are coming here. I believe that this is the first time in eight years that I have left one of your letters unanswered for a month. At first I did not know whether I should write to Zborov or to Braila and you know that in sweltering weather, and given a tendency to idleness, what is not done at once will not get done quickly.

My cousin Heinrich[8] from Cracow was here for a few days.

Looking forward to an exciting reply from you and praying that God's blessing be upon you

With cordial regards, Your
Cipion
perro e.e.h.d.S.

1. Town in Galicia, on the Lvov-Tarnopol railroad line, near the Russian border.

2. The Russo-Turkish War (1877–1878), into which Romania was drawn in the summer of 1877; hence the mention below of Silberstein's father's house, in Braila.

3. Schiller, *Wilhelm Tell*, IV.3: "The milk of pious thought in me / have you to seething dragon's bane transformed."

4. Reference to Alexander II (1855–1881), emperor of Russia, a member of the Romanov dynasty, and to William I (1797–1888), king of Prussia and first emperor of Germany.

5. A fire-bomber at the time of the Paris Commune.

6. "Der Ämter-Jäger" (The job hunter), published in the *Neue Freie Presse* on August 13 and 14. "Eine Episode aus John Oakhurst's, des Spielers Leben" (An episode from the life of the gambler John Oakhurst), described as Harte's latest story, appeared at the same time.

7. S. Andreas, *Die Träumleiter: Ein Märchen* (The dream ladder: A fairy tale), 1832; Berthold Auerbach (1812–1882), *Auf der Höhe* (On the heights), 1865.

8. Heinrich Nathansohn (b. 1858), son of Amalie Freud's older brother Adolf, was a lawyer in Cracow. Tr.

Vienna, September 7, 1877

Querido Berganza,

You will see from the heading of this letter that time is slipping by me unmarked by any special events; I should not have confused

September with August otherwise.[1] I worked hard for a time, but
then I broke off to read Pickwick instead of botany and tutti quanti.
I have read the Macaulay volume[2] you left me at least four times,
opening it somewhere near the middle and going on till fatigue
stopped me. The two essays on Bacon and Temple are quite outstanding. I have no news at all of our friends. Perhaps some of the
rings of our circle were drowned in the lake at Gmunden during the
last storm, but perhaps not, because the papers carried no such
news. I cannot really tell. Only Paneth, who is unsure whether he
should go to Vienna or Berlin, has written to me. Lipiner is here, or
rather in Baden;[3] I have had a fairly long chat with him and, if he
gives me the chance, I may well try to become more closely acquainted. I am not at all sure what to make of him; I have neither
taken the measure of his intellect nor weighed up his personality.
All in all, however, I am not inclined to endorse Wahle's condem-
nation, but have a very favorable opinion of him. I normally consider
Wahle a good observer—personal considerations have perhaps
robbed him of his competency in this instance. Anyway, I care no
more about Lipiner's opinion of Wahle than about Wahle's opinion
of Lipiner, for respect and affection are reciprocated in this case. I
am told that Braun is here but have not seen him. This is an example
of how old attachments can evaporate.

The war is keeping us in tremendous suspense. Unfortunately no
sensible news about the vast scene of carnage has appearing during
the past few days. About a week ago a battle was fought at Pelischat,[4]
and from a comparison of all the reports in the European press it is
impossible to tell who was the actual victor and what really happened. Our Turkophile newspapers keep prophesying a Russian ca-
tastrophe every three days. I suspect that this time History will behave like a diplomat and admit that nothing at all of importance is
taking place.

Nothing much else is happening either. It rains for a few days so
that people can acquire colds, then the weather turns fine for no
good reason, and then it rains again until in the end the misery of
winter will be upon us. Today all the world is preparing for the High
Holiday; I am told we are to have a leap year.[5] There is much cooking
and baking going on at home and the only result will be that I shall
have a worse night's sleep than usual. I remember with pleasure that
the whole spectacle passed me by last year in Trieste. Gorging one-

self on such a scale can be excused only if a large company which does not normally meet at table is gathered together. In that case, good food becomes a means of merrymaking,[6] just like fine clothes, dancing, games, and other entertainment. It is, however, a poor way of celebrating when all it means, caeteris paribus [other things being equal], is burdening the stomach with a greater girth and an increased consumption of acid. We young people who have half left our own families and have not yet found a new one are in fact singularly unsuited to the enjoyment of holidays.

Dolfi is almost completely recovered.

Did you receive the lecture list? I am quite proud of the dedication and also of the new meaning I have attached to the perro e.l.h.d.S. It is one of the last great exploits of the celebrated A.E. I invite you to conjure up a nice winter evening when together we shall burn the archives in a solemn auto-da-fé. Out of boredom, I am keeping a diary once again, but, like my present circumstances, it is rather bleak and uninteresting.

Farewell, write again and report on what you are doing and how your family is, particularly little Adolf.

With cordial regards
Your faithful
Cipion
perro en el hosp. d. Sevilla

P.S. If you cannot read my letter, it doesn't matter. Much luck á la franca.[7]

Minna will be with us tomorrow and the day after.

1. Freud had first written August 7.

2. The *Essays.*

3. A spa south of Vienna.

4. There was heavy fighting at Plevna; on August 31 the Russians beat back a Turkish sortie at Pelischat, a village west of Plevna.

5. In the Jewish calendar, the New Year is in September and the leap year has thirteen months.

6. Freud used the English word. Tr.

7. Means both "with the Franconian woman" (see the following letter) and "in generous measure."

Vienna, August 14, 1878

Querido Berganza,

Your letters are slightly shorter than the intervals between them. I wonder why you do not come here if you are so bored where you are. You would save time that way. Your account of your doings in Braila is presumably incomplete. "Franconian woman" is presumably a generic term.

Your scientific efforts deserve every credit. You would undoubtedly have become a Humboldt[1] had that cursed jurisprudence not diverted your energies from the contemplation of nature. If, with your usual modesty, you should reject this appraisal, please remember your attempts to concoct the great elixir from various organic substances, your unquenchable thirst for closer acquaintanceship with flies' legs under the microscope, and your thorough grasp of my collected works, which are not written for a popular audience. Your latest find seems to concern Xiphias gladius, the swordfish; I offer this opinion with all the caution that experience has taught me to attach to such "actions at a distance."[2] I have enriched the last few weeks by reading tales of exploration in Africa. I have read Baker, Schweinfurth, and Stanley.[3] It is all very charming, but a little like those fairy tales in which the prince, with one stroke of his sword, slays one horrible dragon and invincible sorcerer after another, so much so that even the most horribly hostile monsters cease to frighten us, experience having taught us not to take them too seriously. None of these modern travelers who kills his ration of 100–200 savages is ever wounded by so much as an arrow. One sees that there is still a God above. More recently, of course, a few of them have been killed, and to that extent a certain gravity has entered the picture.

In addition, I have been reading Macaulay and advise you to do likewise. It is not possible that Macaulay should be unobtainable in a port city. The last piece I read was on Bertrand Barère,[4] and I am left with the vivid impression that a man may as soon be executed with words alone as with the sharpest of guillotines.

In two weeks Bettelheim has become as staunch a Macaulayist as I am, and he has been showing a degree of enthusiasm and of simple admiration—unmixed with criticism—of which I would never have thought him capable.

During the holidays, my demon drove me to visit Stricker's[5] laboratory, where I was well received and provided with good research subjects. I am now involved in the microscopic study of the nerves of salivary glands and am quite sure I shall find something. Not so sure that I shall be publishing anything, however, for the subject is highly rewarding and highly popular, and it is quite likely that someone will anticipate me, whereas I cannot be sure when I shall be coming up with anything. Next month I shall finally start to do experimental work, also on salivary secretion in dogs.

As you will have seen in the papers, we buried Rokitansky[6] in July. It was a hot day and the procession long. The Hernals Cemetery is a few minutes from Dornbach, and this prompted us to seek refreshment in Dornbach after the interment. Then we—Bum, Bettelheim, and I—drove to the Prater and, since none of my crowd was there, I allowed myself to be enrolled as a member of the Bettelheimian dinner party. I cannot say that I was amused or found it agreeable. The old man seems to be a very "grobber Jüd."[7] He found nothing better to do the whole time than to jeer at a hunchbacked woman at a nearby table. One of the girls is quite nice, as you may have noticed yourself; she was occupied the whole time by Bum, who ate from her plate and asked her whom she really intended to marry, Rosanes or Kohn. He modestly refrained from mentioning himself, although admiration of his exceptional good looks was shared by the whole family. B. has been sent a touching invitation by Rosanes which he intends to decline. Ros. remarks, just by the way, that Frau B. is, of course, back again and that they must, of course, act as her escorts as before.

With cordial regards
Your Cipion

Remember me to all your family.

1. Alexander von Humboldt (1769–1859).

2. Reference to a poem by Goethe, "Wirkung in die Ferne," which also bears on the remarks about the "Franconian woman."

3. Samuel Baker (1821–1893), *The Albert Nyanza*, 1866, or *Ismailia*, 1874; Georg

Schweinfurth (1836–1925), *Im Herzen von Afrika, 1868–1871* (The heart of Africa, 1874); Henry Morton Stanley (1841–1904), *How I Found Livingstone, 1872,* or *Through the Dark Continent, 1878.*

4. Bertrand Barère de Vieuzac (1755–1841), a member of the French National Convention, played a crucial role in the conviction of Louis XVI.

5. Salomon Stricker (1834–1898), appointed Professor of Pathology at Vienna in 1873; head of the experimental pathology laboratory.

6. Karl von Rokitansky (b. 1804) died on July 23, 1878; appointed Professor of Pathological Anatomy at Vienna in 1834.

7. A coarse, uneducated Jew; a play on the Yiddish *grobber jung,* vulgarian. Tr.

Vienna, March 11, 1879[1]

Dear Berganza,

If your examinations leave you time to spare, please let me have by next post the name and address of your tailor because I urgently need new suits. As a reward[2] I shall not be coming to visit you this week.

I am much better and with best regards

I remain Your Cipion

Postcard; in Spanish

1. Freud wrote *martes* (Tuesday) for *marzo* (March).

2. Probably meaning that he would not be disturbing Silberstein during his preparations for his examinations. The postcard is addressed to Dr. Eduard Silberstein, although he did not obtain his doctorate until the completion of his examinations, on December 23.

Viena, Martes 11.1879

¡Querido Berganza!

Cuando tus ejamines te dejan tiempo libero, te ruego, me hagas saber por el poste projimo, el nome y paradero de tu sastre, porque muy menester me hacen vestidos nuevos. No vendré á verte por agradecimiento esa semana.

Estoy muy mejor y saludandote

soy tu Cipion

Vienna, July 22, 1879

Dear Berganza,

I write today having finished my examinations and started on my
work and holiday assignment. You will want to know first how I got
on in physiology so I shall write about that first. It so happened that
Brücke[1] was in a very bad mood, and I had no chance to shine; nevertheless His Eminence exaggerated [?]. I was the first of the candidates and Brücke greeted me very courteously when I came in and
asked me to go straight up to the laboratory [several illegible words]
to explain the microscope. That was not a very happy choice because I had not bothered about such minor matters, believing that
the larger and more difficult apparatus would fall to me, the kind
that allows one to talk at length and to show off one's profound
knowledge. And so it happened that I was not very inspired and got
muddled at one point during the description of the apparatus, although no one can say that I disgraced myself badly. While I was
busy up at the desk, Brücke noticed that one of the candidates, sitting at the microscope, was doing something completely wrong, and
shouted at him in annoyance, asking him what he thought he was
doing, and from that moment on he was nervous and disagreeable to
all of us. After the apparatus, I was given a very simple chemical
reaction to do and when I was finished with that, seeing Brücke had
not been watching what I was doing but was still being cross with
the others, I stepped down to do my microscopic work. I don't need
to add that everything went well, and when Brücke came over to my
seat I was able to tell him that the result was so-and-so, and that one
of the specimens had been very badly prepared, although one could
still tell what it was. He agreed, and because of its poor quality took
it away. Since I was the last to be seated, and, moreover, in such a
way that the others could not see me, Brücke told me to change
places lest the others think I was doing something different from
them. One of the others did not pass, and the examination ended
after exactly one hour. Next day Fleischl[2] told me that before the
examination Brücke had asked him what he should test me on, and,
not knowing what to reply, Fleischl had told him that I would probably know everything. Had I told Fleischl beforehand that I wanted

this or that, I am certain I would have got it. Which goes to show that it pays to be brazen, and I shall be so from now on.

Next day I took my leave of the laboratory, and spent the evening with Em. Loewy and Paneth. Loewy, a worthy but not very imaginative fellow, speaking of Brücke, Exner,[3] and Fleischl, combined all three names into an amalgam: Brüxl, which amused us no end.

And so the last year of my studies has gone by and I am thinking about what I am going to do during the vacation. My work is going to take up all my time and I shall not be able to go out into the countryside on Sundays. I feel very lonely, like the last rose of summer, which without doubt is a very poetic simile.

Last week I had the great scientific satisfaction of receiving a paper by Professor Schwalbe[4] from Jena, who accepts the results of my work on the spinal ganglia,[5] quotes me many times, and calls me, among other things, the "aforementioned research scientist," which, among people who would take the food from each others' mouths, must be considered a rare courtesy. Schwalbe, incidentally,

Ernst von Brücke

is the man who writes the annual histology report,[6] and so this business has a practical advantage as well.

I have nothing more to say except, perhaps, that I shall write to you again one of these days and that all your letters will elicit replies from me. I trust that you are well, and ask you to convey my respects to your mother and your beautiful aunt.

Believe me, yours as ever,
Cipion

P.S. My brother Emanuel has written to say that he doesn't know the book you asked him for, and that he was unable to procure it from the bookshop.

In Spanish

1. Ernst Wilhelm von Brücke (1819–1892), appointed Professor at Vienna in 1849 and director of the Physiological Institute, was the most important of Freud's science teachers.

2. Ernst von Fleischl-Marxow (1847–1891), one of Brücke's assistants at the time.

3. Sigmund Exner (1846–1926), another of Brücke's assistants.

4. Gustav Schwalbe (1844–1916), "Das Ganglion oculomotorii" (The oculomotor ganglion), *Jenaische Zeitschrift für Naturwissenschaft* (Jena journal of natural science) 13 (1879): 173ff.

5. "Über Spinalganglien und Rückenmark des Petromyzon" (On the spinal ganglia and spinal cord of Petromyzon), *Sb. Ak. d. W. Wien* (Math.-Nat. Kl.) (Proceedings of the Vienna Academy of Science, Mathematics and Natural Science Division) 78 (1878): 81ff.

6. The reference is to *Jahresberichte über die Fortschritte der Anatomie und Physiologie* (Annual reports on the progress of anatomy and physiology); Schwalbe, however, did not write the report on histology.

Viena, Julio 22 1879

Querido Berganza

Hoy te escribo acabado mis examenes y comenzando mi acititud y trabajos de vacaciones. Por lo primero querras saber como he pasado la fisiologia y sea eso lo primero que te escribo. Era el Brücke por casualidad muy mal dispuesto y no tenia yo ocasion de esplandecer, sin embargo exageraba [?] la eminencia. Era yo el primero de los candidatos y el Brücke me saludaba muy cortes entrando me hacia subir en el laboratorio [several illegible words] el microscopo para esplicarlo. No era eleccion favorable, pues esas cosillas no habia cuidado mucho, pensando que á mi caerian los aparatos grandes y dificiles, de los cuales mucho se puede decir y se pueden ostentar profundos conocimientos. Asi era que no era muy animado y en la descripcion del aparato una vez me turbaba, aun no se puede decir que era un gran vitupero. Mientras que yo estaba ocupado en la catedra, notó el Brücke, que uno de los candidatos, que al microscopo eran asentados, hacia una cosa muy mala y enojandose le gridaba, qué era lo que hacia, y desde mismo momento era nervoso y desagradable á todos. Despues del aparato tenia una reaccion química muy ligera y acabada esa el Brücke no habiendo observado a que hacia yo, sino siempre enojandose de los otros bajaba yo para hacer mis obras microscopicas. No es menester decir que todo andaba muy bien de esas cosas y llegando el Brücke en mi lugar le decia, que tal era tal y que uno de los preparados era muy mal hecho aunque se podia conocer lo que era. Consentia el y lo confisco por ser tan malo. Siendo yo el postrero asentado de manera que los otros no me podian ver me decia el Brücke que habia de andar en otro lugar, para que no creyese la gente que yo tenia allí otra cosa que hacer que los otros. Caía uno de los otros y se acababa el ejamen en una hora en punto. El dia projimo me dijo el Fleischl, que antes del ejamen el Brücke le preguntó cual cosa debria el pedir de mí y el Fleischl no sabiendo le decia que por seguro yo sabría todo. Si yo habria dicho al Fleischl antes, que quiero eso ó eso, por cierto que lo habria recibido. De eso sigue, que es lo mejor ser impertinente, y así seré yo de aquí adelante.

El dia projimo me despedió del laboratorio y pasé la tarde con Em. Loewy y Paneth. El Loewy, hombre muy honrado, pero poco ingenioso, hablando de Brücke, Exner y Fleischl mezcló esos tres nombres en un compuesto: Brüxl, lo que nos causé gran entretenimento.

Así se ha pasado el año postrero de los estudios mios y pienso á que hacer en las vacancias. Mis quehaceres piden todo mi tiempo, no podré ir en la campaña en domingo. Me siento muy solitario como la postrera rosa del verano, lo que sin duda alguna es una comparacion muy poetica.

En la semana pasada tenia una grande satisfaccion cientifica, recibiendo un papel del Profesor Schwalbe en Jena quien aceptando los resultos de mi trabajo sobre las ganglios spinales me cita muchas vezes y me llama entre otros "genannter Forscher" lo que con hombres, que se sacan el pan de la boca uno á otro es cortesía escojida. Es ese Schwalbe hombre, quien escribe los relatos anuales de histologia y por eso hay un provecho practico en el afar.

No tengo mas que decir acaso e escribo á V. otra vez en esos tiempos y sus cartillas servirán á provocar las mias respuestas. Espero que V. se halla muy bien y le ruego traer mis respetos á su madre y hermosa tia.

Creame V. el suyo como siempre he sido
Cipion

Vienna, August 10, 1879

Dear Berganza,

At last I have time to write at leisure, having spent the past two weeks working on the translation of the essay by J. S. Mill on Plato and his work.[1] I could not sleep at night because it had to be finished by a certain deadline, which was the same as that for the Russian evacuation of Bulgaria.[2] Now I fear nothing, save that the devil bring me uncles or aunts or cousins making demands on my time, more valuable to me during these months than ever before. I spend part of the morning in the clinic and the rest of the day is all mine. I give priority to studying, there being nobody here I know, no pleasures or any diversions, except that I shall be going to bathe in the Prater when the heavens are kind and send no rain! Up till now it has not been dry; in fact it has been so wet that even I, the arch-enemy of umbrellas, of which I always say that if it rains heavily they give no protection and if it rains moderately they are superfluous, have been forced to buy such a device.

I have some marvelous books to read, two volumes of Macaulay's magnificent essays, two more of his history of England, some short works by Fechner,[3] a great philosopher and wit, Adam Smith's fundamental book on the wealth of nations,[4] splendid new books on physiology, and so on. Thus time passes with reading, studying, and on occasion making plans for next year.

And so it could be said of me that I am feeling deprived of the noble Spanish language, and to remedy this I propose that upon receiving my translation fee (which, as Gomperz[5] has told me, I can claim at any time) I shall buy myself a new Spanish book as a reward.

My family is well, and my sister has asked me to find out from you when you intend to return to Vienna, because she needs the information in order to carry out a task given to her by Your Honor's mother.

I very much hope that you will not leave me without news of your activities and the many delights you will be enjoying in Ischl.[6] In this hope I salute Your Honor and beg you to convey my respects to your mother and aunt.

Always your
Cipion

P.S.   I have no news of Brust. Nor have I written to him because I expect him to visit me one of these Sundays, once the ties that bound him to Baden are loosened.

Should Herr Guzman be in Ischl and in your company, please give him my regards.

In Spanish

1. Freud's translation was published in J. S. Mill, *Gesammelte Werke* (Collected works), vol. 12, Leipzig, 1880.

2. On August 10, the *Neue Freie Presse* published a report from a correspondent in Burgas which stated: "On this day [July 27] the last Russian regiment, the Vladimir Alexandrovich, left Eastern Rumelian soil."

3. The reference is to his humorous essays, mainly published under the pen name of Dr. Mises.

4. Adam Smith (1723–1790), *An Inquiry into the Nature and Causes of the Wealth of Nations*, London, 1776.

5. Theodor Gomperz (1832–1912), appointed Professor of Classical Philology at Vienna in 1873. Gomperz had commissioned the Mill translation from Freud.

6. A fashionable spa in Upper Austria. Tr.

Viena el 10 Austo 1879

Querido Berganza

En fin que tengo tiempo y ocio para escribirte habiendo trabajado las dos semanas anteriores á la traduccion de tal ensayo por J. S. Mill sebre Plato y sus obras. No dormia en los noches por ser necesario acabar en termino fijado, y era el mismo como el de la evacuacion de la Bulgaria por los Rusos. Ahora no temo otra cosa sino que el diablo traiga allá unos tios y tias o primas y primos que pidan mi tiempo el cual mas valor tiene en esos meses que jamas tenia. Parte de la mañana paso en el hospital, el resto del dia es á mi y en primer lugar al estudio no habiendo allí ningun conocido, ningun divertimiento ni aun distraccion cualquiera escepto que iré al baño en el prado cuando placerá al cielo que no llueve! Hasta hoy no era tan seco, y tan humido era que aun yo, enemigo principal de los paraguas, que siempre digo que siendo fuerte la lluvia no protejen y siendo mediocre no se necesitan, me he visto forzado á comprar una tal maquina.

Tengo por lectura á unos libros muy hermosos, dos tomos de los gloriosos ensayos de Macaulay, otros dos de su historia de la Inglatierra, unas obritas de Fechner gran filósofo y hombre burlador, la obra fundamental de Adam Smith sobre las riquezas de las naciones, libros hermosisimos nuevos fisiologicas y tal. Asi leyendo, estudiando y en ocasion haciendo planes por el año viniedro se me pasa el tiempo.

Tal es que se puede decir de mí, que siento, que muy mal se me va mancando el noble idioma castellano, y por pasarme eso me propongo, que recibiendo el salario de mi traduccion (el cual como el Gomperz me dijo, cada dia puedo pedir) compraré un libro español nuevo para recompensamiento.

Lis mios se sienten bueno y hace preguntar mi hermana en cual tiempo volveran Vds á Viena, por ser necesario esa informacion á la ejecucion de un trabajo que de la madre de Vm tiene.

Ahora bien que espero que V. no me dejerá sin nuevas algunas de sus quehaceres y de las muchas amenidades, que debe gozar en Ischl. Con tal esperanza le saludo á Vm y le ruego de traer mis cortesias á su madre y tia.

Siempre el suyo
Cipion

P.S. De Brust nada sé yo, ni le he escrito esperando que venga á verme uno de esos domingos, como los vinculos que le tenian en Baden encerrados, sean sueltos.

Cuando el Señor Guzman sea en Ischl y en su sociedad le traiga V. mi saludacion.

Vienna, February 3, 1880

My dear Edward

I have made up my mind to stay at home and work and to let Mr Hansen[1] puzzle our dear fourteen friends, as he can. I am almost sure the interruption of an evening might put me out and destroy my artificial systematic structure of study. Let my Mr Hansen come when I am rather more independent and give him my best love. Hope you will keep your mind sceptical and remember 'wonderful' is an exclamation of ignorance and not the acknowledgment of a miracle.

Yours for ever
Sigmund Freud

Postcard; in English

   1. Probably the hypnotist Carl Hansen (1833–1897), one of whose demonstrations Freud witnessed as a student.

Vienna, March 26, 1880

Dear Berganza,

What shall I write to you? That I commiserate with you with all my heart; that I already know that my help is not needed, I being a theoretician, especially in matters such as this, when nearly everyone else is a practitioner. Moreover, the event will soon lose its novelty value for you and your fellow dogs, of whom I am one. "It's all happened before," as the wise Rabbi Akiba[1] used to say. He was a very clever man and went to the heart of things.

With which I remain as I always have been
Your Cipion
dog under examination[2]

Postcard; in Spanish

   1. In *Uriel Acosta* (1846), a play by Karl Gutzkow (1811–1878).

   2. The three oral examinations for the doctorate were held between June 9, 1880, and March 30, 1881.

Viena 26to Marzo 1880

¡Querido Berganza!

   ¿Que tengo que escribirle? Que le tengo compasion de todo mi corazon; que ya sé, que no se necesita mi ayuda, siendo yo theorético y mas en tal cosa, en qué casi toda la gente demasiado pratica es. Tambien tal evenimiento perderá su fuerza de noveldad para V. y sus comperros, siendo yo uno de ellos; "Todo ha sido antes" como usaba decir el sabio Rabbi Don Akiba. Era hombre muy cuerdo y miraba en lo profundo de las cosas.

Con qué estoy como he sido
su Cipion
perro ejaminando

Vienna, July 24, 1880

My dear Berganza,

This is to let you know that I have done well in my second theory exam,[1] after quite some effort and very great anxiety, since as I did not have enough time for pharmacology I expected to fail in this subject, and so only got down to it on the day before the examination (ereb,[2] as the Spanish forebears say). But fortune smiled on me, and here I am safe and sound and intending to go up to Semmering[3] tomorrow with two roses (one being my sister [Rosa] and the other the sister of Fräulein Fanny[4]) and to stay there with my ladies for two days or so, until we have spent our meager funds. When I return, I shall write you more, and meanwhile beseech you to answer me, so that your letters will be awaiting me when I return home. I was not slow in replying to you, as I had first to recover from all the work I had done and from which all my limbs are still aching. Enough for the moment; I have to go and see Bettelheim at the hospital and time is getting short and I am also very tired. Please give my respects to your mother and sister, and with kind regards

I remain, as I always have been
your faithful Cipion, dog at the hospital of Seville
and member of the Spanish Academy

In Spanish
1. On July 22, 1880.
2. Hebrew: eve.
3. An Alpine spa on the borders of Lower Austria and Styria.
4. Fanny Philipp, Freud's cousin.

Sevilla Julio 24 1880

¡Querido mio Berganza!

Por eso te annuncio que he pasado bien mi segundo ejamen teorético con unas penas y apresiones muy grandes, porque no alcanzaba el tiempo para la farmacologia y era mi intencion dejarme caer en esa disciplina, de manera que no la estudiaba sino en el dia antes del ejamen (Ereb, como dicen los antiguos Castellaños). Pero me favorecia la dicha y ahí soy sano y salvo y quiero irme mañana sobre el Semmering con dos rosas (una mi hermana y la otra hermana de Señorita Fanny) y estarme con mis doñas allí dos dias ó mas ó menos, hasta que habiamos gastado nuestros escasos dineros. Vuelto te escribiré mas y ahora te ruego, que me respondías, así que halle cartas de ti en casa cuando vuelvo. No era tarda mi respuesto, esperando yo revivir despues de tanto trabajo, que en todos miembros siento. Por ahora basta eso; que iré á ver Bettelheim en el hospital y no tengo mucho tiempo tambien soy muy cansado. Le ruego traer mis respetos á su madre y hermana y le saludo.

quedando como siempre era
su fiel Cipion p.e.e.h.d.S.
y m.d.l.A.E.

Vienna, October 3, 1880

Dear Berganza,

Two of the best teeth in my mouth have just broken, which will cost me a lot of money to repair, and this is one of the reasons why

I did not go to your rendezvous at the café, being very short of cash. Besides, I have taken a vow not to play tarok again before I become a doctor,[1] what with the waste of time and the amount of money I spend on it. Two of my courses begin tomorrow, and in the evenings I shall be at home studying and smoking the pipe I have bought myself. So I expect you any evening that suits you best, except for Tuesday the fifth, for I have been unable to get out of a meeting with Paneth that day.

> With greetings, I am your faithful
> Cipion dog at the hospital of Seville
> member of the Spanish Academy etc.

In Spanish
  1. Freud received his medical degree on March 30, 1881.

Viena, 3ro Octubre 1880

¡Querido Berganza!

Han se me quebrado dos de los mas valientes dientes de mi boca, que mucho dinero me costará el repararlos y es esa una de las razones porqué ayer no vino á su rendezvous en el café, siendo muy estrecho en dineros. Ademas he hecho voto de no jugar taroco antes de ser doctor por el mucho tiempo y tambien dinero, que se me gasta. Mañana empiezan dos de mis cursos y estaré las tardes en casa mia estudiando y fumando de mi pipa que me he comprado. De manera que le espero cuando mas le gusta por la tarde, Martes el 5 escepto que no he podido evitar hallarme con Paneth ese dia.

> Te saludo y soy tu fiel
> Cipion p.e.e.h.d.S.
> m.d.l.A.E.y.o.s.

Correspondence of the Spanish Academy 1881

Vienna, January 24, 1881

Dear Berganza,

I have two pieces of news to report, one from close to home and disagreeable, the other from far away and happier. To start with the sad news, the two noble knights prepared to put fortune to the test by my side[1] could again not be found today, so that I must lose a further week, and, if fate is [not] kinder to me, I shall not be able to call myself Doctor before the middle of next month. I am biting my nails and keep telling myself "Tu l'as voulu, Georges Dandin."[2]

Now for the happier news. My niece Anna from Odessa, whom you know, has married a Russian railway engineer and everyone over there agrees on the suitability of the match. Now you know all the news I know, and you are invited to come over one of these evenings, as I shall always be at home.

> With greetings I remain
> your faithful Cipion
> dog at the hospital of Seville
> member of the Spanish Academy etc.

In Spanish

   1. The two disputants needed for the doctorate examination.

   2. "You asked for it, Georges Dandin," a common slight misquotation from Molière's *Georges Dandin*, I.9.

Corresp. d.l.A.E. 1881

> Sevilla 24 Januar 1881

¡Querido Berganza!

Te hago saber dos nuevas, una de cercano y penible, la otra de muy lejos y mas alegre. Es para comenzar con lo triste que hoy tambien no se han encontrado dos caballeros gallantes, que conmigo aventuren ensayar la dicha así que una semana de mas pierdo, y cuando mas sea favorecido por la fortuna no podré llamarme doctor antés de medio del projimo mes. Me muerdo las uñas y digo "Tu l'as voulu G. D."

Sigue la novela mas gozosa. Es que mi sobrina Ana de Odesa, la cual tu conoces, se ha desposado á un ingeniero de un camino de hierro ruso y juzgan todos de allí ser un partido muy bueno. Así que sabes todo lo que sé yo de nuevo y estas rogado llegar á verme unas de esas tardes, que siempre estaré en casa.

> Saludote y quedo
> tu fiel Cipion
> p.e.e.h.d.S.
> m.d.l.A.E. etc.

APPENDIXES

ILLUSTRATION SOURCES

INDEX

TWO LATER LETTERS

[to Eduard Silberstein]

Vienna, April 28, 1910

Dear Friend,

Forgive me for not replying to your congratulations last year. You may be sure that they made me very happy. We have grown old since we first shared the small pleasures of student life. Now life is running out. I should very much like to hear in detail how things are with you. Of myself I can only say that I have come up against a great many unforeseen difficulties, but that on the whole I am not too dissatisfied with the outcome. My scientific expectations are slowly being fulfilled; I earn enough for our needs and might now be a well-to-do man had I not preferred a large family. The patients you mention are welcome to call; I shall refer them to my many pupils, who will treat them as I will suggest, but I myself cannot take on anything more this season.

I am in the midst of a great movement in the interpretation and treatment of nervous diseases, one that is probably not unknown in Romania either, since it has gained many adherents in Russia, Switzerland, and America. Last September I visited America by invitation, giving a course of lectures at a university in the vicinity of Boston.[1] It is in Germany, of all places, that I still have to overcome a great deal of hostility.

Thanking you cordially for your "sign of life"
Your old
Freud

1. Beginning on September 6, 1909, Freud delivered the *Five Lectures on Psycho-Analysis* at Clark University, in Worcester, Massachusetts. S.E., XI, pp. 3–55.

———————————

[to the President of the B'nai B'rith Lodge in Braila]

Vienna, April 22, 1928

Honored Mr. President and dear Brother,[1]

I was deeply touched to learn of the honor your Lodge has bestowed on my late childhood friend, Dr. Eduard Silberstein. I spent many years of my boyhood and young manhood in intimate friendship, indeed in fraternal fellowship, with him. Without a teacher, we learned Spanish together, read Cervantes, and signed our letters to each other with the names of the two perros en el hospital de Sevilla: Scipione and Berganza. We also shared more serious interests. Later, life and physical distance separated us, but early friendship can never be forgotten.

I would also see him from time to time when he came to Vienna, and once had occasion to attend to his first wife.[2]

You are right to acclaim him as a man of distinction. He was thoroughly kind-hearted and had a gentle sense of humor that must certainly have made it easier for him to bear the vicissitudes of life.

Please be assured of the best wishes of an ailing seventy-two-year-old to you, and to all the Brothers of the Lodge, in W. B. and E.[3]

Yours,
Freud

1. Freud had been a member of the Viennese Lodge since 1897; see his *Address to the Society of B'nai B'rith*, S.E., XX, pp. 273ff.

2. See the Introduction for an account of this incident.

3. *Wohlwollen, Bruderliebe, und Eintracht* (benevolence, brotherly love, and harmony), the motto of the Order.

DRAFT OF EPITHALAMIUM[1]

I [*or* F ?]
un [*or* und ?], unselig Geschick,
reich mir, oh Freund, Deine Muse, denn meine ist [?] längst schon
"gepackt" [?].
Im deutschen Worte zu kleiden [den] garstig entsetzlichen Jammer,
den Dein Brief geworfen so plötzlich ins Innere des Herzens—
sie, das /x/ [*possibly* die Perle ?], ja [*possibly abbreviation for*
    Gisela], die Muse der Academia,
verheiratet [*changed from* hinweggegeben] bereits an einen der
    Enkel Jakobs.—
Weh mir, oh weh; ich rase, der Schmerz versengt mit den Busen.
Kaum zu fassen imstande bin ich das entsetzliche Schicksal.—
Freund, geliebter Du, bin Dir [*or* der ?] /x x x/ [*possibly
    abbreviation for* Ichthyosaura /x/ Fluss].
Sende mir sogleich ein, 2 Zyankalium, 2 grüne,
5 von Äthertropfen, aber keine [?] Pflanze [?] des Schierlings,
9 schöne /x/, ganz frisch, von Dir /x/ bereitete,
Arsenik, ganz weißen und echten sende mir heute.—
[*deleted*] Stelle [mir] einen scharfes Rasier[messer],
einen Revolver dazu, von 6 gezogenen Läufen—
bleierne Kugeln mit Schrot, doch alles gut und solide—
denn nicht länger ertrag ich das garstige Schicksal.
Sie, die getreue Braut, [*deleted:* zu sehen in] in eines anderen Arm
    zu schauen.
Alles Glück und die Wonne der glücklichen Liebe genießend.—
Wenn ich denke daran, wie sie dem geliebten Gatten
jetzt gleich das Kinn umstreichelt mit leisem [?] Geflüster,

/x/ ihm gibt, /x/, die Liebe nur ersinnt,
die Lippe ihm küßt und die Stirn, die /x/, oh weh mir,
weh mir,
auch das, obschon /x/, lange das alte /x/.
Oh, mein Gott Abraham, wie wurde so grausam zunichte [?]

I [or F ?]
un [or and ?], unhappy fate,
hand me, oh friend, your Muse, for mine has [?] long since "packed
    up" [?].
To put into German words [the] wretched, abominable despair,
your letter so suddenly cast into the depths of the heart—
she, the /x/ [possibly the pearl ?], indeed [possibly abbreviation for
    Gisela], the Muse of Academia,
married [changed from given away] already to a descendant of
    Jacob.—
Woe is me, woe; I rage, pain sears my breast.
Scarce can I grasp the abominable fate.—
Friend, loved one, to you [or to the ?] I am /x x x/ [possibly
    abbreviation for Ichthyosaura /x/ Fluss].
Send me forthwith two potassium cyanides, two green ones,
five drops of ether, but no [?] plant [?] of hemlock,
nine lovely /x/, quite fresh, prepared by you /x/,
Arsenic, all white and pure, send me today.—
[deleted] Provide [me] with a sharp razor[blade],
a revolver as well, with six rifled barrels—
lead bullets with shot, good and sound one and all—
for no more can I bear this wretched fate.
Her, the faithful bride, [deleted: to be seen in] in another's arms to
    behold.
All happiness and the bliss of happy love enjoying.—
When I think how she, even now,
caresses her adored spouse's chin with soft [?] whispers,
gives him /x/, /x/, thinks only of love,
kisses his lip and his brow, the /x/, oh woe, woe is me,
even that, though /x/, long the old /x/.
Oh, my God Abraham, how was so cruelly destroyed [?]

1. The difficult transcription of the original draft was the work of Dr. Reinhold N. Smid and Dr. Ursula Panzer, of the Husserl Archive at the University of Cologne. The draft, on a sheet of paper folded both lengthwise and crosswise, is written in the old Gabelsberger shorthand, with some personal idiosyncrasies. Edmund Husserl's unpublished papers are written mainly in this sort of shorthand, and only a few specialists are now familiar with it. The transcribers' glosses are in brackets; /x/ represents an untranscribable shorthand symbol.

BIOGRAPHICAL NOTES
ON DR. EDUARD SILBERSTEIN

by Rosita Braunstein Vieyra

I remember my grandfather, Eduard Silberstein, as a quiet and gentle man, with a short grey beard and blue eyes. He possessed a keen sense of humor and could, on occasion, be the "life of the party."

He was born in Jassy, Romania, in 1857, one of four children of Orthodox Jewish parents. His father, Osias, a prosperous merchant banker, sent his sons to a Cheder, a Jewish religious school. My grandfather and his brother Adolf (Dolfi) rebelled very early against this rather narrow and Talmud oriented education. They aspired to a more secular view on the world.

When came the time to go to a university, Eduard chose Vienna, and Leipzig or Heidelberg. (I am unsure about which of the two latter schools). He studied Law and Philosophy and graduated with degrees in both disciplines. His brother Dolfi went to Germany, studied Medicine, married a "suitable" German Jewish young lady, and practiced medicine in Berlin until Hitler's rise to power.

My grandfather's student days seemed happy. He was known to remark that he lent money to fellow students to pay their tailor, but that they always turned out to be more elegantly dressed than he was; he, the "rich" lender!

He spoke fluent Romanian, German, French (with me), Greek, (he read ancient classical Greek as well), Spanish. He had, however, great difficulty learning English; this in spite of his many travels to

Eduard Silberstein with his first wife, Pauline,
née Theiler, about 1890

England, where he loved to stay with Quakers and even attend their meetings.

He fell deeply in love with Paula (or Pauline) Theiler, a young girl from Jassy. Sadly, their marriage was a short one. She soon became mentally ill, was treated unsuccessfully by his friend Sigmund Freud, and threw herself from a window in Freud's apartment building. This tragedy was corroborated by Anna Freud, who invited me to visit her in 1982, a few months before her death. My understanding and intelligent grandmother, Anna Sachs (native of Kovno, Lithuania), was his second wife.

They settled in Braila, an active commercial port town on the Danube. After a child dead in infancy, my mother, their only daughter, was born in 1895. They named her Theodora, after the empress of Byzantium. They sent her to a catholic convent school, probably the only good girls school in Braila. E. S. was very much for a modern education for women: "Less embroidery, more chemistry, mathematics and science."

Upon her marriage to my father, Elias Braunstein, the young couple went to live in Antwerp, Belgium. This separation was especially painful for E. S. who adored his daughter.

Dr. Silberstein became a prominent member of the community. He took an active part in Jewish communal affairs, although not in their religious aspects. He was president of H.I.A.S. (Hebrew Immigrant Assistance Society), Alliance Israélite Universelle, B'nai B'rith, and a Free Mason. (The Braila lodge was named after him and Dr. Peixotto). In those days, some poor young members of the Jewish "intelligentia" travelled to the port of Braila on foot, from remote parts of the Balkans, on their way to America, to escape antisemitism. My grandparents offered them shelter, and my grandfather collected moneys among his friends for their passage to the New World, "where the streets were paved with gold." One such young man became president of B'nai B'rith in New York, and a prominent Jewish leader.

The reason Eduard Silberstein believed in their future in America was that he always expressed misgivings about the possible founding of a Jewish State in Palestine. He foresaw difficulties with the Arabs, regardless of Herzl's ideals of Zionism.

World War I was a difficult time for him. Because of his thorough knowledge of German, he was appointed to work at the city hall, with the occupying military and civilian German forces (billeting, etc.). He dreaded the possible appearance of his beloved brother Dolfi, now an officer in the German army. Fortunately, this did not happen. Nevertheless, after the war, the antisemitic element in town found a way to accuse him of treason. At the trial which followed he was completely exonerated, but he used to say that the pain and aggravation of this slander shortened his life.

He became involved with the struggle for Jewish civil rights in Romania, and instrumental in obtaining citizenship and the right for Jews to vote, rights which were nonexistent until then. At the Treaty of Versailles, Clémenceau and Sonnino among others worked towards establishing rights for minorities. Who knows, his correspondence with them or with their offices may still be in existence somewhere? Singlehandedly, he obtained the abolition of what was called the Jew's Oath. (Disraeli had achieved this in England.)

He was an intellectual, totally unsuited for the business world. However, the suicide of a brother, after he had lost the family fortune, forced him to enter the grain trade. His responsibilities towards parents and family left him no alternative. There was no one else to pick up the pieces of what had been a considerable fortune. There was a time when my grandmother Anna feared that he would follow his brother's example. She used to trail him everywhere.

He was a socialist in the sense that he was for workers' rights and the common man. When he died the shops in Braila were kept closed during his funeral.

His literary tastes were: Anatole France, Upton Sinclair, Lafcadio Hearn. (He always admired the Japanese). He was the kind of person who would send Maeterlinck's *La vie des abeilles* as a birthday gift to my mother in Belgium. This, I thought with amusement, was like "sending coals to Newcastle."

He liked the Yiddish language. He had a correspondence with Shalom Aleichem, whom he was supposed to meet in Corfu, to discuss translation of one of his books. Nothing came of it, but those letters may also be found somewhere someday.

He had a special admiration for Saint Francis of Assisi. His favorite place was Piazza San Marco in Venice, where he went as often as he could, while my grandmother went to Marienbad for the "waters."

My grandfather, Eduard Silberstein, was a modest, learned, unpractical, aristocratic, dear man. I have childhood memories of him which I cherish. I remember his love for me, the charming ditties he composed for me in Spanish, and the stories he used to tell me.

He died in Braila in 1925.

New York, May 8, 1988

DER ICHTHYOSAURUS

by Josef Victor von Scheffel

Es rauscht in den Schachtelhalmen,
Verdächtig leuchtet das Meer,
Da schwimmt mit Tränen im Auge
Ein Ichthyosaurus daher.

Ihn jammert der Zeiten Verderbnis,
Denn ein sehr bedenklicher Ton
War neuerlich eingerissen
In der Liasformation.

"Der Plesiosaurus, der Alte,
Er jubelt in Saus und Braus,
Der Pterodaktylus selber
Flog neulich betrunken nach Haus.

Der Iguanodon, der Lümmel,
Wird frecher zu jeglicher Frist,
Schon hat er am hellen Tage
Die Ichthyosaura geküßt.

Mir ahnt eine Weltkatastrophe,
So kann es ja länger nicht gehn;
Was soll aus dem Lias noch werden,
Wenn solche Dinge geschehn?"

So klagte der Ichthyosaurus,
Da ward es ihm kreidig zumut';

Sein letzter Seufzer verhallte
Im Qualmen und Zischen der Flut.

Es starb zu der selbigen Stunde
Die ganze Saurierei,
Sie kamen zu tief in die Kreide,
Da war es natürlich vorbei.

Und der uns hat gesungen
Dies petrefaktische Lied,
Der fand's als fossiles Albumblatt
Auf einem Koprolith.

The horsetails all were a-rustle,
Suspiciously gleamed the abyss,
When, swimming with tears brimming over,
An Ichthyosaurus said this:

"How depraved are the times that we live in,
How deplorable is the new tone
That has recently caused such upheaval
In the Lias formation alone.

The Plesiosaurus, the Ancient,
He leads such a riotous life,
And even the staid Pterodactyl
Flies home sozzled each night to his wife.

Iguanodon, the rapscallion,
No pleasures he ever resists,
For e'en in the broadest of daylight
The Ichthyosaura he kissed.

Catastrophic the world's latest progress,
We've allowed things to go much too far;
What is to become of the Lias,
If we carry on just as we are?"

Thus lamented the Ichthyosaurus,
His mood turned Cretaceous again;
The last of his sighs rose and faded
In the hiss of the flood and the rain.

So perished that very same hour
The whole of the Saurian age,
Too deep in the chalk[1] they had fallen,
So now we must turn their last page.

And he who has sung us this epic,
The song petrified herewith,
In a fossilized album he found it,
Inscribed on a coprolith.

1. The German *Kreide*, chalk, indicates the Cretaceous era; to be "deep in the chalk" is to be deeply in debt. Tr.

ILLUSTRATION SOURCES

page

xxix Ernst Freud, Lucie Freud, and Ilse Grubrich-Simitis, eds., *Sigmund Freud: His Life in Pictures and Words,* trans. Christine Trollope, New York and London, 1978

15 Mary Evans, Sigmund Freud Copyrights Ltd., Colchester, England

65 Copper etching by Franz Schütz, Bildarchiv des Instituts für Geschichte der Medizin, Vienna

100 Archiv der Universität Wien, Vienna

103 Bildarchiv der Österreichischen Nationalbibliothek, Vienna

132 Rosita Braunstein Vieyra, New York

148 Sigmund Freud Copyrights Ltd.

158 Sigmund Freud Copyrights Ltd.

172 Bildarchiv der Österreichischen Nationalbibliothek

191 Rosita Braunstein Vieyra

Permission to reprint is gratefully acknowledged.

INDEX

Library of Congress Cataloging-in-Publication Data
Freud, Sigmund, 1856–1939.
[Sigmund Freud, Jugendbriefe an Eduard Silberstein, 1871–1881.
English & Spanish]
The letters of Sigmund Freud to Eduard Silberstein, 1871–1881 /
edited by Walter Boehlich ; translated by Arnold J. Pomerans.
p.   cm.
Translation of: Sigmund Freud, Jugendbriefe an Eduard Silberstein,
1871–1881.
Includes index.
ISBN 0-674-52827-1 (alk. paper)
1. Freud, Sigmund, 1856–1939—Correspondence. 2. Silberstein,
Eduard, 1856–1925—Correspondence. 3. Psychoanalysts—Austria—
Correspondence.   I. Boehlich, Walter, 1921–   II. Title.
BF173.F85A4   1990
150.19'52—dc20
[B]   90-39119
CIP